RAISING THE BAR

FOR PRODUCTIVE CITIES
IN LATIN AMERICA AND
THE CARIBBEAN

RAISING THE BAR

FOR PRODUCTIVE CITIES IN LATIN AMERICA AND THE CARIBBEAN

MARÍA MARTA FERREYRA AND MARK ROBERTS, EDITORS

 WORLD BANK GROUP

Contents

Foreword . . . . *xiii*
Preface . . . . *xv*
Acknowledgments . . . . *xvii*
About the Authors . . . . *xix*
Abbreviations . . . . *xxi*

Overview 1
    The Productivity of LAC Cities Is Slightly above Average but below the Global Frontier . . . 2
    What These Findings Might Mean for Policy 18
    Annex OA: Productivity Measures Used in the Book to Assess LAC Cities 19
    Annex OB: The Need for Policy 20
    Notes 21
    References 23

Part I. Urbanization and Productivity in Latin America and the Caribbean 25

Chapter 1. Urbanization, Economic Development, and Structural Transformation 27

Paula Restrepo Cadavid and Grace Cineas

    Introduction 27
    The Origins of Cities in Latin America and the Caribbean 28
    Urbanization in the LAC Region and the Rest of the World: Discrepancies between
        Consistent and Official Measures 30
    Urbanization, Economic Development, and Structural Transformation: How Does the
        LAC Region's Performance Stack Up? 38
    Conclusions 42
    Notes 43
    References 45

Chapter 2. The Many Dimensions of Urbanization and the Productivity of Cities in
Latin America and the Caribbean 49

Mark Roberts

    Introduction 49

Defining a Global Data Set of Urban Areas 51

Urban Areas in the LAC Region Are More Densely Populated Than Those Elsewhere . . . 52

A Significant Share of Latin America and the Caribbean's Urban Population
Lives in Large MCAs 59

A Third of LAC Countries Analyzed Suffer from Potentially Excessive Primacy 62

Implications for National Productivity: Density and MCAs Matter,
but Urban Primacy Does Not 65

International Benchmarking of LAC Urban Areas' Productivity: Better
Than Average, but Lagging the Global Frontier 67

Productivity is Highly Dispersed across LAC Urban Areas 72

Conclusions 75

Annex 2A: List of Comparator Countries for Each LAC Country 77

Annex 2B: Statistical Tests of Differences in Population, Area, and Population Density
between LAC Countries and Their Comparators 78

Annex 2C: List of Multicity Agglomerations in the LAC Region 79

Annex 2D: Cross-Country Regression of Log(GDP per Capita) on Different
Dimensions of Urbanization: Alternative Definition for a Multicity Agglomeration 81

Notes 81

References 84

**Part II. The Determinants of City Productivity in Latin America and
the Caribbean** **87**

Chapter 3.   The Empirical Determinants of City Productivity 89

Mark Roberts

Introduction 89

Cities Are More Productive Than Rural Areas 91

Large Subnational Variations in Productivity, Explained Partly by Sorting 96

Explaining Underlying Variations in Productivity: The Three Theories 98

What about Firms? Evidence from World Bank Enterprise Surveys 104

Conclusions 109

Annex 3A: Results of Regressions on the Determinants of Underlying
Productivity Variations Based on the Single-Stage Approach 110

Notes 111

References 114

Chapter 4.   Transport Infrastructure and Agglomeration in Cities 117

Harris Selod and Souleymane Soumahoro

Introduction 117

Transport, Agglomeration, and Productivity: A Brief Review 118

Transport in Latin America and the Caribbean: History, Current State, and Challenges . 119

Roads and Agglomeration Economies: Evidence from Mexico 129

Conclusions 135

Notes 135

References 136

Chapter 5. Human Capital in Cities. 141

María Marta Ferreyra

Introduction 141
Some Stylized Facts 143
Returns to Aggregate Human Capital. 151
Attracting Skilled Individuals to Cities 156
Conclusions. 160
Annex 5A: Areas Used in the Stylized Facts. 161
Annex 5B: Percentage of Employment in Services, by Educational Attainment 162
Annex 5C: Probability of Working in the Service Sector for Skilled and
   Unskilled Workers, by Area Size 163
Annex 5D: Percentage of Urban Population Born Abroad 163
Notes 164
References 165

Chapter 6. Urban Form, Institutional Fragmentation, and Metropolitan Coordination . . 167

Nancy Lozano Gracia and Paula Restrepo Cadavid

Introduction 167
Urban Form and Productivity. 168
Institutional Fragmentation, Metropolitan Coordination, and Productivity. 180
Conclusions. 187
Annex 6A: Seventy-Three Cities in Institutional Fragmentation and
   Coordination Analysis. 188
Annex 6B: Urban Form Indicators 189
Annex 6C: Correlation Matrix between Urban Form Variables. 190
Notes 190
References 192

Boxes
O.1   Form, Skill, and Access 10
1.1   Precolonial Densities, Location Fundamentals, and the Persistence
      of Subnational Population Densities 29
1.2   Location Fundamentals and the Distribution of Economic
      Activity in Latin America and the Caribbean versus the Rest of the World 31
1.3   The Agglomeration Index and the Cluster Algorithm 35
1.4   Comparing the Population of Urban Areas: Cluster Algorithm
      versus Official Data. 36
2.1   Comparing Apples with Apples: Selecting Comparators for LAC Countries 55
2.2   Congestion Forces in LAC Urban Areas 56
2.3   VIIRS Nighttime Lights Data 68
2.4   Cities and Aggregate Growth: United States and Brazil. 75
3.1   SEDLAC: A Treasure Trove of Harmonized Data 92
3.2   Which Groups of Workers Benefit More?. 103
3.3   The Determinants of Manufacturing Firm Productivity across
      Colombian Municipalities. 108

4.1   History of Road Development in Mexico 121
4.2   Measuring Industrial Concentration: The Ellison and Glaeser Index. 130
4.3   Measuring Municipality Specialization: The Krugman Specialization Index 131
4.4   Market Access. 132
5.1   An Equilibrium Model of Household Sorting for Brazil 156
6.1   Outlining Urban Extents Using Nighttime Lights 173
6.2   Constructing Institutional Fragmentation and Metropolitan
       Coordination Variables 182

Figures

O.1   LAC Countries Exhibit Average Productivity Given Their Urbanization Levels. . . . 3
O.2   Productivity of LAC Cities Is above Average but Lags the Global Frontier 3
O.3   A High Percentage of LAC Cities Have Population Densities above the
       Global Median 4
O.4   LAC Cities Are Dense Because Their Areas Are Small. 5
O.5   Productivity Varies Widely across Cities and Countries in Latin America
       and the Caribbean. 6
O.6   Within-Country Productivity Dispersions Are High in LAC Countries 7
O.7   More Populous LAC Cities Have Higher Shares of Skilled Labor 8
O.8   Rail Is Not Prevalent in Latin America 9
O.9   Paved Road Density Has Been Stagnant in Latin America and the Caribbean. . . . 9
O.10   Unconditional and Conditional Effects of Density on Productivity
       Provide Insights into the Mechanisms for Agglomeration Effects 11
O.11   The Effects of Form, Skill, and Access on Productivity 12
O.12   In Most Countries, a City's Population Density Does Not Have a
       Positive Significant Effect on Its Productivity. 13
O.13   Across Countries, Returns to Skill Are U-Shaped in Average City Skill 15
O.14   Individual Returns to Skill Fall and Then Rise with Own Education. 16
O.15   Market Access Is Associated with City Productivity in Some Countries 17
O.16   Countries with Better Road Coverage Have More Efficient
       Systems of Cities 18
1.1   Strong Persistence in Subnational Population Densities in the
       LAC Region 30
1.2   Urban Shares for Latin America and the Caribbean and Other
       World Regions, 1960–2015. 32
1.3   Urban Shares for LAC Subregions, 1960–2015. 33
1.4   Annual Growth of Urban Population, Worldwide and by
       Region, 1960–2005. 33
1.5   Urban Shares: Official versus Consistent Measures of Urbanization 35
B1.4.1 Comparison of Cluster Algorithm and WUP City Population Values,
       by Region 36
B1.4.2 Between and within Variation of the Relocation Fraction per Region 37
1.6   Relationship between Economic Development and the Urban Share
       on Official Measures. 38
1.7   Change in the Structural Composition of the Economy, 1960–2009 42
2.1   Percentage of Urban Areas with Population Densities Higher
       Than the Global Median, by Region 53
2.2   Distribution of Area Size and Population across Urban Areas,
       Selected Regions 54

2.3   Percentage of Urban Areas with Population Densities Higher Than
          the Global Median, by LAC Country 54
B2.2.1   Relationship between Traffic Congestion and Population Density,
          LAC Cities versus Non-LAC Cities 57
B2.2.2   Air Pollution in Cities in Latin America and the Caribbean and
          Other Regions. 58
2.4   Percentage of Urban Population Living in Multicity Agglomerations,
          by Region 61
2.5   Multicity Agglomerations, by LAC Country 62
2.6   Cross-Country Relationship between Urban Share and Share of
          National Population Living in Multicity Agglomerations 63
2.7   Urban Primacy, by Region. 63
2.8   Urban Primacy, LAC Countries and Comparators. 64
2.9   Relationship between Log(Nighttime Lights) and Log(Population),
          All Urban Areas Globally 70
2.10   Mean Urban Area Productivity in LAC Countries Benchmarked
          against International Comparators 71
2.11   Distribution of Productivity across Urban Areas, Selected Regions 73
2.12   Productivity Dispersion (Measured by the Coefficient of Variation) across
          Urban Areas in LAC Countries Benchmarked against High-Income
          International Comparators 74
2.13   Productivity Dispersion across Urban Areas in a Country Is
          Negatively Correlated with National Road Density, 112 Countries. 75
3.1   Ratio of Nominal Mean Urban to Nominal Mean Rural Wage in
          15 LAC Countries, 2000–14. 92
3.2   Urban and Worker Premiums in 15 LAC Countries 95
3.3   Subnational Variations in Underlying Productivity in
          16 LAC Countries. 98
3.4   Correlation between Underlying Productivity and Population
          Density, Average Number of Years of Schooling, and Market Access 99
3.5   Cross-Country Heterogeneity in Estimated Elasticities of Underlying
          Productivity with Respect to Population Density, Average
          Number of Years of Schooling, and Market Access. 102
3.6   Different Dimensions of a City's Business Environment. 105
3.7   Security Costs Incurred by Firms in Cities, Latin America and the
          Caribbean and Other Regions. 107
4.1   Length of Railroad Track in Service and Urban Share in Latin
          America and the Caribbean, 1900–2007. 120
4.2   Export Density and Railroad Density in Selected Latin American
          Countries, 1900–30. 120
4.3   Length of Roads and Urban Population Share in Latin America
          and the Caribbean, 1950–2000 122
4.4   Modal Split of Surface Freight in Latin America and the Caribbean, 2012 124
4.5   Investment in Transport Infrastructure in Latin America
          and the Caribbean, 2000–13. 124
4.6   Change in Transport Investment as a Share of GDP, 2008–15. 125
4.7   Evolution of Paved Road Density, Selected Regions, 1961–2000. 126
4.8   Average and Per Capita Road Length in a 100-Kilometer Radius
          around Cities with at Least 1 Million Inhabitants. 127

4.9   Average Road Length in a 100-Kilometer Radius around Cities
      with at Least 1 Million Inhabitants 127
4.10 Ad Valorem Freight and Real Tariffs for Intraregional Exports and
      Exports to the United States, 2005 128
5.1   Distribution of Human Capital at the Area Level, circa 2014 144
5.2   Population and Human Capital in the Largest Areas, circa 2014 145
5.3   Percentage of the Adult Population Living in Urban Areas, circa 2014 145
5.4   Percentage of Skilled Population, by Area Size, circa 2014 146
5.5   Average Gini Coefficient, by Area Size, circa 2014 147
5.6   Percentage of Skilled Migrants, by Area Size, circa 2014. 148
5.7   Percentage of Skilled Individuals Who Are Migrants, by Area
      Size, circa 2014 148
5.8   Percentage of Employment in Services, by Area Size, circa 2014 149
5.9   Percentage of Service Workers, by Sector in Large Areas and by
      Skill Level, circa 2014 150
5.10 Returns to Aggregate Human Capital, 2000–14 153
5.11 Returns to Aggregate Human Capital, by Individual's Own
      Education, 2000–14. 154
6.1   Urban Form in Latin America and the Caribbean Shows Great Variability 176
6.2   Change in Urban Form Indicators, 1996–2000 177
6.3   What Levels of Fragmentation Are Needed to Reap the Benefits? 186

Maps
O.1   Multicity Agglomerations in Latin America and the Caribbean
      Span Multiple Municipalities 5
2.1   Examples of Multicity Agglomerations in Latin America and the
      Caribbean That Span Multiple Municipalities. 60
3.1   Subnational Variations in Nominal Wages in South America 97
3.2   Subnational Variations in Nominal Wages in Central America and
      the Caribbean 97
4.1   The Evolution of the Road Network in Mexico, 1985–2016 122
4.2   Spatial Distributions of Formal Establishments and Manufacturing
      Firms in Mexico, Overlaid on the Road Network, 2014 130
4.3   Output Locality Specialization, Overlaid on the Road Network, 2014 132
4.4   Changes in Market Access in Mexico, 1986–2014 133
B6.1.1 Examples of Urban Extents over the DMSP-OLS Radiance-Calibrated
      2010 Composite 174
B6.2.1 Examples of Metropolitan Areas. 182

Tables
B1.2.1 *R*-Squared Results for Relationship between Log(Radiance-Calibrated
      Nighttime Lights) and Base, Agriculture, and Trade Fundamentals 31
1.1   Regression Results for Relationship between Log(GDP per Capita)
      and the Official Urban Share. 39
1.2   Regression Results for Relationship between Log(GDP per Capita)
      and the Urban Share, Using Consistent Measures 40
2.1   Summary Statistics for Global Sample of Urban Areas 52
2.2   Number of Multicity Agglomerations, by Region 61

2.3   Cross-Country Regression of Log(GDP per Capita) on Different
        Dimensions of Urbanization 66
B2.3.1 Regression of Log(GDP) on VIIRS Nighttime Lights Data, 2015 68
2.4   The 15 Urban Areas in the LAC Region with the Highest Estimated
        Economic Activity, as Measured by Nighttime Lights Data, 2015 69
2.5   Relationship between Log(Nighttime Lights) and Log(Population),
        All Urban Areas Globally 70
3.1   Differences in Characteristics between Urban and Rural Workers in
        15 LAC Countries. 93
3.2   Results of Regressions on the Determinants of Underlying Productivity
        Variations across Subnational Areas 100
B3.2.1 Heterogeneous Effects of Determinants on Underlying Productivity
        across Worker Subgroups 104
3.3   The Effects of a City's Business Environment on Firm Productivity. 106
3A.1   Results of Regressions on the Determinants of Underlying Productivity
        Variations Based on the Single-Stage Approach. 110
4.1   Density of All Roads (Paved and Nonpaved) in Regions of the
        World, 1961–2000 123
4.2   Modal Share of Surface Freight, by Region, 2015 124
4.3   Transport Infrastructure Investments, by Sector, 2008–15 125
4.4   LAC Cities Are among the Top 100 Congested Places in the World 128
4.5   The Effects of Market Access on Employment 134
4.6   The Effects of Market Access on Local Specialization. 135
4.7   The Effects of Market Access on Nighttime Lights 135
5.1   Returns to Aggregate Human Capital, 2000–14 152
5.2   Local Labor Demand, Brazil, 2010 158
5.3   The Effects of Raising Labor Demand for Higher Education
        Graduates in Feira de Santana, Brazil, 2010 159
6.1   Examples of Urban Areas with High, Medium, and Low
        Values of the Indexes That Describe Urban Form 170
6.2   Descriptive Statistics of Urban Form in LAC Cities. 175
6.3   Regression Results for Urban Form and City Productivity
        with Outliers. 179
6.4   Institutional Fragmentation and Metropolitan Coordination 181
6.5   Institutional Fragmentation and Metropolitan Coordination,
        LAC Region versus OECD 183
6.6   Top 15 Fragmented Metropolitan Areas, LAC Region
        versus OECD 183
6.7   Regression of a City Productivity Premium (ln) on Institutional
        Fragmentation and Metropolitan Coordination Variables. 185

Foreword

Since the early days of civilization, human beings have come together in cities. Cities (from the Latin *civitas*) and civilization (from the Latin *civilis*) are inextricably linked. Throughout human history, cities have been centers of civilization, culture, and human achievement. They have also been powerful hubs of economic activity, entrepreneurship, and innovation. As firms and workers gather in cities, opportunities emerge for employment and business. As cities within a country become better connected, further opportunities emerge for production and trade among cities.

These opportunities, however, do not always come to full realization. Such is the case when cities are overwhelmed by congestion, or when people, goods, and services do not flow freely across cities. Cities can only realize their potential and their contribution to national productivity when policy makers implement an enabling environment through a combination of policies at the local, state, and national level.

These issues are critical for the Latin America and the Caribbean (LAC) region today. Since almost three-quarters of LAC's population lives in cities, LAC countries cannot be productive unless their cities are also productive. Further, the region is in need of greater productivity, as the high growth rates of the first decade of the new millennium have given way to low and uneven growth rates. Reviving growth is thus at the top of policy makers' agenda.

Despite the importance of LAC cities' productivity, surprisingly little is known about it. The novel research conducted for this report tells us that while the productivity of LAC cities is on par with the world's average, it lags the world's frontier, which is where LAC policy makers would wish to be. Not only does the region lag other countries, but some cities lag others within the same country. While human capital makes key contributions to cities' productivity, other mechanisms, such as access to a larger market, seem rather muted. Closing these productivity gaps calls for an enabling environment of adequate infrastructure, urban planning, public services, and metropolitan governance. It also requires further investments in human capital and an economy that facilitates the flow of people, goods, and services across cities.

In its quest for greater productivity, LAC must seek to develop the full potential of its cities. We hope that the research presented in this report will enhance our knowledge and stimulate the type of insights and food for thought that leads to sound and progressive policy making.

Jorge Familiar, Vice President
Carlos Végh, Chief Economist
Latin America and the Caribbean Region
The World Bank Group

Preface

This book investigates the contribution of cities to productivity in Latin America and the Caribbean (LAC), a topic about which surprisingly little is known. The rapid economic growth that prevailed in the region during the first decade of the new millennium has, since the collapse of global commodity prices, given way to low, uneven growth in recent years. In this context, boosting productivity is critical to reviving economic growth in the region. And the potential of that great engine of growth—cities—cannot be left untapped.

The book has two parts. Part I documents overall urbanization patterns across the LAC region and their relationship to productivity outcomes at the national and subnational levels, compared with the rest of the world. Part II conducts a deeper, more rigorous analysis of the underlying determinants of productivity differences across LAC cities focusing on three key factors: city form, skills, and access to markets through transportation networks.

Acknowledgments

This book was prepared by a team led by María Marta Ferreyra and Mark Roberts. The core team also consisted of Nancy Lozano Gracia, Paula Restrepo Cadavid, and Harris Selod, and received excellent research assistance from Angelica Sanchez Diaz, Grace Cineas, Jane Park, and Souleymane Soumahoro. The work was conducted under the general guidance of Augusto de la Torre, former Chief Economist for the Latin America and the Caribbean (LAC) region of the World Bank, and Carlos Végh, current LAC Chief Economist of the World Bank, with substantial inputs from Daniel Lederman, former Deputy LAC Chief Economist, and Ming Zhang, LAC Practice Manager for the Social, Urban, Rural and Resilience Global Practice of the World Bank.

Preparation of the book was informed by a series of background papers. Authors of these background papers who have not already been named include Jorge Balat, Paulo Bastos, Brian Blankespoor, Theophile Bougna, Maria Camila Casas, Chandan Deuskar, Juan Carlos Duque, Lin Fan, Rafael Garduno, Jorge Patino, Luis Quintero, Daniel Reyes, Benjamin Stewart, Christopher Timmins, and Lixin C. Xu. Empirical work for the book was underpinned by an extensive geospatial database for LAC that was developed in collaboration with a research team at the University of Southampton's GeoData Center led by Julia Branson and Chris Hill. Further support on data was generously provided by the World Bank's Geospatial Operations Support Team, as well as by Siobhan Murray.

The team was fortunate to receive excellent advice and guidance from four distinguished peer reviewers: Uwe Deichmann, Gilles Duranton, William Maloney, and Forhad Shilpi. While the authoring team is very grateful for the guidance received, these reviewers are not responsible for any remaining errors, omissions, or interpretations. Additional insights from Judy Baker, Matias Busso, Walker Hanlon, Maria Flavia Harari, Adam Storeygard, Daniel Sullivan, Matthew Turner, Daniel Xu, and other participants of a workshop on May 11 and 12, 2017, are gratefully acknowledged.

In preparing the book, the team benefitted from discussions with Peter Ellis, Somik Lall, and Horacio Cristian Terraza, while Anna Wellenstein and Catalina Marulanda played an important role in early discussions relating to scoping out the book. The team is also grateful for the support provided by senior management of the World Bank's Social, Urban, Rural, and Resilience Global Practice, including not only Anna Welleinstein but also Senior Director Ede Jorge Ijjasz-Vasquez and Director Sameh Naguib Wahba Tadros.

Bruce Ross-Larson was the principal editor, and Joe Caponio, Mike Crumplar, and John Wagley were the copyeditors. Additional editing work was performed by Joseph Coohill. Patricia Katayama (acquisitions editor), Rumit Pancholi (production editor), and Deborah Appel-Barker (print coordinator), of the World Bank's Formal Publishing Program, were responsible for managing the design, typesetting, and printing of the book. Last, but not least, the authors thank Ruth Delgado, Ruth Eunice Flores, Jacqueline Larrabure, and Michelle Chen for unfailing administrative support.

About the Authors

María Marta Ferreyra is a senior economist in the Office of the Chief Economist for Latin America and the Caribbean of the World Bank. Her research specializes in the economics of education, with special emphasis on the effects of large-scale reforms. She has conducted research on charter schools, private school vouchers, public school accountability, and school finance reform for primary and secondary education in the United States and on higher education in Latin America and the Caribbean. Her research has been published in journals such as the *American Economic Review*, the *Journal of Public Economics*, and the *American Economic Journal: Economic Policy*. She was the lead author of *At a Crossroads: Higher Education in Latin America and the Caribbean*. Before joining the World Bank, she served as a faculty member at the Tepper School of Business at Carnegie Mellon University. She holds a PhD in economics from the University of Wisconsin–Madison.

Mark Roberts is a senior urban economist in the Social, Urban, Rural, and Resilience Global Practice of the World Bank, where his work primarily focuses on the East Asia and Pacific, and Latin America and the Caribbean regions. Before joining the World Bank, Mark was a lecturer in spatial economics at the University of Cambridge and a Fellow of Murray Edwards College in Cambridge, United Kingdom. Mark has published widely in leading peer-reviewed journals on spatial economic development and is a former coeditor of the journal *Spatial Economic Analysis*. He is the coauthor of the World Bank's South Asia region's flagship book, *Leveraging Urbanization in South Asia*, and the Latin America and the Caribbean region's flagship report, *Raising the Bar for Productive Cities in Latin America and the Caribbean*. He is also currently leading the World Bank's Indonesia flagship report on urbanization. Mark holds a PhD in land economy and an MA in economics from the University of Cambridge, United Kingdom, as well as an MSc in economics from Warwick University, United Kingdom.

Grace Cineas is a consultant in the Social, Urban, Rural, and Resilience Global Practice of the World Bank, where her work has focused primarily on urban development and resilience in Europe and Central Asia. She has also contributed to work in Latin America and Sub-Saharan Africa. Grace holds a master of international economics and international relations from The Johns Hopkins University School of Advanced International Studies.

Harris Selod is a senior economist in the Development Research Group of the World Bank. His research focuses on the role of transport, property rights, and land markets on economic development. His papers have been published in academic journals such as the *American Economic Journal: Economic Policy*, the *Economic Journal*, the *Journal of Development Economics*, the *Journal of Public Economics*, and the *Journal of Urban Economics*. He currently coordinates the World Bank's research program on Transport Policies for Sustainable Growth and Poverty Reduction and is the co-organizer of the annual World Bank/George Washington University Urbanization and Poverty Reduction Research Conference. Before joining the World Bank, he served as an associate professor at the Paris School of Economics and as a researcher at the French National Institute for Agricultural Research (Institut national de la recherche agronomique, or INRA). He holds a PhD in economics from Sorbonne University, an MSc in statistics from the Paris Graduate School of Economics, Statistics, and Finance (École nationale de la statistique et de l'administration économique, or ENSAE), and an MBA from ESCP Europe (École supérieure de commerce de Paris).

Nancy Lozano Gracia is a senior economist in the Social, Urban, Rural, and Resilience Global Practice of the World Bank, where she has worked extensively on designing and using diagnostic tools to improve the understanding of the challenges of rapid urbanization and city development and to help identify priorities for action. As part of these efforts, she has led work using innovative data collection methods such as satellite imagery, new survey designs, and big data approaches, to build a better understanding of within-city challenges. As a core member of the Global Solutions Group on Territorial Development, her work has recently focused on using spatial analysis to identify priorities for action in lagging regions. She holds a doctorate in applied economics from University of Illinois,

where she worked on models for measuring capitalization of the value of local amenities into housing prices. Her areas of work include urban and regional economics, spatial economic analysis, and spatial econometric applications.

Paula Restrepo Cadavid is a senior urban economist in the Social, Urban, Rural, and Resilience Global Practice of the World Bank, where her work has primarily focused on the Eastern Europe and Central Asia and Latin America and the Caribbean regions. At the World Bank, her work focuses on areas related to urban and territorial development, municipal finance, and housing. She is the lead author of the World Bank's *Cities in Eastern Europe and Central Asia: A Story of Urban Growth and Decline*. She has also led or contributed to investment projects in Albania, Azerbaijan, Colombia, Georgia, Honduras, Kyrgyz Republic, Moldova, Peru, Tajikistan, and Uzbekistan. She holds a master's degree in environmental and development economics from Ecole Polytechnique and a PhD in economics from Ecole de Mines de Paris, where she worked on assessing the welfare effects of slum-upgrading policies. Her areas of research span from urban and regional economics to infrastructure financing and environmental economics.

Souleymane Soumahoro is an economist and consultant in the Development Research Group of the World Bank. His research focuses on the political economy of development, access to infrastructure, and public service delivery. His research has been published in peer-reviewed academic journals such as *Economic Development and Cultural Change* and *Applied Economic Letters*. Before joining the World Bank, he worked as a postdoctoral fellow at the Center for Global Development, a leading development think tank in Washington, DC. Also, he holds a PhD in economics from the University of Oklahoma and a master's degree in international economics from the University of Auvergne Clermont-Ferrand 1 in France.

Abbreviations

AAA	American Automobile Association
AI	Agglomeration Index
BE	business environment
CEDLAS	Center for Distributive, Labor and Social Studies
DENUE	*Directorio Estadístico Nacional de Unidades Económicas* (National Statistical Directory of Economic Units)
DMSP-OLS	Defense Meteorological Satellite Program–Operational Linescan System
EAP	East Asia and Pacific
ECA	Europe and Central Asia
GDP	gross domestic product
GGDC	Groningen Growth and Development Center
GHSL	Global Human Settlement Layer
GIS	Geographic Information System
HCE	human capital externality
IBGE	*Instituto Brasileiro de Geografia e Estatística* (Brazilian Institute of Geography and Statistics)
INEGI	*Instituto Nacional de Estadísticas y Geografía* (National Institute of Statistics and Geography)
IV	instrumental variable
IPUMS	Integrated Public Use Microdata Series
LAC	Latin America and the Caribbean
MCA	multicity agglomeration
MENA	Middle East and North Africa
NTL	nighttime lights
OECD	Organisation for Economic Co-operation and Development
OLS	ordinary least square
PM	particulate matter
PPP	purchasing power parity
R&D	research and development
SA	South Asia
SEDLAC	Socio-Economic Database for Latin America and the Caribbean

SSA	Sub-Saharan Africa
TFP	total factor productivity
VIIRS	Visible Infrared Imaging Radiometer Suite
WAP	working-age population
WBES	World Bank Enterprise Survey
WDI	World Development Indicators
WHO	World Health Organization
WUP	World Urbanization Prospects

Overview

In modern economies, cities can be formidable engines of productivity and economic growth. By bringing people and firms together in close geographic proximity, cities facilitate production, innovation, and trade. Historically, urbanization has accompanied the productive transformation of economies—with the decline in low-productivity agricultural employment and the rise of high-productivity manufacturing and services. Falling transportation costs—by facilitating trade by cities, both with one another and with rural areas—have accelerated this process, further stimulating both urbanization and development.

Today, almost three-quarters of the population of Latin America and the Caribbean (LAC)—or 433 million people—live in the region's 7,197 cities.[1] Some are mega-cities, such as São Paulo and Mexico City, each boasting populations of about 20 million.[2] Others are small settlements in the gray area between urban and rural. Some cities date back to precolonial times (Bogotá, Cuzco, Mexico City). Others were established by Spanish and Portuguese *conquistadores* during colonial times (Asunción, Buenos Aires, São Paulo) or by the newly independent countries in postcolonial times (La Plata). Still others were established a few decades ago (Brasilia, Puerto Ordaz).

The productivity of LAC cities is on par with the world average but lags the world productivity frontier, where LAC policy makers want their cities to be. What accounts for the failure of LAC cities to reach the global frontier? First, although LAC cities benefit from strong positive agglomeration effects associated with skills, they may lack the "enabling environment" needed to fully leverage the wider benefits of agglomeration and mitigate congestion costs. Thus, urban infrastructure management and urban planning may not be adequate to curb the congestion of roads, basic urban services, and land and housing markets associated with the high urban density in most LAC countries. Included in this is inadequate coordination across local governments within fragmented metropolitan areas. Second, a lack of integration among cities within countries is associated with underinvestment in national transport networks, opening wide productivity gaps across cities and undermining the aggregate contribution of cities to national productivity.

The evidence also shows that human capital is a bedrock source of productivity across cities throughout the LAC region, but that the skilled—who form a smaller share of the workforce than in, say, the United States—are also heavily concentrated in the largest cities. This makes it a priority to close the region's shortfall of skills relative to the most developed countries, and to ensure that both small and large cities can be attractive places for the skilled to live and work. Investing in infrastructure, transport, and human capital in cities of all sizes, as well as developing efficient local governance institutions, will thus prove crucial to raising the bar for productivity in the region's cities—and ultimately in the region's countries as well.

The proximity of people and firms in cities can give rise to many benefits. The concentration of individuals, particularly the skilled, can facilitate the exchange of ideas and the sharing of knowledge, boosting innovation and productivity. Firms located in a city enjoy the privilege of having access to a large local market, which may also be well connected to the markets of nearby cities. Access to a larger market can encourage a wider variety of products and services, many of which are inputs into the production of other firms. The proximity of people and firms in cities also creates thick labor markets, which give firms access to larger and more diverse pools of workers, and workers access to a greater number and variety of potential employers, leading to better job matches. The proximity of people and firms also spreads the cost of large-scale investments in transport and infrastructure for basic services over many individuals. Cities thus generate productivity-enhancing agglomeration effects.

But cities also give rise to negative congestion effects. As the number of people and firms within a city grows, so does the demand for land, housing, and labor, raising the costs of living and conducting business. Without additional investments in infrastructure, or improvements in urban policy and management, the city becomes more congested, roads and other public infrastructure more crowded, and crime and grime more prevalent.

All cities are subject to the opposing forces of agglomeration and congestion, but their net outcomes depend, at least in part, on a city's enabling environment for spurring beneficial agglomeration effects and mitigating negative congestion effects. The enabling environment depends, in turn, on the extent and quality of infrastructure provision within cities (such as roads, bridges, and utility and communications networks), on urban planning and management, and on policies that influence the quality of the local business environment, including protection from crime.

Because no city exists in isolation, its productivity is related to that of other cities in the country. Any one city is part of a country's system of cities, where cities are connected by transport and other networks. So policies that affect the productivity of one city will also have repercussions on other cities. The easier the flow of goods, resources, and people across cities, the greater the contribution of cities to national productivity. That is why maximizing the contribution of cities to a country's productivity and growth requires taking the whole system of cities into account.

The Productivity of LAC Cities Is Slightly above Average but below the Global Frontier

To compare LAC cities with those in the rest of the world, an important complication is that countries differ in defining "urban." Overcoming this complication is critical for cross-country comparisons. One crucial contribution of this book is to apply an algorithm (the "cluster algorithm") that allows for a globally consistent definition of urban areas. Rather than define urban areas on the basis of their official administrative boundaries, which often fail to accurately delineate the actual extent of a city, this algorithm identifies cities as spatially contiguous dense clusters of population, whose total population surpasses a well-defined threshold.[3] With this definition, we calculate a variety of country-level urbanization metrics, the most basic of which is a country's urban share (the percent of its population that lives in cities). We also use the individual cities as units of observation in their own right, which allows us to benchmark the productivity of LAC cities against those in the rest of the world.

The story of productivity in LAC cities in relation to the rest of the world has good news and bad. Historically, the joint processes of economic development and urbanization have given rise to a positive association between a country's aggregate productivity (measured by gross domestic product [GDP] per capita) and the share of its population that lives in urban areas (its urban share).[4] Across countries in the world, a 1 percentage point increase in the urban share is associated with a 3.8 percent increase in GDP per capita. Without implying causality, this relationship, shown by the solid line in figure O.1, establishes a country's expected productivity given its urban share. A country falling below the solid line underperforms, given its urban share, and a country above it overperforms.

As it turns out, LAC countries (indicated by the orange, green, and red markers) on average perform as expected given their urban shares. This is true for the region, and for the South America, Central America, and Caribbean subregions. Nonetheless, LAC countries underperform relative to countries in North America and Western Europe (blue markers). The good news, then, is that LAC countries perform as predicted given their urban shares; the bad news is that they are below the global productivity frontier.[5]

A similar conclusion emerges from using city-level productivity measures. Figure O.2 depicts the global relationship between a city's level of economic activity—as proxied by the intensity of the light it emits at night—and its level of population. As it turns out, LAC cities overall perform above the global average—in other words, they are more productive than expected given their populations.[6] This result is driven by South American and Mexican cities (red markers); cities in the rest of the region tend to perform around the global average. Yet, once again, LAC cities fail to reach the global frontier, given by the outer envelope of points in the figure, representing mainly North American and Western European cities (blue markers).

To summarize, LAC cities perform at or above the global average, but they perform below the global frontier. To provide insights into why LAC cities lag the global frontier, we examine the distinctive features of LAC cities relative to others in the world, and the role of

FIGURE O.1 LAC Countries Exhibit Average Productivity Given Their Urbanization Levels

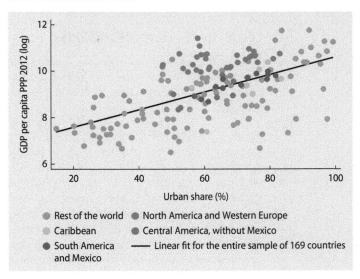

Source: Calculations based on WDI data and cities defined using the cluster algorithm of Dijkstra and Poelman (2014), as applied to Landscan 2012 gridded population data.
Note: GDP per capita is measured in constant international dollars at 2012 PPP exchange rates. It is expressed in natural logs on the vertical axis. GDP = gross domestic product; LAC = Latin America and the Caribbean; PPP = purchasing power parity; WDI = World Development Indicators.

FIGURE O.2 Productivity of LAC Cities Is above Average but Lags the Global Frontier

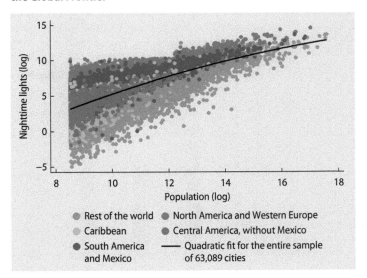

Source: Calculations based on nighttime lights data from the 2015 VIIRS annual composite product (https://ngdc.noaa.gov/eog/viirs/download_dnb_composites.html). Cities are defined using the cluster algorithm of Dijkstra and Poelman (2014), as applied to Landscan 2012 gridded population data.
Note: Nighttime lights on the vertical axis is the sum of nighttime lights luminosity values within a given city. LAC = Latin America and the Caribbean; VIIRS = Visible Infrared Imaging Radiometer Suite.

three critical, proximate determinants of city productivity—form, skill, and access.

Distinctive Features of LAC Cities

Several features distinguish LAC cities from others in the world—and can help in understanding why they perform below the global frontier.

Feature 1. LAC cities are relatively dense. In Bogotá, Colombia, almost 13,500 people occupy each square kilometer of land, while in Lima, Peru, nearly 9,000 people populate each square kilometer. More generally, with an average density of almost 2,400 people per square kilometer across all 7,197 of its cities, the LAC region exhibits urban densities that are well above the world average of just over 1,500. Although density is highest in South American cities, followed by Central American and Caribbean cities, it is high by international standards in all three subregions. Further, 80 percent of LAC cities have a population density above the global median, well above the percentage in regions such as Europe and Central Asia (ECA) and North America (NAC) (figure O.3).[7]

Two factors can contribute to a city's high density. The first is a large population relative to the geographic area. The second is a small

area relative to the population size. In relation to the rest of the world, LAC cities are dense not because their populations are large but because their geographic areas are small, particularly compared with cities in ECA and NAC (figure O.4). Given its potential to generate strong positive agglomeration effects, high density can be a blessing. However, in the absence of an adequate enabling environment to help manage congestion costs and foster these agglomeration effects, this blessing can become a curse—which may help explain why LAC cities lag the global productivity frontier.[8]

Feature 2. Multicity agglomerations are unusually prevalent. The administrative definition of a city can differ quite radically from the "true" urban extent of a city using the cluster algorithm. Indeed, a city as defined in this book can span multiple "cities" as defined from an administrative or jurisdictional viewpoint. We refer to such areas as multicity agglomerations (MCAs).[9] By definition, MCAs span multiple local government jurisdictions. Take Mexico City and Santo Domingo: Mexico City's urban area encompasses 34 municipalities, and Santo Domingo's covers 19 (map O.1).[10]

Of the world's 295 MCAs, 54 are in the LAC region second only to East Asia

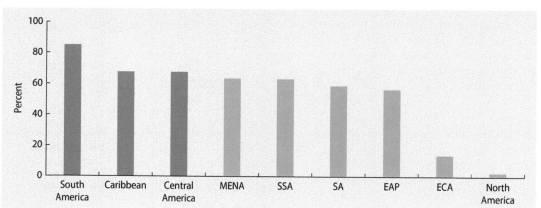

FIGURE O.3   **A High Percentage of LAC Cities Have Population Densities above the Global Median**

Source: Calculations based on an analysis of cities defined using the cluster algorithm of Dijkstra and Poelman (2014), as applied to Landscan 2012 gridded population data.
Note: A city is classified as dense if its mean population density exceeds the global median of 1,180 people per square kilometer. Central America includes Mexico. EAP = East Asia and the Pacific; ECA = Europe and Central Asia; LAC = Latin America and the Caribbean; MENA = Middle East and North Africa; SA = South Asia; SSA = Sub-Saharan Africa.

FIGURE O.4   **LAC Cities Are Dense Because Their Areas Are Small**

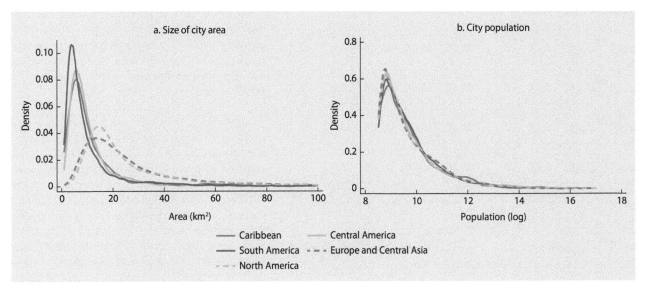

Source: Calculations based on analysis of cities defined using the cluster algorithm of Dijkstra and Poelman (2014), as applied to Landscan 2012 gridded population data.
Note: Panels a and b show, for different regions, the distribution of area (in square kilometers) and population (log), respectively, of cities using an Epanechnikov kernel.
For expositional purposes, the distributions of area are trimmed at 100 square kilometers. Central America includes Mexico. LAC = Latin America and the Caribbean.

MAP O.1   **Multicity Agglomerations in Latin America and the Caribbean Span Multiple Municipalities**

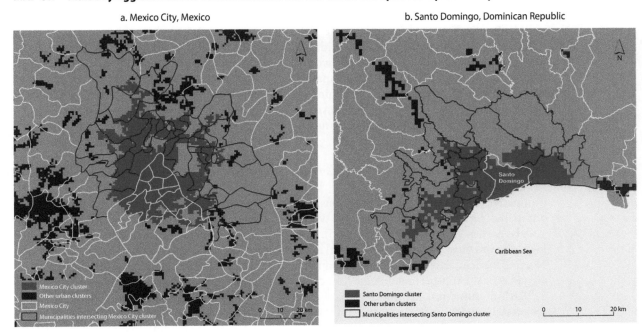

Source: Calculations using Geographic Information Systems software and administrative boundary data from the LAC Geospatial Database (Branson et al. 2016).
Note: In the maps, the red areas correspond to cities as defined using the cluster algorithm of Dijkstra and Poelman (2014), as applied to Landscan 2012 gridded population data.
The yellow lines represent subnational administrative boundaries at the municipality level that belong to a city as officially defined. The dark blue lines represent the boundaries of
municipalities that intersect with the city but that do not belong to the officially defined city. In the case of Mexico City, the officially defined city comprises several municipalities.
LAC = Latin America and the Caribbean.

FIGURE O.5   Productivity Varies Widely across Cities and Countries in Latin America and the Caribbean

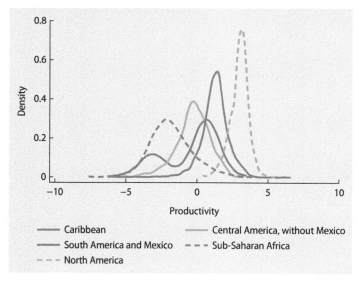

Caribbean

South America and Mexico

North America

Central America, without Mexico

Sub-Saharan Africa

Source: Calculations based on nighttime lights data from the 2015 VIIRS annual composite product (https://ngdc.noaa.gov/eog/viirs/download_dnb_composites.html).
Note: The figure shows density plots of the residuals from a regression at the city level where the dependent variable is the sum of nighttime lights (in logs) and the independent variable is the population (in logs). These residuals measure city-level productivity; cities have been identified by applying the cluster algorithm of Dijkstra and Poelman (2014) to Landscan 2012 gridded population data. VIIRS = Visible Infrared Imaging Radiometer Suite.

and the Pacific (EAP). About 40 percent of the LAC region's urban population resides in MCAs, compared with a third of the world's urban population. Thus, LAC cities may be particularly vulnerable to the shortcomings of MCAs, which arise when their local jurisdictions fail to coordinate governance and the provision of public goods and services.

Feature 3. Within countries, productivity varies widely across cities.   City labor productivity, measured by the (log) intensity of nighttime lights net of population, varies widely across LAC cities (figure O.5). The LAC region's most productive cities rival many North American cities, but the least productive are close to the top-performing African cities.

Within countries, productivity is widely dispersed across cities. In a well-integrated system of cities, the flow of goods, people, and resources across cities closes productivity gaps among cities and maximizes the contribution of the system of cities.

Compare the productivity dispersion in LAC countries with that of high-income countries. For each LAC country, the within-country productivity dispersion is relatively high (figure O.6). So LAC systems of cities are not well integrated and thus not fully productive.[11]

Feature 4. Within countries, the skilled are unusually concentrated in large cities.   Skilled people tend to sort into larger cities (figure O.7).[12,13] This sorting takes place in the United States as well but is stronger in the LAC region. In the United States, a 10 percent increase in a city's population is associated with a 1.2 percent increase in the share of the city's population that is skilled (Behrens and Robert-Nicoud 2015), but with a 2.9 percent increase in the LAC region.[14] This indicates that, compared with the United States, skilled people are relatively more concentrated in a few large cities. This concentration of skills may help to explain, at least partly, the high productivity dispersion across cities in LAC countries.

Feature 5. Inequality in LAC cities is unusually high.   Not only are large LAC cities more skilled but they are also more unequal. On average in the LAC region, a 10 percent increase in city population is associated with a 0.29 percent increase in income inequality, measured by the Gini coefficient.[15] The corresponding increase in the United States is lower (0.12 percent), indicating a stronger tendency toward income inequality in large LAC cities.

Of the greater income inequality in the LAC region's larger cities, 43 percent is due to skills. Put differently, relative to smaller cities, large cities are more unequal because they are more skilled and have a greater share of high-earning individuals.[16] A similar, yet weaker, finding holds for the United States, where skills explain only 25 percent of the association between city population and income inequality.[17]

That city population, skills, and inequality are more strongly associated in the LAC region than in the United States may reflect the LAC region's scarcity of skills. For example, the share of individuals with some higher education in the average LAC country (18 percent) is roughly one-third of that in the United States (59 percent), and returns to higher education are concomitantly higher (104 percent for the average LAC country, and more than twice that in the United States).[18,19] The stronger associations in the LAC region may also reflect a more unequal distribution of amenities and public services—which serve to attract skilled people—across cities in the LAC region than in the United States.

Feature 6. National transport networks remain quite undeveloped. In NAC, Asia Pacific, and Europe, about 40 percent or more of surface freight is shipped by rail, reflecting well-developed and well-used national rail networks. But, in Latin America, rail captures only 22 percent of surface freight, close to the 19 percent captured by rail in Africa (figure O.8).

A low share of freight shipped by rail would not be problematic if national road networks were of high quality. But LAC roads are not, and the paved road density has been rather stagnant in the LAC region for four decades (figure O.9). Although paved road density in South Asia was only slightly above that of the LAC region in the early 1960s, it is now much higher. Although EAP and the Middle East and North Africa (MENA) regions started at virtually the same level as did the LAC region they too are ahead of the LAC region today.

FIGURE O.6   Within-Country Productivity Dispersions Are High in LAC Countries

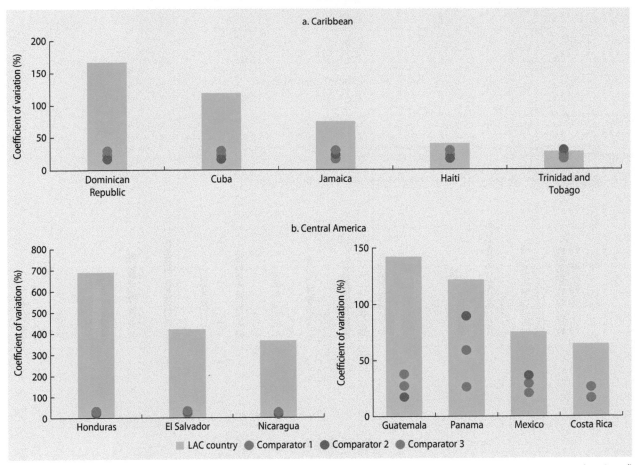

(continued)

FIGURE O.6 Within-country Productivity Dispersions Are High in LAC Countries *(continued)*

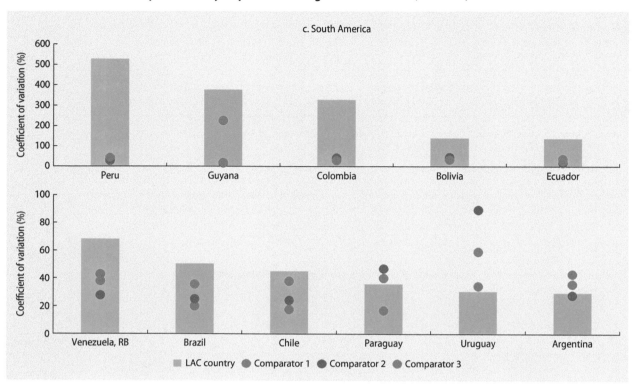

Source: Calculations based on nighttime lights data from the 2015 VIIRS annual composite product (https://ngdc.noaa.gov/eog/viirs/download_dnb_composites.html).
Note: City productivity is measured using the residuals from a regression at the city level where the dependent variable is the sum of nighttime lights (in logs) and the independent variable is the population (in logs). Productivity dispersion across a country's cities is measured by the coefficient of variation (in percent). Comparators for each LAC country are restricted to high-income countries, but with no restrictions on the regions their comparators are drawn from. The methodology for selecting comparators is described in detail in box 2.1 in chapter 2. A full list of comparators for each LAC country is in annex 2A in chapter 2. LAC = Latin America and the Caribbean; VIIRS = Visible Infrared Imaging Radiometer Suite.

FIGURE O.7 More Populous LAC Cities Have Higher Shares of Skilled Labor

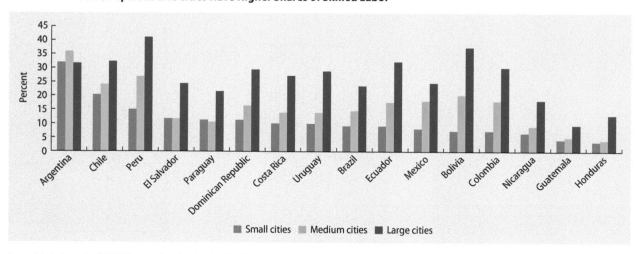

Source: Calculations using SEDLAC for countries other than Brazil and IPUMS International for Brazil.
Note: The figure shows the average percentage of adult population (age 25–64 years) with some higher education, by area size. The area size classification follows country-specific population thresholds, as explained in annex 5A of chapter 5. IPUMS = Integrated Public Use Microdata Series; LAC = Latin America and the Caribbean; SEDLAC = Socio-Economic Database for Latin America and the Caribbean.

The underdevelopment of national transport networks in the LAC region reflects the lack of integration among cities in LAC countries. Together with the unusually high concentration of skills in large cities, this underdevelopment may contribute to the wide dispersion of productivity across cities in LAC countries.[20]

To summarize, LAC cities have distinctive features. They are relatively dense, perhaps exacerbating congestion forces given prevailing infrastructure and policies. MCAs, with their potential coordination and governance problems, are unusually prevalent. Skilled human capital is highly concentrated in large cities. Productivity dispersions across cities in LAC countries are very high, indicating that their systems of cities are not efficient. Such dispersions may be linked to the underdevelopment of national transport networks. The spatial concentration of skills also means that two issues—a deficit of skills in small cities, and inequality in large cities—may be particularly acute in the LAC region. These distinctive features of LAC cities help explain why these cities lag the global productivity frontier. To further expand our understanding of this question, we turn to empirical evidence on the proximate determinants of city productivity in the LAC region.

FIGURE O.8   Rail Is Not Prevalent in Latin America

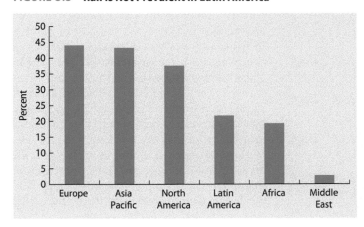

Source: International Transport Forum 2017.
Note: The figure shows the percentage of goods transported by rail (as opposed to road).

FIGURE O.9   Paved Road Density Has Been Stagnant in Latin America and the Caribbean

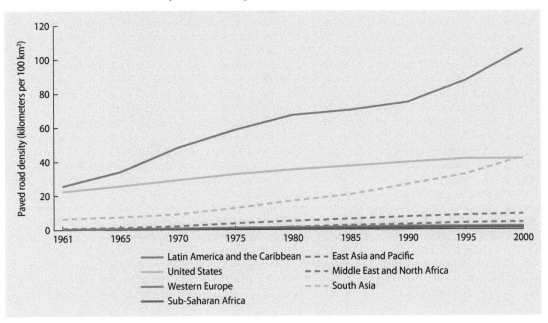

Source: Calculations based on data from the World Development Indicators.

The Role of Form, Skill, and Access in the Productivity of LAC Cities

A city may be more productive than others because of sorting, as skilled and talented people gravitate toward it. But its greater productivity can also be due to agglomeration effects, which operate through various mechanisms enabled by the proximity of firms and individuals. For example, the greater number of firms and workers that characterize cities can generate better matches between them. The greater number of customers and firms can support a large and diversified array of suppliers of final and intermediate goods and services, an effect facilitated by connections to other cities and the markets they provide. It can also spread the cost of large-scale investments in transport and infrastructure that underlie the supply of basic services. And the interaction of workers within and across

firms can contribute to knowledge spillovers and allow all workers to learn from the most skilled ones.

As a result of these mechanisms, agglomeration effects are associated with city form, skill, and access (box O.1). Form refers to the size and configuration of a city, skill to how skilled individuals contribute to the productivity of others, and access to a city's connectedness to other cities in the country through the transportation network. Figure O.10 shows that, if we look at form alone (measured by population density), LAC cities experience positive agglomeration effects.[21] Controlling for features of a city's physical geography, a 1 percent increase in population density is associated with a 0.049 percent increase in productivity (and nominal wages).[22] This "unconditional" estimate is close to that for the United States (0.046 percent), using a comparable regression specification, but far

---

BOX O.1   Form, Skill, and Access

As the net outcome of the tussle between agglomeration and congestion forces, a city's productivity depends on form, skill, and access.

Form refers to the size and configuration of a city. A city's size (usually measured by population or density) influences the likelihood of interactions among individuals and firms. These interactions can stimulate a wide array of positive, productivity-enhancing agglomeration effects. But they can also generate negative congestion effects, such as increased crime and a heightened probability of spreading communicable diseases. In the absence of offsetting investments and policies, density also brings other negative congestion effects as markets and infrastructure become crowded.

A city's configuration, meanwhile, encompasses several dimensions. The first dimension is whether a city is, in fact, a broader metropolitan area or multicity agglomeration. In an agglomeration, the boundaries between one administratively defined "city" and another blur to such an extent that it becomes difficult to tell where one ends and the other begins. A distinctive aspect of multicity

agglomerations is the governance challenges that they face in coordinating the provision of infrastructure and basic services in a space fragmented by local government administrative boundaries.

The second dimension is geometric shape. For example, in a perfectly circular city, the average distance between two locations is lower than in an elongated city of the same area. All else being equal, therefore, interactions take place more easily in a circular city than in an elongated city.

The third dimension of form is internal structure, which depends on a city's road network among other things. For example, mobility is easier in cities with well-planned road networks that follow a regular pattern, such as a grid, than in cities with more haphazard networks.

The fourth dimension is land use. For example, building restrictions may favor sprawl, which in turn can increase the journey to work as well as other travel times. Similarly, although land zoning is necessary—for example, to keep a chemical plant from locating in a residential area—overly stringent zoning requirements may create unnecessary

(continued)

Form, Skill, and Access *(continued)*

distance between the places where people live and the places where they work.

Skill refers to a city's aggregate stock of human capital, or aggregate skill. When individuals choose where to live in a country, they compare locations on the basis of such attributes as wages, job opportunities, housing values, natural amenities, manmade amenities—including, for example, cultural attractions—and the demographic composition of the population. Given their preferences and personal characteristics (such as age, education, and place of birth)—they thus sort into different cities. A city that attracts more skilled individuals could be more productive simply because its residents are on average more productive—yet this is not the meaning of "skill" as it relates to city productivity.

Instead, skill refers here to the productivity contribution of skilled individuals above and beyond their own productivities. This contribution arises because a person's human capital benefits not only her but others in the city as well. For example, workers in a city with a higher share of college-educated individuals will likely be more productive because they will have greater opportunity to interact with such individuals and learn from them, regardless of their own skill level.

Access refers to a city's connectedness to other cities through the transportation network.[a] When a city is well connected to others, transporting people or goods to and from other cities is not costly. In such a city, firms have access to markets that extend beyond that of the city itself. By promoting trade with other cities both domestically and internationally, this allows firms in a city to expand, become more specialized, and benefit from economies of scale. And, when firms and workers become freer to move between cities, they flock to more productive cities. In a system of well-connected cities, the dispersion of productivity across cities is minimized, and cities maximize their overall contribution to national productivity.

a. In this book, we focus mainly on access to other cities and areas in the same country. Hence, the results in both figures O.10 and O.11 are based on a measure of *domestic* market access. Some discussion of the importance of international market access through ports and airports, as well as the road and rail networks that connect cities to them, is contained in chapter 4.

weaker than that for China (0.192 percent) or India (0.076 percent).[23]

However, both skill and access are positively correlated with population density because more densely populated cities tend to have higher average levels of human capital and better access to other cities' markets through transportation networks. Figure O.10 shows "conditional" estimates of agglomeration effects. When we control for skill (measured by average years of schooling), the estimated agglomeration effect shrinks to 0.013 percent. When we control for access (measured by a market access index) as well as skill, it becomes almost zero.[24]

Comparing "conditional" agglomeration effects for LAC and other regions is difficult because conditional estimates for other regions do not control for both skill and market access. Yet, those that control for skill (measured by percent of the working-age population with higher education), without controlling for access, paint a similar picture because the estimated agglomeration effect

FIGURE O.10 **Unconditional and Conditional Effects of Density on Productivity Provide Insights into the Mechanisms for Agglomeration Effects**

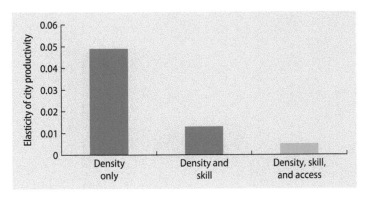

Source: Quintero and Roberts 2017.
Note: The figure shows the sensitivity (elasticity) of city productivity to population density for different regression specifications in which cities from 16 LAC countries are pooled. Productivity is measured as (log) city average nominal wage, controlling for worker characteristics. The first bar ("Density only") shows the effect of population density on city productivity without controlling for skill and access; the second bar ("Density and skill") the effect of population density on city productivity when controlling for skill, but not access; the third bar ("Density, skill, and access") the effect of population density on city productivity when controlling for both skill and access. Skill is measured as log average years of schooling. All three regression specifications control for features of a city's physical geography (mean air temperature, terrain ruggedness, and total precipitation) and include country fixed effects. The orange bar represents coefficients that are not significantly different from zero at the 10 percent level.

for LAC (0.023 percent) is similar to that of the United States (0.024 percent), but lower than that for China (0.112 percent) or India (0.052 percent). The LAC effect is, however, less precisely estimated than that for China, India, or the United States.[25]

This analysis indicates that agglomeration effects in the LAC region operate mainly through skill (as workers in a city learn from skilled workers), and much less through access (as cities gain access to the markets of other cities). By contrast, other positive agglomeration effects in LAC cities that might be associated with population density seem to be largely absent—such as those that might arise from better job matches, the growth of a large and local diversified array of specialized suppliers, spreading costs of large investments in infrastructure and transport, and more general knowledge spillovers beyond those associated with skilled workers.

To gain insight into the relative importance of form, skill, and access, figure O.11 shows the sensitivity of productivity to form (density), skill, and access when all three are included in the same regression specification (along with features of a city's physical geography).

Form. Holding skill and access constant, density has, at best, no impact on productivity; at worst, it has a negative impact. An increase in density is associated with almost no change in city productivity. The response of productivity to density varies across countries, but its effect is significantly positive only for Brazil, Dominican Republic, Ecuador, and Peru. For Chile and Nicaragua, the effect of density on productivity is significant but negative (figure O.12).

Other findings are also consistent with the notion that, under current infrastructure and

FIGURE O.11   **The Effects of Form, Skill, and Access on Productivity**

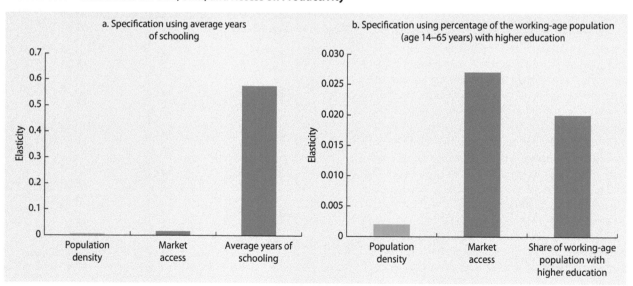

Source: Quintero and Roberts 2017.
Note: The figure shows the sensitivity (elasticity) of city productivity to density, skill, and access when all three are included in the same regression specification in which cities from 16 LAC countries are pooled. Productivity is measured as the (log) city average nominal wage, controlling for worker characteristics. Density, market access, and average years of schooling are in logs. For example, an increase in average years of schooling equal to 1 percent raises productivity (and thus wages) by 0.57 percent. The regression specification controls for features of a city's physical geography (mean air temperature, terrain ruggedness, and total precipitation) and also includes country fixed effects. Orange represents coefficients that are not significantly different from zero at the 10 percent level. Panel a shows coefficients using average years of schooling as a measure of aggregate skill; in panel b, aggregate skill is measured through the percentage of the working-age population with higher education.

FIGURE O.12   **In Most Countries, a City's Population Density Does Not Have a Positive Significant Effect on Its Productivity**

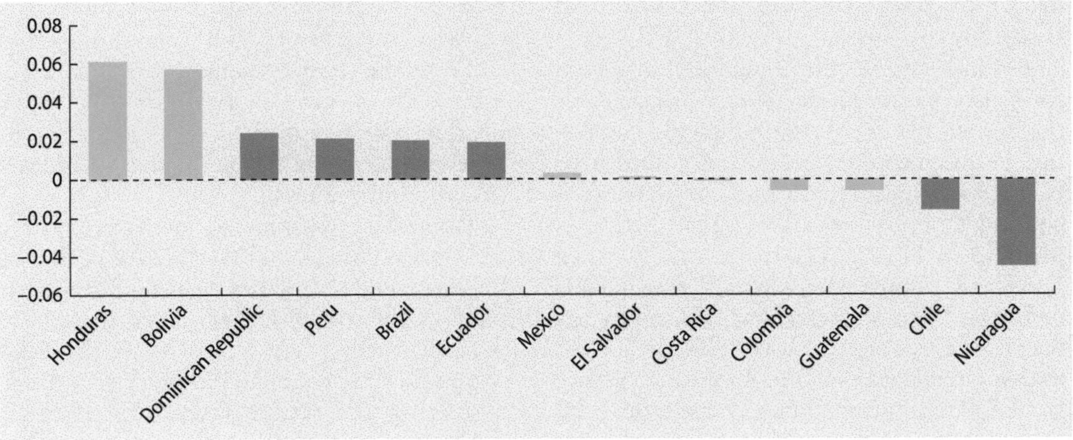

Source: Quintero and Roberts 2017, background paper for this book.
Note: The figure show the estimated elasticities to population density for each country derived from regressing, in country-level regressions, estimates of city productivity (measured in natural logs) on the following variables, expressed in natural logs: population density, average years of schooling, market access, mean air temperature, terrain ruggedness, and total precipitation. Productivity is measured as (log) city average nominal wage, controlling for worker characteristics. The orange bars represent coefficients that are not significantly different from zero at the 10 percent level. This figure excludes Argentina, Panama, and Uruguay because these countries lack a sufficient number of subnational locations (that is, observations for the regressions) to permit reliable estimation.

policy conditions, density does not contribute to city productivity in the LAC region. A study for this book finds that, opposite to what is found for the rest of the world, the LAC region's labor productivity is lower in large cities than in its smaller cities, after controlling for elements of a city's business environment and firm characteristics such as industry, size and ownership structure, age, and whether the firm is an exporter (Reyes, Roberts, and Xu 2017).[26] And, when considering all countries in the world, there is either no association, or a negative one, between national levels of productivity, measured by GDP per capita, and density.[27]

As mentioned above, the weak (or even negative) contribution of density to city productivity in the LAC region suggests the absence of positive agglomeration effects beyond those associated with skill and access. Because the region has relatively dense cities, they may be suffering from negative congestion effects, which more than offset positive agglomeration benefits. Congestion, in turn, may be aggravated by

an inadequate enabling environment associated with a lack of infrastructure investment, poor planning, and more generally poor urban management in cities. For example, even if they have the same density, cities with fewer vehicles on the road (perhaps because of better public transportation) or with better traffic management systems will be less congested. Indeed, four LAC cities—Buenos Aires, Mexico City, Rio de Janeiro, and Santiago de Chile—are among the world's most congested, and Mexico City tops the chart.[28]

Congestion effects in the form of crime might also be aggravated by there being little basic protection from theft, kidnapping, and other criminal activity. Across the world, labor productivity and firm total factor productivity (TFP) are lower in cities with higher private security costs, perhaps because firms must pay for private security to fill the void left by local police (Reyes, Roberts, and Xu 2017). A case study of Colombia for this book finds that high levels of crime and violence have large, negative, and statistically significant effects on firm TFP, with large productivity losses associated with the presence of paramilitary and drug-trafficking groups in a city (Balat and Casas 2017).

Beyond density, other dimensions of a city's form also bear on productivity. Most salient is the presence of MCAs. Although the association between country productivity (measured by log GDP per capita) and the share of a country's population that lives in MCAs is positive in North American and Western European countries, it is virtually zero in LAC countries. This suggests that LAC countries may not handle effectively the difficult coordination challenges that MCAs pose. Evidence from 73 large metropolitan areas in the LAC region indicates that, although half of them have a metropolitan-level governance body, the mere existence of such a body does not yield productivity gains, pointing to the need for better institutional arrangements.

Lower productivity is also a feature of LAC cities with a long irregular shape (as opposed, say, to "round" cities). And it is a feature of cities where segments of the street network are poorly connected (due, say, to dead ends, circular streets, and few street intersections).

Skill. In the productivity race between density, skill, and access, skill emerges as the clear winner. Holding density and access constant, a 1 percent increase in skill (measured as average years of schooling) is associated with a 0.57 percent increase in city productivity, much higher than the associated increase for density or access (figure O.11, panel a). While the contribution of skill to productivity varies across countries, it is significantly different from zero[29] and positive for all of them, which is not the case for density or access.

To understand the responsiveness of productivity to skill, note that, when a LAC worker acquires an additional year of schooling, his or her salary rises by 8.9 percent on average;[30] when a city's average years of schooling rises by one year, salaries in the city rise by 9.2 percent on average. This means that, if all people within a city were to acquire an extra year of education, this would

(approximately) raise their salaries by a remarkable 20 percent, coming in equal parts from own and aggregate human capital.

Returns are not as high when skill is measured by the share of higher education graduates in a city's population, with productivity rising by 2 percent for every 1 percentage point rise in share of graduates (figure O.11, panel b).

Regardless of the metric, returns to skill in cities are relatively high in the LAC region by international standards. Although in other parts of the world they are equal to 50–100 percent of the private returns, in the LAC region they are equal to 100 percent or more, reflecting the region's scarcity of skills (Duranton 2014).

Although returns to skill in cities are positive for all LAC countries, they vary across countries depending on average skill in the average city. The relationship is U-shaped, indicating that, when a country's cities have a low average skill level, returns fall as average skill rises yet increase after the cities reach a critical skill level (figure O.13).

Returns to city skill are also U-shaped for an individual's own level of education (figure O.14), indicating that, as an individual's skill rises, the return she or he enjoys from city skill first falls and then rises. This pattern likely reflects the interplay between the two sources of social returns to human capital: complementarities and human capital externalities. Complementarities arise when skilled workers in a firm raise the productivity of other workers (usually unskilled ones) and are paid for it. For example, skilled workers in a firm may streamline the production process and thus enhance the productivity of the firm's unskilled workers. Complementarities also arise when the greater presence of skilled individuals in a city raises demand for unskilled workers (who work at restaurants and drive cabs, for example). In contrast, human capital externalities arise when skilled workers in a firm raise the productivity of workers, perhaps in other firms, but are not paid for it. For example, skilled workers may exchange knowledge and ideas with workers from

FIGURE O.13   **Across Countries, Returns to Skill Are U-Shaped in Average City Skill**

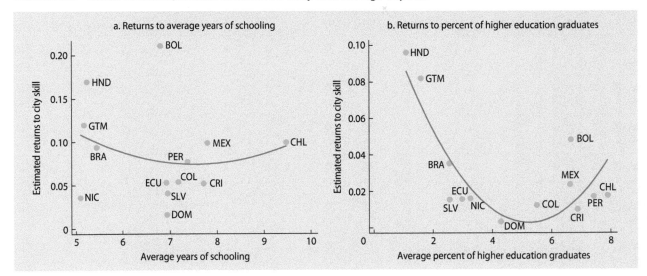

Source: Calculations using SEDLAC for countries other than Brazil and IPUMS International for Brazil.
Sample covers 2000–2014.
Note: The vertical axis shows, for each country, the estimated returns to city skill. The horizontal axis shows, for each country, the average of the corresponding variable; the average is calculated over the country's cities. Average years of schooling, and percent of higher education graduates, correspond to individuals age 14–65 years. Returns can be expressed in percent if multiplied by 100. To obtain these returns, for each country we regress city-level productivity on the corresponding measure of city skill. These regressions control for area density, market access, air temperature, terrain ruggedness, and precipitation. City-level productivities are estimated by regressing, for each country, log wages on individual-level characteristics (age, age squared, years of schooling, gender, and marital status) and year fixed effects. We do not run these regressions for Argentina, Panama, and Uruguay because of their low number of cities. Coefficients from the quadratic specification in panel b are significantly different from zero. Coefficients from the quadratic specification in panel a are not significantly different from zero. IPUMS = Integrated Public Use Microdata Series; SEDLAC = Socio-Economic Database for Latin America and the Caribbean. For a list of country abbreviations, see annex 2A.

other firms, either in formal settings such as conferences and public presentations or in informal settings such as school meetings, civic associations, or neighborhood interactions.

In general, an increase in city skill will raise salaries for unskilled workers because of both complementarities and human capital externalities, yet it will have two opposing effects on the salaries of skilled individuals: a negative effect due to greater relative supply of skilled individuals, and a positive effect due to human capital externalities. So an increase in city skill that leads to higher salaries *for skilled workers* can be regarded as evidence of human capital externalities.

The U-shaped pattern in figure O.14, panel a, provides evidence of human capital externalities. The positive return to the share of higher education graduates among individuals with complete higher education suggests the existence of human capital externalities.

Meanwhile, the least educated individuals enjoy the highest returns to the share of college graduates because, in addition to human capital externalities, they may benefit from complementarities as well.

The U-shaped pattern in figure O.14, panel b, likely reflects a different balance of complementarities and human capital externalities. Because average years of schooling is about seven years (close to where returns reach a minimum in the figure) for the average LAC city, the average worker in this city is unskilled. Thus, his or her impact on the productivity of others is more likely to come from complementarities than from externalities. Additional schooling for the average worker may hurt individuals with the least amount of schooling, with whom he or she competes. However, it may benefit individuals with more schooling, by allowing them, for example, to specialize in more complex tasks and leave other tasks to the average worker.

FIGURE O.14 **Individual Returns to Skill Fall and Then Rise with Own Education**

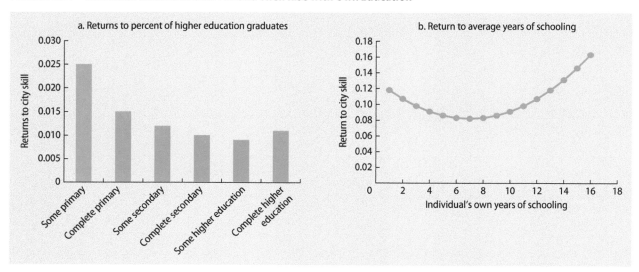

Source: Calculations using SEDLAC for countries other than Brazil and IPUMS International for Brazil. Sample is the same as that used by Quintero and Roberts (2017), covering 2000–14.
Note: To construct panel a, we pool data from all countries and regress log wages on individual characteristics (age, age squared, indicators of educational attainment, gender, and marital status) interacted with country dummies, city-level characteristics (density, share of college graduates, market access, air temperature, terrain ruggedness, and precipitation), country-year fixed effects, and the interaction between indicators of individual educational attainment and the city share of college graduates. Individuals with complete primary (secondary) have not started secondary (higher) education. To construct panel b, we pool data from all countries and regress log wages on individual characteristics (age, age squared, years of schooling, years of schooling squared, gender, and marital status) interacted with country dummies, city-level characteristics (density, average years of schooling, market access, air temperature, terrain ruggedness, and precipitation), country-year fixed effects, the interaction between own years of schooling and average years of schooling, and the interaction between own years of schooling squared and average years of schooling. All relevant coefficients for these panels are significantly different from zero.
IPUMS = Integrated Public Use Microdata Series; SEDLAC = Socio-Economic Database for Latin America and the Caribbean.

Access. Access to the markets of other cities in the same country through transportation networks has a statistically significant association with city productivity. Holding density and skill constant, a 1 percent increase in access is associated with a 0.015–0.020 percent increase in productivity, well below the increase associated with skill but above the increase associated with density. The responsiveness of productivity to access varies among countries and is significantly different from zero in 6 out of 13 countries (figure O.15).

Multiple factors may explain the low impact of access on the productivity of LAC cities. First, our estimate of access impact may be biased downward. This may be the case, for example, if transport investments have targeted cities in lagging regions,

with low economic potential. Indeed, a case study of Mexico for this book finds a stronger effect of market access on city productivity when adopting an estimation strategy that controls for this potential bias (Blankespoor et al. 2017).[31] It also finds that Mexico's road investment in recent decades was associated with local job growth and output, and with increasing specialization among manufacturing firms. In other words, market access holds the promise of raising city productivity.

Second, even if cities have access to other cities through the transportation network, using the network may be costly in money (due, say, to high toll prices, or to a noncompetitive transportation sector that limits supply and raises prices) or in difficulty (due, for example, to low road safety or to frequent traffic disruptions created by protests).

FIGURE O.15   **Market Access Is Associated with City Productivity in Some Countries**

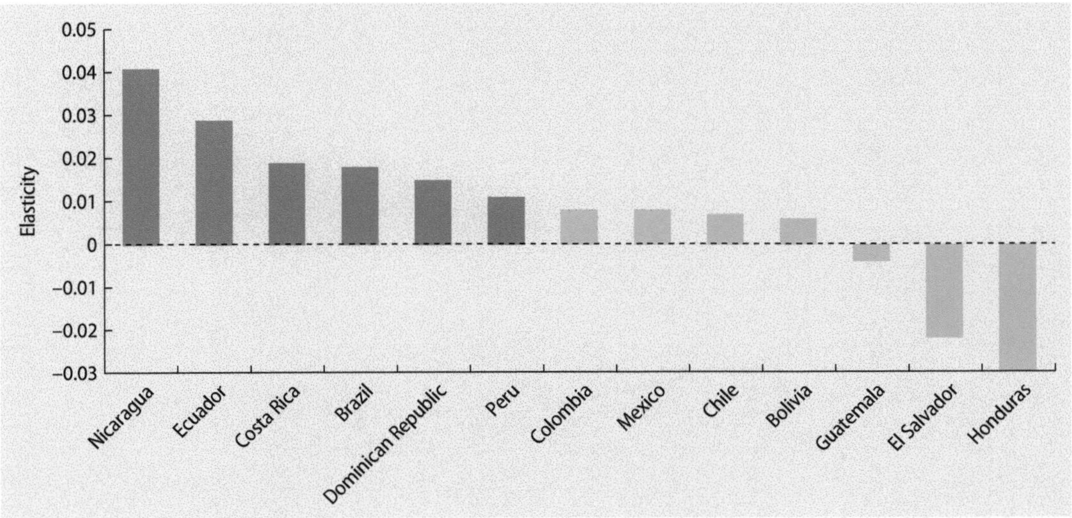

Source: Quintero and Roberts 2017.
Note: Figures show the estimated elasticities to market access for each country derived from regressing—in country-level regressions—estimated city productivity (measured in natural logs) on the following variables, measured in natural logs: population density, average years of schooling, market access, mean air temperature, terrain ruggedness, and total precipitation. Productivity is measured as (log) city average nominal wage, controlling for worker characteristics. The orange bars represent coefficients not significant at the 10 percent level. This figure excludes Argentina, Panama, and Uruguay because these countries lack a sufficient number of cities (that is, observations for the regressions) to permit reliable estimation.

Access holds the promise of raising the productivity not only of individual cities but also of the whole system of cities. Indeed, improvements in national transport networks can help create a more integrated system of cities—with lower productivity dispersion across cities and with a higher contribution to national productivity. Evidence from countries throughout the world shows that the within-country productivity dispersion across cities is lower in countries with higher road density (figure O.16).

To summarize, agglomeration effects driven by skill—and, to much less extent, by access—are strong in LAC cities. Skill, which has a positive effect in all countries, operates through complementarity between skilled and unskilled workers, and through human capital externalities, mostly from skilled workers. Market access has a small estimated positive impact, driven by only some of the countries, although its estimated effect may be biased. These results suggest that other types of agglomeration effects associated with population density are largely absent in LAC cities, which may not have the necessary enabling environment. For example, current levels of infrastructure, urban management practices, and transportation policies may not adequately support LAC cities' relatively high densities, resulting in congestion forces that overwhelm positive agglomeration effects. Institutional weaknesses that limit coordination across local governments in metropolitan areas may also dampen agglomeration effects. And the high within-country productivity dispersion indicates that LAC city systems are not efficient and do not maximize their contribution to national productivity, likely because of poor intercity connectivity through the transportation network.

FIGURE O.16   Countries with Better Road Coverage Have More Efficient Systems of Cities

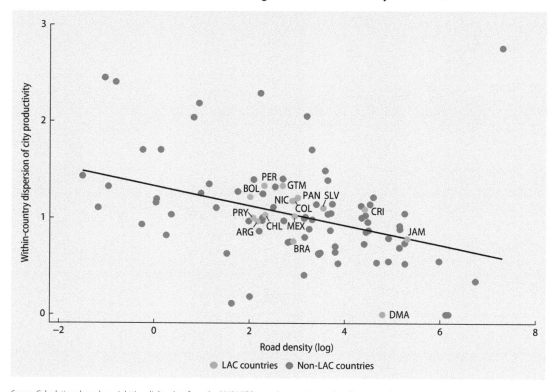

Source: Calculations based on nighttime lights data from the 2015 VIIRS annual composite product (https://ngdc.noaa.gov/eog/viirs/download_dnb
_composites.html) and road density data from the World Bank's World Development Indicators database (http://data.worldbank.org/data-catalog
/world-development-indicators).
Note: Productivity is measured using the residuals from a regression at the city level where the dependent variable is the sum of nighttime lights (in logs)
and the independent variable is the population (in logs). Productivity dispersion across a country's cities is measured by the interquartile range of the
distribution of productivity. Road density is the ratio of the length of the country's total road network to the country's land area and is measured in
kilometers per 100 km² of land area. VIIRS = Visible Infrared Imaging Radiometer Suite. For a list of country abbreviations, see annex 2A.

What These Findings Might Mean for Policy

Although this book is intended primarily as a research piece, its rich results can provide food for thought for policy makers. As with any piece of applied research that makes use of diverse data sets and a variety of methods, extracting this food for thought is not necessarily straightforward. As might be expected, not all results are consistent across the different methods and data sets. Even when methods and data are consistent, not all results apply to all countries. In stepping back and viewing the body of research presented in this book as a totality, several policy-relevant insights emerge.

That LAC cities lag the world's productivity frontier might be due not only to market failures, but also to policy failures.[32] For example, although LAC cities benefit from positive agglomeration effects, these effects are mainly associated with city skill—with complementarities between skilled and unskilled workers, as well as with spillovers of knowledge from skilled workers. By contrast, LAC cities largely lack other positive agglomeration effects—such as those that might arise from good job matches, a large and diversified array of local suppliers of intermediate inputs, the cost-sharing of large-scale infrastructure and transport, and other knowledge spillovers. Policy makers may thus need to improve the enabling environment for these broader agglomeration effects. Improvements may include carefully planned infrastructure and public services to mitigate the congestion created by current density. They may also include stronger coordination among municipalities in large metropolitan areas or MCAs, as well as effective policies for deterring crime and improving security.

LAC systems of cities do not seem to operate efficiently. Within countries, cities seem to be poorly integrated, and resources do not seem to flow to their most productive uses. Skilled people are strongly concentrated in the largest cities—even more than in the United States. The concentration is in part due to a relative shortage of skilled people at the national level, which makes investing in human capital across the board a priority. But it may also be due to an unequal distribution of basic services across areas that disproportionately favors large cities. Although improving this distribution would help in principle, great care must be exercised in the design of relevant programs aiming to do so—to make sure that gains for one city do not merely come at the expense of others.[33]

The inefficiency of city systems also appears related to the underdevelopment of national transport networks and to barriers to mobility across cities. Expanding transportation networks, and lowering the pecuniary and nonpecuniary costs of their use, would in principle raise cities' productivity. Eliminating obstacles that might constrain people from moving to the cities where they would be most productive might also help. For example, a city's inelastic housing supply can mean that, as the city grows, housing prices rise rapidly but the housing stock does not, which limits people's ability to move to the city even if they would be more productive there than in other places. Similarly, a city's high crime rates might discourage people from moving to that city, even if they would be more productive there.[34]

Whereas almost all skilled individuals in the region live in cities, many unskilled individuals do not. Going forward, any additional urbanization that LAC may experience will most likely be driven by the migration of the unskilled to cities. Because migration will increase the population (and probably density) of cities, it may also increase their congestion. It is all the more critical, then, for cities to create an enabling environment for strong agglomeration effects.

At the same time, unskilled populations in cities mostly work in low-productivity, often local, services such as retail, hotels, and restaurants.[35] Under prevailing conditions, further urbanization of unskilled workers may just continue shifting workers from agriculture and manufacturing into low-productivity sectors. A better enabling environment for agglomeration effects, which operate more strongly for the formal sector, and for tradable goods and services may reduce that effect.[36] To be productive, cities also need the enabling environment of sound macroeconomic policies and efficient markets for goods and services, which are critical to the existence of productive firms, good jobs, and high national productivity. Without this wider enabling environment, LAC cities are not likely to reach the world's productivity frontier.

Cities thus are lenses to consider a whole host of policies, including education, infrastructure, transportation, and urban planning. Cities are the immediate context in which people live and work. And, because almost three-quarters of the LAC population live and work in this context, raising the bar for the productivity of LAC cities is crucial. Although this book cannot provide all the policy answers, we hope that, by taking a stride forward in our knowledge of the determinants of productivity in LAC cities, the book can raise the bar for productive cities in the region.

Annex OA: Productivity Measures Used in the Book to Assess LAC Cities

- Per capita GDP at the national level proxies average labor productivity at the national level and is relevant to the aggregate contribution of urbanization and cities to national productivity.

- Nighttime lights (NTL) at the city level measures output at the city level. Because city-level GDP is typically not available, researchers have used the intensity of an area's NTL as a proxy for its level of economic activity.[37]
- NTL net of (log) population at the city level measures average labor productivity at the city level.
- Average nominal wages at the city level is a commonly used measure of a worker's productivity in the urban economics literature, especially in literature that estimates the strength of agglomeration economies (for example, see Duranton 2016 and Chauvin et al. 2017). All other things equal, a city that pays a higher average nominal wage can be considered to have a higher average level of labor productivity.
- Average nominal wages net of individual worker characteristics at the city level measures a city's labor productivity, having controlled for differences in the composition of its workforce. If workers with the same observable characteristics (such as age, education, marital status, and gender) who live in different cities within a country earn different wages, it must be because their cities have different productivity levels.[38]
- TFP at the firm (establishment) level captures firm productivity, net of the capital, labor, and intermediate inputs used in the production process.

Annex 0B: The Need for Policy

Cities represent potential engines of productivity and growth. But, if cities are left to markets alone, this potential cannot be realized—for several reasons.

Externalities arise when a decision by an economic agent, such as a worker or firm, has consequences for other agents, yet the agent's decision does not take such consequences into account. In these cases, what is best for the individual is not best for society as a whole. Externalities are pervasive in cities. Some of these are positive, whereas many

others are negative. Aggregate skill, for example, is subject to positive externalities. Although many workers in a city gain when aggregate skill rises, any one worker regards his or her contribution to the aggregate skill level as negligible. Thus, when deciding whether to acquire more skill, individuals do not consider the benefit of their actions for the whole city and are thus less likely to acquire additional skill. As a result, aggregate skill in the city is below the socially optimal level. Meanwhile, traffic congestion and pollution externalities represent classic textbook cases of congestion effects that are negative externalities.

Cities are also notorious for their *public good* problems. Cities typically contain infrastructure (such as bridges and roads) and public spaces (such as parks and town squares) that can be enjoyed by many individuals at once, without an easy mechanism to exclude users. No individual is willing to pay for public goods because all have an incentive to free ride by letting others pay. As a result, no private firm is willing to provide public goods.

Cities also suffer from *coordination failures*. Within a city, individual firms and workers may fail to coordinate. For example, although all individuals may desire clean air, which could be more easily accomplished if more of them used public transportation rather than driving their own vehicles, many individuals may find it more convenient to drive. Given the practical difficulties of coordinating among themselves, individuals may end up driving, thus raising pollution above the socially optimal level. Similarly, many firms might benefit from moving to a given location within the city if a sufficiently large group of them moves there, yet no individual firm might gain from moving alone. In the absence of a mechanism to coordinate their actions, firms might remain where they are, and might all be worse off.

Cities may fail to coordinate as well. The cities of an MCA can fail to coordinate, as discussed in the main text. More broadly, the cities in a system can fail to coordinate. They may not have incentives to invest in human capital when workers are mobile across cities, because they may not reap the return to their investment if the workers move. And, if a public transit link benefits two cities, neither city has an incentive to invest in the link because the other city will benefit as well.

More broadly, systems of cities can suffer from *barriers to mobility* that raise the cost of moving resources across cities. Whereas some of these barriers can be natural (a mountain range), others arise from policy regulations (overly restrictive building and planning regulations), or from coordination failures among cities (the two cities that could benefit from a connecting transport link).

Such market failures justify policy intervention, both for cities and for systems of cities.

Notes

1. These figures are based on the globally consistent definition of urban areas that we introduce in chapter 1. They differ from corresponding figures based on official national definitions of urban areas, which, as discussed in detail in chapter 1, vary widely not only across countries within LAC but also across countries globally. On the basis of national definitions of urban areas, the share of the LAC region's total population living in cities in 2016 was 80.1 percent.
2. A mega-city is generally defined as a city that has a population in excess of 10 million.
3. The algorithm that we use is from Dijkstra and Poelman (2014). In total, we identify almost 64,000 urban areas globally, of which just under 7,200 belong to LAC. For ease of exposition, we refer to urban areas as "cities" throughout this overview, even though the smaller and less densely populated urban areas may perhaps be more aptly referred to as "towns." To be classified as an urban area, a cluster must have a minimum density of 300 people per square km, and the cluster's total population must be at least 5,000.
4. Multiple measures of productivity are used in this book. See annex OA for a list of such measures.
5. The concept of a global productivity frontier, as presented here, is a purely empirical one in which the frontier is implicitly defined by the set of countries that exhibit the highest levels of GDP per capita at given levels of urbanization. Similar comments apply to figure O.2, where the frontier is defined by the set of cities that exhibit the highest levels of economic activity at given levels of population.
6. This statement is based on the average performance of LAC cities—so LAC cities, on average, exhibit higher output than we would expect based on their populations. However, as also shown in figure O.2, LAC cities show considerable variation around the average, with some exhibiting levels of output much lower than we would expect based on their populations. We discuss the dispersion of productivity levels across LAC cities later in the overview.
7. Argentina, Barbados, and Grenada provide the most notable exceptions to the finding that LAC countries have unusually dense cities. Antigua and Barbuda, the Bahamas, Guyana, Jamaica, and St. Kitts and Nevis all have a roughly 50:50 split between dense and not dense cities.
8. Just as important as a city's average density from the perspective of fostering positive agglomeration effects and mitigating congestion is likely to be how that density is organized. This is discussed more in chapter 6.
9. In this book, MCAs are defined as urban areas identified by the cluster algorithm that encompass two or more cities as given by countries' own definitions. Each component city must have at least 100,000 people. Nevertheless, as discussed in chapter 2, our main regression results relating national productivity and the share of population in MCAs also hold when allowing for smaller component cities.
10. In the case of Mexico City, several of the municipalities in the officially defined city (shown in map O.1 by the yellow lines) only overlap partially with its "true" urban extent.
11. Within-country productivity dispersion does not necessarily indicate inefficiency in the system of cities; it could also indicate a disparity in the presence of amenities. For example, some individuals may choose to live and work in a city where they do not maximize productivity or wages simply because the city is close to the beach. In these cases, productivity in the country is not maximized, yet welfare is. However, assuming that the disparity in amenities accounts for a similar fraction of

productivity dispersion in LAC countries and their comparators, we can view the high productivity dispersion within LAC countries (relative to their comparators) as indicative of inefficient systems of cities in the LAC region.

12. An individual is defined as skilled who has at least some higher education.

13. From figure O.7, Argentina is an exception to this pattern.

14. We obtain this result by regressing (log) share of the city population that is skilled on (log) city population, pooling data for all LAC countries. Results are very similar when country fixed effects are included, or when we run a separate regression per country and average the country-specific coefficients.

15. The Gini coefficient is a measure of inequality in the income distribution. It ranges between zero and 1. The larger the coefficient, the greater the inequality. We obtain the LAC elasticity (equal to 0.029) by regressing (log) city Gini coefficient on (log) city population, pooling data for all LAC countries. When including country fixed effects, the coefficient of this regression rises from 0.029 to 0.042. The U.S. elasticity (equal to 0.012) comes from Behrens and Robert-Nicoud (2015).

16. Income inequality can be decomposed into two components: between-group and within-group inequality. These correspond to income inequality among individuals with different skill levels, and among individuals with the same skill level, respectively. Even if all individuals in a city are skilled, income might be unequally distributed if income for the skilled is dispersed. In the LAC region, however, the greater inequality of larger cities is driven by between-group inequality—by income inequality among individuals with different skill levels.

17. The elasticity of the Gini coefficient with respect to population falls from 0.012 to 0.009 for the United States when controlling for city education (Behrens and Robert-Nicoud 2015). On average (across countries), this elasticity in the LAC region falls from 0.03 to 0.017.

18. These are private returns to higher education, accruing to the individual who attains it. Percent of skilled population is calculated relative to the population ages 25–65 years in each country. Sources for LAC: SEDLAC for all countries other than Brazil; IPUMS for Brazil.

Source for the United States: U.S. Census Bureau, Current Population Survey 2010. Returns to higher education correspond to complete higher education. Source for LAC is Ferreyra et al. (2017); estimates for the United States are based on Card (2001) and Heckman, Lochner, and Todd (2006).

19. Following Ferreyra et al. (2017), "higher education" encompasses both bachelor's programs (akin to the bachelor's programs in the United States) and short-cycle programs (akin to associate degree programs in the United States).

20. The high concentration of skills in large cities may itself be a symptom of the underdevelopment of national transport networks and, more generally, of a lack of integration between cities. Hence, high migration costs associated with a lack of integration may limit migration for the unskilled more than for the skilled, rendering the skilled more likely to migrate than the unskilled—as is the case in Brazil (Fan and Timmins 2017).

21. This discussion is based on the regressions, which cover subnational areas in 16 LAC countries, reported in chapter 3. These regress city productivity (in logs), as measured net of individual worker characteristics, on (log) population density, (log) mean air temperature, (log) terrain ruggedness, and (log) total precipitation.

22. To assess the role of form, skill, and access in city productivity, we measure productivity through average nominal wages, net of worker characteristics. See annex OA for further details on productivity measures used in this book. For a discussion of why nominal wages provide an appropriate measure of productivity, see Combes and Gobillon (2015).

23. Estimates from China, India, and the United States come from Chauvin et al. (2017), who do not control for cities' physical geographic attributes (such as climate and terrain). As in our case, they use individual-level data and use density as a right-hand side variable. Using aggregate data, Ciccone and Hall (1996) and Rosenthal and Strange (2008) estimate agglomeration effects for the United States of 0.04–0.05 percent.

24. For each city, the market access index reflects the number of cities to which the city is connected through the road network, the time it takes to travel to those cities, and those cities' population. See chapters 3 and 4 for further details.

25. Although the effects for China, India, and the United States reported by Chauvin et al. (2017) are all statistically significant at the 1 percent level, the effect that we estimate for LAC is significant at only the 10 percent level.
26. A large city here is defined as one that has a population of more than 1 million or is a national capital.
27. Country-level productivity is measured by (log) GDP per capita, and average density is measured in two ways: as the weighted average of density levels across cities in a country or as the percent of the population that lives in dense cities. Findings are based on regressions that also control for a country's urban share. For further details, see chapter 2.
28. This congestion ranking is based on TomTom data. See chapters 2 and 4 for further details.
29. At the 5 percent significance level.
30. This is the average of country-specific Mincerian returns to schooling, controlling for individual characteristics.
31. The bias associated with the endogenous placement of transport infrastructure also has the potential to go in the opposite direction. Hence, the estimated coefficient on access may be biased upward if transport investments have been targeted at better connecting cities that policy makers anticipate will grow rapidly.
32. Annex OB describes the market failures associated with cities.
33. For example, place-based policies aiming at boosting employment or economic activities in specific areas have a mixed track record (World Bank 2009).
34. In his case study of Brazil for this book, Bastos (2017) finds that the productivity dispersion among workers in the formal sector, who made up two-thirds of the total Brazilian workforce in 2013 (Messina and Silva 2018), has fallen in recent decades. This might have been prompted by the reduction of crime rates in the most productive metropolitan areas, which has served to attract workers from other, less productive, areas. At the same time, productivity dispersion among cities in Brazil remains higher than in the United States. One possible explanation is the shortage of affordable housing in Brazil's most productive cities. On average, housing deficits have risen more in high-wage than in low-wage metropolitan areas. Although informal housing presumably filled the gap

for some migrants to high-wage metro areas, the poor quality of such housing may have deterred would-be migrants, thereby keeping them "trapped" in less productive cities.
35. See chapter 5 for further details on the employment of skilled and unskilled individuals in cities. As is well known, measuring productivity in the service sector is remarkably difficult, partly because of the difficulties in measuring output.
36. Chapter 3 presents evidence that agglomeration effects are stronger in formal than in informal economic activities.
37. Among economists, the use of NTL to proxy for levels of economic activity has become widespread since the work of Henderson, Storeygard, and Weil (2011, 2012). Before this, the ability of NTL to proxy for levels of economic activity had been highlighted in the field of remote sensing by, for example, Elvidge et al. (1997).
38. Of course, the difference could also be due to systematic differences in their unobserved characteristics. We assume that controlling for our set of observed individual characteristics minimizes the role of such differences.

References

Balat, J., and C. Casas. 2017. "Firm Productivity and Cities: The Case of Colombia." Background paper for this book, World Bank, Washington, DC.

Bastos, P. 2017. "Spatial Misallocation of Labor in Brazil." Background paper for this book, World Bank, Washington, DC.

Behrens, K., and F. Robert-Nicoud. 2015. "Agglomeration Theory with Heterogeneous Agents." In *Handbook of Regional and Urban Economics, Volume 5,* edited by Gilles Duranton, J. Vernon Henderson, and William C. Strange, 171–87. Amsterdam: Elsevier.

Blankespoor, B., T. Bougna, R. Garduno-Rivera, and H. Selod. 2017. "Roads and the Geography of Economic Activities in Mexico." Policy Research Working Paper 8226, World Bank, Washington, DC.

Branson, J., A. Campbell-Sutton, G. M. Hornby, D. D. Hornby, and C. Hill. 2016. "A Geospatial Database for Latin America and the Caribbean: Geodata." Southampton, U.K.: University of Southampton.

Card, D. 2001. "Estimating the Return to Schooling: Progress on Some Persistent

Econometric Problems." *Econometrica* 69 (5): 1127–60.

Chauvin, J. P., E. Glaeser, Y. Ma, and K. Tobio. 2017. "What Is Different about Urbanization in Rich and Poor Countries? Cities in Brazil, China, India, and the United States." *Journal of Urban Economics* 98: 17–49.

Ciccone, A., and R. Hall. 1996. "Productivity and the Density of Economic Activity." *American Economic Review* 86 (1): 54–70.

Combes, P. P., and L. Gobillon. 2015. "The Empirics of Agglomeration Economies." In *Handbook of Regional and Urban Economics, Volume 5,* edited by Gilles Duranton, J. Vernon Henderson, and William C. Strange, 247-348. Amsterdam: Elsevier.

Dijkstra, L., and H. Poelman. 2014. "A Harmonised Definition of Cities and Rural Areas: The New Degree of Urbanization." Regional Working Paper, Directorate-General for Regional and Urban Policy, European Commission, Brussels.

Duranton, G. 2014. "Growing through Cities in Developing Countries." *World Bank Research Observer* 30 (1): 39–73.

———. 2016. "Agglomeration Effects in Colombia." *Journal of Regional Science* 56 (2): 210–38.

Elvidge, C., K. Baugh, E. Kihn, H. Kroehl, E. Davis, and C. Davis. 1997. "Relation between Satellite Observed Visible-Near Infrared Emissions, Population, Economic Activity and Electric Power Consumption." *International Journal of Remote Sensing* 18 (6): 1373–79.

Fan, L., and C. Timmins. 2017. "A Sorting Model Approach to Valuing Urban Amenities in Brazil." Background paper for this book, World Bank, Washington, DC.

Ferreyra, M. M., C. Avitabile, J. Botero, F. Haimovich, and S. Urzua. 2017. *At a Crossroads: Higher Education in Latin America and the Caribbean.* Washington, DC: World Bank.

Heckman, J., L. Lochner, and P. Todd. 2006. "Earnings Functions, Rates of Return, and Treatment Effects: The Mincer Equation and Beyond." In *Handbook of the Economics of Education*, Volume 1, edited by E. A. Hanushek and F. Welch, 307–458. Amsterdam: Elsevier.

Henderson, J. V., A. Storeygard, and D. N. Weil. 2011. "A Bright Idea for Measuring Economic Growth." *American Economic Review* 101 (3): 194–99.

———. 2012. "Measuring Economic Growth from Outer Space." *American Economic Review* 102 (2): 994–1028.

ITF (International Transport Forum). 2017. "Capacity to Grow: Transport Infrastructure Needs for Future Trade Growth." Organisation for Economic Co-operation and Development, Paris.

Messina, J., and J. Silva. 2018. *Wage Inequality in Latin America: Understanding the Past to Prepare for the Future.* Washington, DC: World Bank.

Quintero, L., and M. Roberts. 2017. "Explaining Spatial Variations in Productivity: Evidence from 16 LAC Countries." Background paper for this book, World Bank, Washington, DC.

Reyes, J., M. Roberts, and L. C. Xu. 2017. "The Heterogeneous Growth Effects of the Business Environment: Firm-Level Evidence for a Global Sample of Cities." Policy Research Working Paper 8114, World Bank, Washington, DC.

Rosenthal, S., and W. Strange. 2008. "The Attenuation of Human Capital Spillovers." *Journal of Urban Economics* 64: 373–389.

World Bank. 2009. *World Development Report: Reshaping Economic Geography.* Washington, DC: World Bank.

Urbanization and Productivity in Latin America and the Caribbean

Cities in Latin America and the Caribbean (LAC) are, on average, more productive than those in many other regions of the world. But they lag the global "frontier" of productivity performance, defined by North American and Western European cities. Considerable scope thus exists for "raising the bar" for productive cities in the region, as well as increasing the contribution that cities, in aggregate, make to national gross domestic product (GDP) per capita. Part I of the book provides an overview of major urbanization trends and the productivity performance of LAC cities. Chapter 1 analyzes urbanization and related trends of structural transformation at the national level. It also assesses whether GDP per capita levels among the region's countries are higher or lower than might be expected given prevailing levels of urbanization. Chapter 2 looks beyond the share of a country's population that lives in cities to examine additional dimensions of urbanization within the region and their links to national productivity performance. It also benchmarks the productivity of individual LAC cities against those in the rest of the world, and analyzes the dispersion of productivity across the region's cities.

Urbanization, Economic Development, and Structural Transformation

1

Paula Restrepo Cadavid and Grace Cineas

Introduction

This chapter presents an overview of urbanization trends in the Latin America and Caribbean (LAC) region and, where possible, their links to productivity. Unlike East Asia, many of the LAC region's largest urban centers are inland, possibly a disadvantage for international trade (Saavedra- Chanduvi and Sennehauser 2009). LAC countries also appear to have lower than expected productivity, given their high urbanization levels.

Some analysts argue that policy distortions have favored population concentrations in urban areas and capital cities, exacerbating congestion forces and limiting the benefits of agglomeration (Davis and Henderson 2003; Ades and Glaeser 1994; Krugman and Elizondo 1996). But most analysts use *official* (national) measures of urbanization to support these findings, and these measures are not consistent across countries. For example, some countries use a minimum population size to identify urban areas, but others do not use any explicitly stated

criteria, relying instead on official lists of cities. "Urban areas" mean different things in different countries, and at least some of the apparent "underperformance" of LAC urbanization might result from data artifacts.

The chapter begins by briefly exploring the historical origins of population and economic concentration in the region, reviewing the role of natural geographic endowments or *location fundamentals*.[1] To do this, it builds on previous work by Maloney and Caicedo (2016) and Henderson et al. (2016). When possible, it assesses whether there are visible differences in the way location fundamentals have influenced the location of population and economic activity in the LAC region and in the rest of the world.

Focusing on national outcomes, the chapter analyzes the relationship between a country's level of urbanization, as measured by the share of its population that lives in urban areas, and its overall productivity, as measured by gross domestic product (GDP) per capita. Drawing on, and

---

The second section of this chapter, on the origins of cities, draws heavily on Maloney and Caicedo (2016) and on Henderson et al. (2016). The third and fourth sections draw heavily on a background paper by Roberts et al. (2017) produced for this book. Angelica Maria Sanchez Diaz also contributed to this chapter.

extending, a background study by Roberts et al. (2017) undertaken for this book, it aims to establish how LAC cities are performing in relation to international benchmarks. The analysis first uses *official measures of urbanization* compiled by the United Nations in its World Urbanization Prospects (WUP) database, which are not consistent across countries. It then proposes an alternative method, the cluster algorithm,[2] which allows constructing urbanization measures that are *consistent* across countries.

This chapter has two main findings.

First, unique historical features influence the location of cities in the LAC region today. Compared with the rest of the world, *location fundamentals* (natural advantages) are not as relevant in determining where people and economic activity concentrate. Globally, such fundamentals explain 57 percent of the variation in the location of population, but this falls to 39 percent in the LAC region. In addition, *agriculture fundamentals* (such as having a fertile hinterland) better explain the concentration of population in the LAC region than *trade fundamentals* (such as being close to the coast). This might, however, be due to the inertia of density: once a city is created, it tends to persist in time (Henderson et al. 2016), and many LAC countries urbanized before the fall in global transport costs (when *trade* fundamentals were not as relevant).[3] Many LAC cities might therefore be in suboptimal locations, based on location fundamentals.

Second, LAC clearly is highly urbanized, independent of the measures (official or consistent) used to define urbanization. Using consistent urbanization measures, GDP per capita in LAC countries no longer appears low for given prevailing levels of urbanization. But substantial room for improvement remains. The largest LAC economies are even seeing their distance from the North American productivity frontier widen, possibly because of below-average productivity gains from the LAC region's structural transformation.

The Origins of Cities in Latin America and the Caribbean

The Origins and Persistence of Cities: Location Fundamentals and Historical "Accidents"

The locations where cities emerge often have underlying natural advantages favorable to production. These natural advantages are usually referred to as *location fundamentals* and might include a favorable coastal location or access to potentially navigable waterways (or both), the presence of favorable terrain and climatic conditions, a (relative) lack of vulnerability to natural disasters, and the (relative) absence of disease vectors.

Because of historical "accidents," however, cities can also emerge in locations that lack strong fundamentals (Arthur 1994; Krugman 1991a, 1991b). Cities can, for example, be founded in certain places for administrative purposes or to exert military control over a territory.

Furthermore, historical evidence from around the world suggests that, once a city is founded, it tends to persist through time (Wahl 2016; Diamond 1997; Davis and Weinstein 2002; Olsson and Hibbs 2005; Comin, Easterly, and Gong 2010; Spolaore and Wacziarg 2013; Maloney and Caicedo 2016). City persistence can result from the permanence of strong location fundamentals, such as a still-fertile hinterland. Cities can also persist, however, in locations that have lost their fundamentals (perhaps because of the depletion of nearby natural resources) or where the fundamentals that originally underpinned development are no longer relevant. For example, because of the increasing returns of agglomeration, a small settlement that emerged in an isolated and arid region for administrative or, originally, resource-extraction purposes can be "locked in" to that location and grow to be a large city. Such "inertia of density" can lead cities to persist even when they are in places whose location fundamentals are poor or no longer relevant. Cities' persistence in such places has long-term consequences for economic performance and overall productivity (Michaels and Rauch 2013).

The Historical Origins and Persistence of LAC Cities

Myriad factors influenced the location and consolidation of LAC cities before, during, and after colonial times. The emergence of precolonial settlements in the LAC region can be traced to the adoption of sedentary agriculture, a shift from nomadic subsistence, and technological progress (Diamond 1997; Bairoch and Braider 1988).[4] Driven by these factors, early settlements located in places that had underlying natural advantages, including major bodies of water, fertile land, and terrain configurations that provided natural defense from hostile tribes (Saavedra-Chanduvi and Sennehauser 2009). Following the same approach as Maloney and Caicedo (2016)—described in box 1.1—we find that a small set of location

fundamentals explains 43 percent of the variation of subnational precolonial population densities in the LAC region.[5] The remaining variation could be explained by unmeasured location fundamentals (such as some natural resources) or by historical "accidents" of the time. Some legends even suggest, as with the origins of Tenochtitlan (today's Mexico City), that arbitrary forces might have played a role in the emergence of some precolonial settlements.[6]

During colonial times, cities often consolidated on top of existing settlements. This allowed European colonizers to benefit from local labor and the existing infrastructure—as well as, often, strong location fundamentals (Maloney and Caicedo 2016). Some colonial cities, however, were created from scratch in places that the colonists deemed

---

BOX 1.1   Precolonial Densities, Location Fundamentals, and the Persistence of Subnational Population Densities

Maloney and Caicedo (2016) study the persistence of subnational population density in the LAC region and North America using an innovative set of historical data that include subnational data on precolonial population density, recent population density, and a set of location fundamentals. As part of their study, they assess the role of location fundamentals in determining precolonial population densities, whether there are strong indications of persistence—by comparing precolonial and recent population densities in the region—and the role that extractive institutions (such as slavery) play in reducing persistence. We use the same approach and data set as Maloney and Caicedo (2016) but restrict the sample to cover only LAC.[a] Here is a description of the main variables used for the analysis:

- Precolonial population density is the number of indigenous people before the arrival of Columbus divided by the area of the state or province in square kilometers.

- Current population density refers to the total population in the year 2000 divided by the area of the state or province in square kilometers.

- Location fundamentals include an index for cultivable land, the density of rivers as a share of area, temperature, altitude, rainfall, presence of malaria, terrain ruggedness, and distance to nearest coast.

- The units of observation are subnational administrative units that correspond to provinces, departments, or states depending on the country. The sample includes 17 LAC countries. Historical information on precolonial densities is not available at a lower scale (such as city level). For the purpose of our analysis, we run the following regressions: (i) the log of precolonial density on a set of location fundamentals and (ii) the log of current population density on the log of precolonial density, with a set of locational fundamentals used as controls.

a. The authors are grateful to Maloney and Caicedo for sharing their data and code to facilitate this analysis.

strategic for military or administrative reasons (Saavedra-Chanduvi and Sennehauser 2009). Colonial cities were also often founded with the aim of facilitating commerce with Europe (not with cities in the region).[7]

Although there are more recent examples of cities that have been created from scratch in the region (such as Brasilia), the origins of most of the LAC region's present-day cities can be traced back to precolonial or colonial times.[8] The reasons for this persistence may vary from city to city. For some, it may reflect persistence or strengthening of location fundamentals.[9] For others, it likely stems from "lock-in" effects, as cities continue to prosper thanks to the accumulated returns to agglomeration, even in locations that never possessed, or have lost, good location fundamentals. It is difficult to estimate the relative importance of each of these factors or, more important, to assess the economic implications of this persistence; but two recent studies and the data sets developed by their authors can provide us with some insights.

Using the same data and approach that Maloney and Caicedo (2016) used, but restricting the analysis to LAC countries,

we find that location fundamentals explain 40 percent of the variation in subnational population densities in the region in 2000. The existence of precolonial settlements, which captures persistence not explained by location fundamentals, explains 11 percent of the variation. Furthermore, we find that subnational precolonial densities in the region are positively and significantly correlated with subnational population density in 2000, even when controlling for location fundamentals. This confirms that one of the central findings from Maloney and Caicedo (2016), the strong persistence of subnational population density, is maintained when restricting the analysis to LAC countries (figure 1.1).[10]

The analysis of a second data set compiled by Henderson et al. (2016; see box 1.2), also suggests that there might be unique features that explain the location of economic and population density in the LAC region today. Current economic activity in the LAC region is less likely to be in places with strong location fundamentals than it is in the rest of the world. The location of economic activity in the LAC region is also explained to a greater extent by agriculture location fundamentals than by trade location fundamentals, partly because of the region's early urbanization process (before the fall of transport costs). It is therefore possible that, if the LAC region's urban systems were to emerge today, many cities would be in different places. These results do not, however, mean that some cities in the region should be relocated—rather that policy makers should focus their efforts on maximizing cities' productivity given their location.

Urbanization in the LAC Region and the Rest of the World: Discrepancies between Consistent and Official Measures

In this section, we explore how the share of the population that lives in urban areas (the *urban population share*) in the LAC region compares with that in the rest of the world by examining some stylized facts,

FIGURE 1.1   Strong Persistence in Subnational Population Densities in the LAC Region

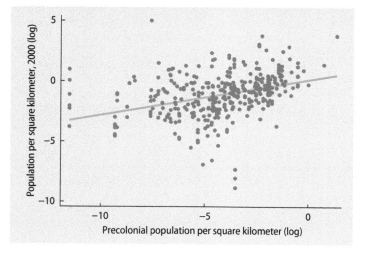

Source: Estimated using the same database and approach as Maloney and Caicedo (2016), but restricting the sample to the 17 LAC countries included in their sample.
Note: The units of observation are subnational units (provinces, departments, or states). LAC = Latin America and the Caribbean.

BOX 1.2   Location Fundamentals and the Distribution of Economic Activity in Latin America and the Caribbean versus the Rest of the World

Henderson et al. (2016) seek to determine how much of the present spatial distribution of economic activity, at the global scale, is explained by what they call base, agriculture, and trade location fundamentals. *Base fundamentals* include elements such as malaria and terrain ruggedness; *agriculture fundamentals* include elements related to agriculture viability, and *trade fundamentals* include variables focusing on access to water transport. They construct a global gridded sample of 250,000 cells (of about 1 km^2 at the equator). The location of economic activity is proxied by nighttime lights (specifically, by the log of nighttime light radiance in 2010). Using the R^2 statistic, they find that base, agriculture, and trade fundamentals alone (see table B1.2.1 note), explain 57 percent of the variation in the location of economic activity worldwide (column a, row 4, in table B1.2.1). We expand Henderson et al.'s analysis to explore whether there are differences in the factors driving population and economic concentration in the LAC region (column b). We also conduct a subregional analysis for the Caribbean, Central America, and South America (the last includes Mexico; columns c, d, and e, respectively.).

Three results stand out. First, there are subtle differences in the features that influence the location of economic activity in the LAC region compared with the rest of the world. As noted earlier, base, agriculture, and trade fundamentals, although still statistically significant, explain only 39 percent of the variation in the location of economic activity in the LAC region but 57 percent worldwide. Second, agriculture fundamentals are better than trade fundamentals at explaining the location of economic activity. As described by Henderson et al. (2016), however, this is expected to apply to countries that urbanized when transport costs were still high—the case of most LAC countries. In these countries, cities often located (and persist) in agricultural regions; however, in countries that urbanized when transport costs fell, cities often located in places with favorable trade fundamentals (such as near the coast). Third, in the LAC region, South America is the subregion where location fundamentals provide the least explanation for location of economic activity.

TABLE B1.2.1 *R*-Squared Results for Relationship between Log(Radiance-Calibrated Nighttime Lights) and Base, Agriculture, and Trade Fundamentals

		(a) All	(b) LAC	(c) Caribbean	(d) Central America	(e) South America
(1)	Base + FE	0.355	0.222	0.275	0.221	0.200
(2)	Agriculture + base + FE	0.566	0.343	0.381	0.386	0.328
(3)	Trade + base + FE	0.369	0.283	0.376	0.256	0.264
(4)	Base + Agriculture + trade + FE	0.568	0.386	0.433	0.456	0.373

Source: Column a presents results by Henderson et al. (2016); columns b through e show World Bank calculations.
Note: The table presents the estimated R^2 of different regressions where the dependent variable is the log (natural) of the radiance-calibrated nighttime lights; the independent variables are combinations of base, agriculture, and trade fundamentals. The unit of observation is the individual grid cell. Fixed effects (FE) are country fixed effects. Base location fundamentals include malaria and ruggedness; agriculture and trade covariates include 14 biome indicators (for agriculture) and five trade variables that focus on access to water transport. LAC = Latin America and the Caribbean.

for which the choice of urbanization measures—official or otherwise—is critical. We begin by showing these facts as documented by official measures compiled by the United Nations in its WUP database.[11] These official measures rely on national definitions of urban areas, and thus vary across countries. Drawing on the background paper by Roberts et al. (2017), we then revisit these facts by using urbanization measures that are consistent across countries.

On Official Measures, LAC Is Highly Urbanized Relative to Other Regions

By 1960, according to official urbanization measures, half of the LAC region's population lived in urban areas, a milestone achieved globally only in 2008 (figure 1.2). By 2015, more than 80 percent of the region's population lived in urban areas, making it the most urbanized developing region and giving it urban population shares similar to those in North America.

The LAC region shows considerable heterogeneity in urban population shares. Some of its countries, like Argentina and Uruguay, have very high levels (with more than 90 percent of the population living in officially defined urban areas). Others, such as Antigua and Barbuda and Guyana, remain predominantly rural (with 30 percent or less

of the population living in urban areas). Among LAC subregions, South America (which we define in this chapter to include Mexico) urbanized earlier and closely mirrored regional urbanization trends.[12] Countries in the Caribbean were predominantly rural in the 1960s but underwent rapid urbanization and reached the 50 percent watershed by the late 1970s, well before their counterparts in Central America, which reached it only in the late 1990s (figure 1.3).

Since 1960, the rate of growth of the region's urban population has been declining from 4.49 percent annually between 1960 and 1965 to 1.61 percent between 2005 and 2010 (figure 1.4).[13] The decline in the urban population growth rate is similar to that observed in countries elsewhere in the world

FIGURE 1.2   **Urban Shares for Latin America and the Caribbean and Other World Regions, 1960–2015**

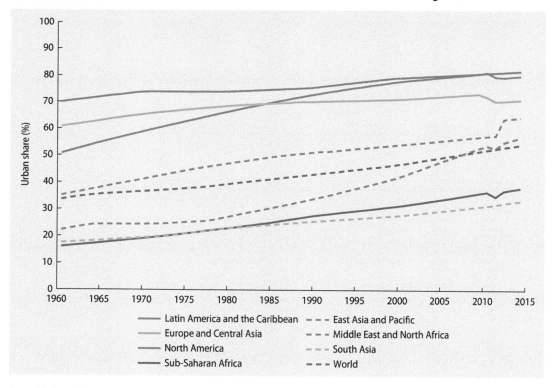

Source: Calculations based on World Development Indicators, July 2017 (https://data.worldbank.org/data-catalog/world-development-indicators), derived from World Urbanization Prospects.
Note: On the y axis, the urban share is the total urban population, as defined by national statistics offices, as a percentage of the total population in each region.

FIGURE 1.3   Urban Shares for LAC Subregions, 1960–2015

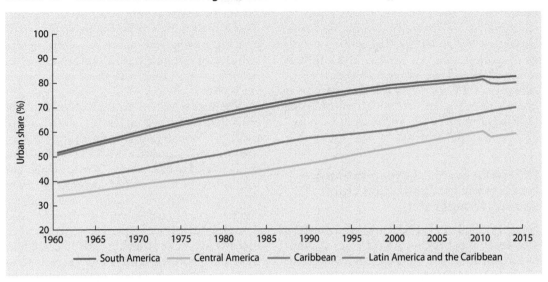

Source: Calculations based on World Development Indicators, July 2017 (https://data.worldbank.org/data-catalog/world-development-indicators), derived from World Urbanization Prospects.
Note: On the y axis, the urban share is the total urban population, as defined by national statistics offices, as a percentage of the total population in each region. LAC = Latin America and the Caribbean.

FIGURE 1.4   Annual Growth of Urban Population, Worldwide and by Region, 1960–2005

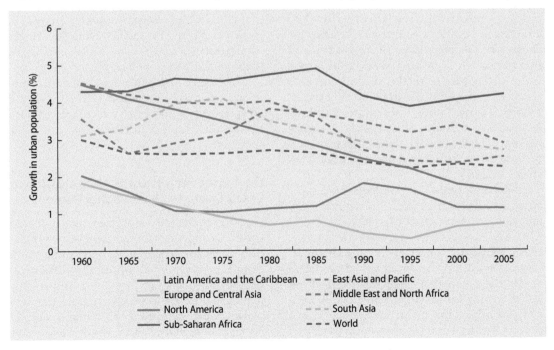

Source: Calculations based on World Urbanization Prospects, July 2017 (https://esa.un.org/unpd/wup/CD-ROM/).
Note: The figure presents regional annual growth rates of the urban population, as defined by national statistics offices. Growth is calculated as the compound annual growth rate between year x and year x+5 (World Urbanization Prospects estimates are available at five-year intervals).

when they attain high urban shares.[14] However, the absolute size of urban population growth in the region remains large: between 1960 and 1987, 181 million people were added to LAC cities, and slightly more—216 million—were added during the subsequent 28 years. As a reference, this is greater than the entire population of Brazil (207 million in 2016), the fifth most populous country in the world.

Official Measures of Urbanization Are Problematic for Conducting Cross-Country Comparisons

Most published research on urbanization and development relies on official measures of urbanization based on national definitions of urban areas (World Bank 2008; Chen et al. 2014; Spence, Annez, and Buckley 2009). As highlighted by Roberts et al. (2017), these definitions vary widely by country. From the 232 countries and territories included in the WUP database, 133 use one or more of four basic types of criteria to define their urban areas. By far the most common is a minimum population size threshold (103 countries). For some countries, the criterion consists of the availability of certain types of infrastructure (such as schools or piped water), structure of the local economy, or a minimum population density threshold. Finally, a large number of countries (99) do not use any explicitly stated criteria, simply listing urban areas by name or stating a designation of administrative units that constitute cities.[15]

In general, non-LAC countries have more stringent criteria than LAC countries for designating areas as urban (World Bank 2008; Ellis and Roberts 2015), with the upshot that, among the countries that use the minimum population threshold to define urban areas, the mean threshold stands at about 2,000 people for LAC but about 5,000 people globally. This mean difference is not driven by the small island nations of the Caribbean because that subregion's mean population threshold is almost identical to that for the LAC region.[16] Instead, on average, LAC countries include smaller settlements in their urban population figures. These variations are problematic for cross- and intracountry comparisons, limiting the validity of comparing official measures of urbanization in LAC with those in the rest of the world.

The growing recognition of such problems has spawned methods that aim to establish consistent definitions of urban areas across countries, and so consistent measures of urbanization. For example, the Agglomeration Index (AI) originally developed by Uchida and Nelson (2008) and the cluster algorithm developed by Dijkstra and Poelman (2014) can be used, together with recently available global, gridded population data, to produce consistent estimates of urban areas for a large global cross-section of countries (box 1.3). In their background paper for this book, Roberts et al. (2017) implement both the cluster algorithm and the AI using three different sources of globally gridded population data.[17] In doing so, they show that the two algorithms generate similar maps of urban areas, both for LAC and globally. For consistency with chapter 2, we focus mainly on results using the cluster algorithm as applied to Landscan 2012 globally gridded population data.

To see how different our urban area population estimates are with those produced by national definitions, we compared data for a global sample of cities from the WUP (box 1.4).

On Consistent Measures, Urbanization in LAC Is Closer to That in Other Regions

Using the cluster algorithm, we revisited the cross-regional comparison of urbanization levels conducted using official measures of urbanization.[18] We found that urbanization levels in the LAC region, using consistent measures, are lower than those estimated using official definitions but remain high, at about 73 percent in 2012 (figure 1.5).[19] We also found that, when we use consistent urbanization measures, the LAC region's level of urbanization (as measured by its urban

FIGURE 1.5   **Urban Shares: Official versus Consistent Measures of Urbanization**

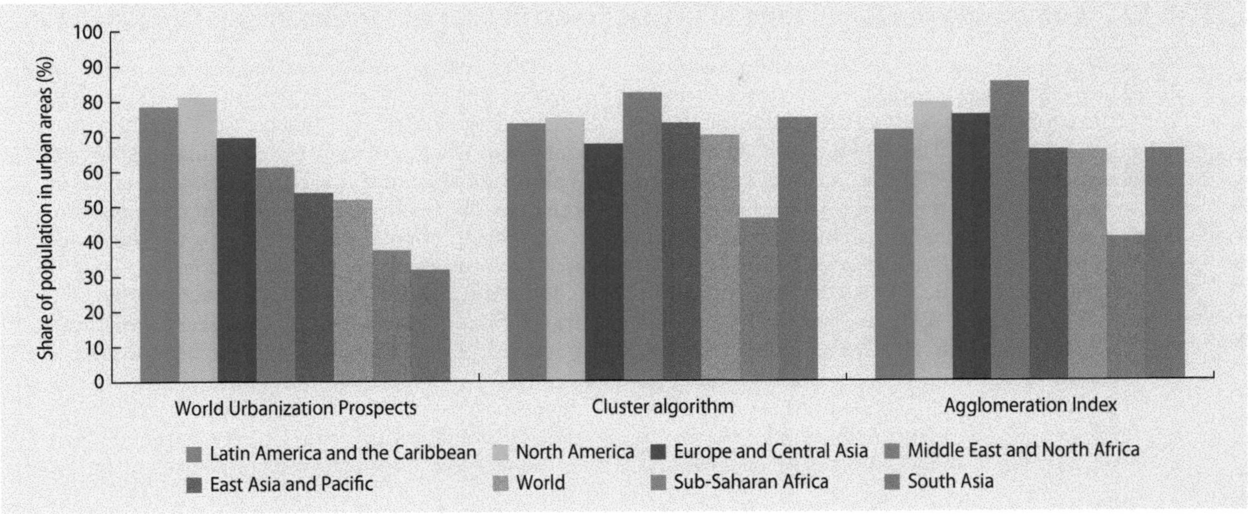

Source: Calculations based on Roberts et al. 2017.
Note: The results correspond to the combination of using the cluster algorithm and the Agglomeration Index with LandScan 2012 gridded population data. The background paper by Roberts et al. (2017) also presents comparisons of urban shares using GHS–Pop gridded population data, and their results are broadly consistent with those here. Data are for 2012.

BOX 1.3   The Agglomeration Index and the Cluster Algorithm

The Agglomeration Index (AI). The AI algorithm defines urban areas from a labor market perspective. It is similar to that proposed by the Organisation for Economic Co-operation and Development (OECD) (2012), and the one used by Duranton (2015). AI algorithms define functional urban areas as the spatial extent of the labor market. Approaches to delineating these areas typically involve identifying an "urban core" and a "commuting shed" around it.

Our AI algorithm starts from a database of settlements and identifies those that are "sizable" on the basis a population threshold. Around each urban core, the algorithm then identifies the commuting shed as the areas located within a given radius (defined by travel time) of the urban core and meeting a population density threshold. Both the urban core and the commuting shed are thus considered urban areas. A country's urban share is then defined as the share of the overall national population living in such urban areas.

To implement the AI, we used estimated, not actual, commuting times (used by OECD) or minimum commuting thresholds (used by Duranton), because they are available globally. Following Uchida and Nelson (2008) and World Bank (2008), an area in the commuting shed is defined as urban if it has a population density of at least 150 people per square kilometer and is located within a 60-minute travel time radius of a settlement, which itself has a population of at least 50,000.

The cluster algorithm. This algorithm adopts a spatial-demographic approach to identifying urban areas. More specifically, it classifies cells in a population grid according to their density, and then groups them into "urban clusters." A spatially contiguous group of grid cells is classified as constituting an urban cluster if each of these cells has a population density of at least 300 people per square kilometer and if the aggregate population of the cells exceeds 5,000 inhabitants. A country's urban share is then defined as the share of the overall national population living in "urban clusters."

Note: For more details on these two methodologies and their implementation for this book, see Roberts et al. (2017).

BOX 1.4   Comparing the Population of Urban Areas: Cluster Algorithm versus Official Data

We compared estimates of city population data produced using the cluster algorithm with figures from the World Urbanization Prospects (WUP) report "World Urbanization Prospects: The 2014 Revision" for a global sample of cities. The WUP's figures provide the most up-to-date estimates of population for the largest cities in the world (cities with more than 300,000 inhabitants in 2014) and are based on city populations reported by national statistics offices. We used the city location points provided by the WUP and matched them with the location of cities identified by the cluster algorithm. We matched virtually all cities in the WUP data set with our urban areas (the sample for this comparison is formed by 1,301 urban areas covering 1,484 cities in the WUP data set).[a] A small number of urban areas (less

than 5 percent) were matched with more than one WUP city. We compared the cluster algorithm city population with the largest WUP city matched, and with the total population when several WUP cities matched with a single cluster algorithm city. The results were similar in both cases. We mainly focused on the first comparison. In comparing population, we proxied the degree of discrepancy using the "relocation fraction."[b]

What do we learn from this comparison? For the largest cities in the world, our cluster algorithm–estimated population sizes are not very different from those estimated by national statistics offices. The global correlation between both populations is 80 percent and increases to 90 percent when we include the population of all matched cities.

FIGURE B1.4.1   Comparison of Cluster Algorithm and WUP City Population Values, by Region

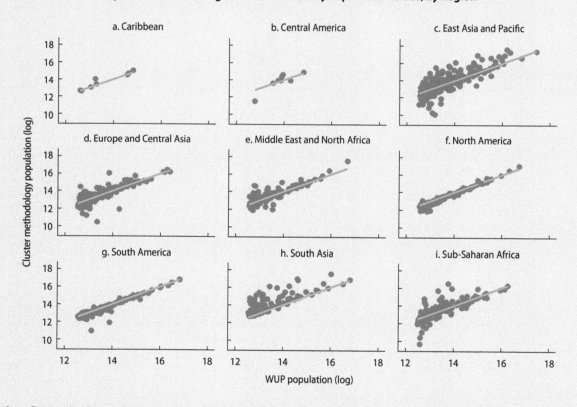

Source: Cluster methodology populations are based on urban areas defined using the cluster algorithm of Dijkstra and Poelman (2014), as applied to LandScan 2012 gridded population data. WUP population figures are from the World Urbanization Prospects: The 2014 Revision.
Note: We calculate the WUP population in 2012 using a linear interpolation of the WUP data in 2010 and 2015. The orange line is a 45-degree line, thus the closer to the line each point is, the lower the difference between the two sources of population data.

(continued)

BOX 1.4   **Comparing the Population of Urban Areas: Cluster Algorithm versus Official Data**
(continued)

Moreover, the relocation fraction is low: on average, only 12 percent of the population in cities would have to be relocated to equalize the populations in both data sets.

Regional variations. As shown by figure B1.4.1, there are, however, important regional differences in the disagreement between the two measures, underscoring the different criteria countries have for defining cities and the need for a globally consistent measure. The Americas tend to have the highest agreement of all regions globally. For example, the correlation coefficients for South and North America between the populations of cluster algorithm cities and their corresponding WUP cities are 99 and 98 percent, respectively; and their average relocation fractions are as low as 5 and 8 percent, respectively. Asian countries have less agreement, with correlations of 66 and 78 percent for South Asia and East Asia and the Pacific, respectively. They have relocation fractions of 19 and 16 percent, respectively.

National variations. There is also considerable inconsistency in national delimitation of urban areas. If countries defined their own cities consistently, we would expect to have a constant bias in the estimation of the population within countries. We find the contrary when we compute, per region, the variation in the relocation fraction between and within countries. For example, the coefficient of variation *between* countries is lower than that *within* countries in East Asia and the Pacific, Europe and Central Asia, and South America.

This means that we would expect to see a larger difference in the disagreement between our calculation of population and that given by the WUP if we choose two cities in the same country than if we choose the average disagreement of two different countries in those regions (figure B1.4.2 presents the data for all regions). The WUP compilation recognizes this discrepancy and classifies each city on three statistical concepts: urban agglomeration, metropolitan area, and "city proper." For almost 60 percent of the countries with more than one large city, their statistical concepts differ among their cities.

These results show that having a consistent measure to define urban areas permits better comparisons of cities not only across countries or regions but also within countries.

FIGURE B1.4.2   **Between and within Variation of the Relocation Fraction per Region**

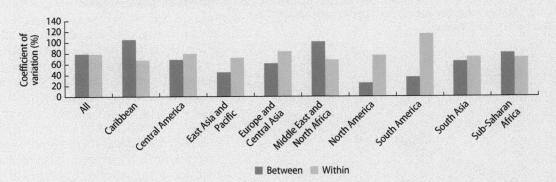

Source: Calculations based on urban areas defined using the cluster algorithm of Dijkstra and Poelman (2014), as applied to LandScan 2012 gridded population data. WUP population figures are from the World Urbanization Prospects: The 2014 Revision.
Note: The figure shows the coefficient of variation of the relocation fraction between and within countries for each region and for the whole sample. The relocation fraction is calculated for each of the 1,301 cities matched.

a. As in the "Defining a Global Data Set of Urban Areas" section of chapter 2, this sample excludes nine implausibly large urban extents formed by the cluster algorithm.
b. In similar fashion to Rozenfeld et al. (2011), the relocation fraction R_i is defined as the fraction of population that needs to be relocated from a cluster city S_i^{clus} to the corresponding WUP city S_i^{WUP} (or vice versa), so that their populations are equalized: $R_i \overset{def}{=} \dfrac{\left| S_i^{WUP} - S_i^{clus} \right|}{\max(S_i^{WUP}, S_i^{clus})}$

population share) is closer to that of the rest of the world. In fact, whereas the overall estimated urban share does not change much for LAC, it does for other regions, notably the Middle East and North Africa and South Asia (SA), where urbanization levels on consistent measures are much higher than on official measures. Thus, using consistent measures, urban shares in the LAC region are more aligned with those of other regions.

In the LAC region, Central America and the Caribbean's urban shares do not change much.[20] However, we find changes in South America where urban shares seem overestimated by official measures.

Urbanization, Economic Development, and Structural Transformation: How Does the LAC Region's Performance Stack Up?

On Conventional Measures, LAC Subregions Systematically Depart from the Global Relationship between Urbanization and Economic Development

Urbanization, economic development, and structural transformation have long been

viewed in the literature as bound together. Consistent with such findings, an analysis of cross-country data exhibits a strong and significant positive correlation between a country's development (measured by GDP per capita) and its urban share (on official measures) (figure 1.6). This correlation is often attributed to the structural change, associated with the movement of labor out of agriculture and into manufacturing and services, that accompanies urbanization (Henderson 2003; Chenery and Taylor 1968). The estimated elasticity between productivity (as measured by GDP per capita) and the share of urbanization is so high, however, that it is questionable whether the relationship can be attributed solely to structural transformation.[21]

Similar to what is observed in the rest of the world, there is a strong and positive correlation between urban shares in the LAC region (on official measures) and GDP per capita. But is the relationship between the urban share and economic development systematically different from the global one?

To find out, we regressed GDP per capita values (purchasing power parity, or PPP) on the urban share defined using official measures (table 1.1). We find that LAC countries are, on average, not behaving differently from those in the rest of the world (column b in table 1.1). However, there appear to be systematic departures at the subregional level (column c). Countries in South America appear to have lower GDP per capita than one would predict from their urban share. On the contrary, countries in the Caribbean appear to have higher GDP per capita than predicted by their urbanization levels. Countries in Central America present no systematic departure from the global relationship.

Although these results suggest that South American cities are "underproductive" (and Caribbean cities are "overproductive") compared with the rest of the world, they were obtained from official measures and so may simply reflect data artifacts arising from the inconsistent definition of urban areas across countries. To examine this notion,

FIGURE 1.6 Relationship between Economic Development and the Urban Share on Official Measures

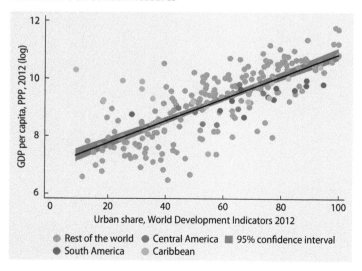

Source: Calculations based on World Urbanization Prospects data and World Development Indicators.
Note: Data are for 2012. GDP = gross domestic product; PPP = purchasing power parity.

TABLE 1.1   Regression Results for Relationship between Log(GDP per Capita) and the Official Urban Share

	(a)	(b)	(c)	(d)
Urban population share	4.200***	4.242***	4.346***	3.067***
	(0.284)	(0.288)	(0.284)	(0.299)
Latin America and the Caribbean		−0.153		−0.868*
		(0.166)		(0.457)
Caribbean			0.603*	
			(0.305)	
Central America			−0.274	
			(0.284)	
South America			−0.480**	
			(0.226)	
Sub-Saharan Africa				−1.590***
				(0.465)
South Asia				−0.821
				(0.520)
Middle East and North Africa				−0.610
				(0.479)
Europe and Central Asia				−0.338
				(0.449)
East Asia and Pacific				−0.614
				(0.468)
Constant	6.769***	6.772***	6.714***	8.245***
	(0.173)	(0.173)	(0.171)	(0.500)
No. of observations	146	146	146	146
R^2	0.603	0.606	0.629	0.740

Source: Calculations using World Development Indicators.
Note: The table shows the results of a regression at the country level where the dependent variable is the GDP per capita PPP in log, and the independent variable is the urbanization share (0–1) in column a and the urban share and regional dummies in columns b through d. Data are for 2012. In columns b and c, the base category is the rest of the world. In column d, the base category is North America. Standard errors are in parentheses. A white test for heteroscedasticity shows that we do not reject the null (homoscedasticity) at α = 0.10. We use normal standard errors. GDP = gross domestic product; PPP = purchasing power parity.
***p < 0.01. **p < 0.05. *p < 0.1.

we revisited the analysis, using consistent measures of urbanization.

On Consistent Measures, LAC Subregions Perform Economically as Predicted by the Global Relationship but Could Do Better

To establish whether the systematic departure of LAC subregions stems from the use of official urbanization measures, we conducted a second set of regressions using consistent measures. Results can be found in table 1.2.[22]

To start, we found that the statistical significance in the global relationship between urbanization and economic development is maintained—a country's development level is, to a significant degree, positively correlated with its urban share (column a in table 1.2). However, the fit of the relationship between urbanization and economic development is not as strong (R^2 values are much lower) as when using official measures, and the estimated coefficient on the urban population share is smaller (compare results in column a of table 1.2 with those in column a of table 1.1).

In addition, and unlike when we used official urbanization measures, we find that neither LAC (see column b in tables 1.1 and 1.2) nor its subregions (see column c in tables 1.1 and 1.2) appear to depart from the global relationship when we use consistent

TABLE 1.2   Regression Results for Relationship between Log(GDP per Capita) and the Urban Share, Using Consistent Measures

	(a)	(b)	(c)	(d)
Urban population share	3.743***	3.771***	3.752***	2.195***
	(0.459)	(0.468)	(0.475)	(0.435)
Latin America and the Caribbean		−0.074		−1.235**
		(0.220)		(0.555)
Caribbean			0.046	
			(0.420)	
Central America			−0.146	
			(0.385)	
South America			−0.088	
			(0.303)	
Sub-Saharan Africa				−2.223***
				(0.561)
South Asia				−2.291***
				(0.605)
Middle East and North Africa				−0.937
				(0.585)
Europe and Central Asia				−0.559
				(0.547)
East Asia and Pacific				−1.119*
				(0.567)
Constant	6.861***	6.857***	6.868***	9.094***
	(0.294)	(0.295)	(0.299)	(0.625)
No. of observations	146	146	146	146
R^2	0.316	0.316	0.317	0.613

Source: Calculations based on World Development Indicators and urban population share based on urban areas defined using the cluster algorithm of Dijkstra and Poelman (2014), as applied to Landscan 2012 gridded population data.
Note: The table shows the results of regressions at the country level where the dependent variable is the GDP per capita PPP in log (ln), and the independent variable is the urban share (0–1) in column a and the urban share and regional dummies in columns b through d. Data correspond to year 2012. In columns b and c, the base category is the rest of the world. In column d, the base category is North America. Standard errors are in parentheses. A white test for heteroskedasticity shows that we do not reject the null (homoscedasticity) at alpha = 0.10. We use normal standard errors. GDP = gross domestic product; PPP = purchasing power parity.
***$p < 0.01$. **$p < 0.05$. *$p < 0.1$.

urbanization measures. South America as a group no longer appears to be "underproductive" and the Caribbean does not appear to be "overproductive" for their urbanization levels. This finding suggests that the narrative of underperforming cities in South America might be partly due, as suspected, to data artifacts.

Having established that neither LAC nor its subregions differ from the global relationship between urbanization and economic development, the task is to determine where LAC falls relative to other regions. It is quite possible that the global relationship between urbanization and economic development is being "pushed down" by underperforming countries in some regions.[23] We find that the LAC region seems to be performing worse than North America (see column d of table 1.2, which compares all regions of the world; North America is the omitted category). Similar results are obtained with official urbanization measures (see column d in table 1.1).

One hypothesis to explain the LAC region's underperformance relative to the global productivity frontier (consisting of North America in this case) is that the productivity gains expected from the reallocation of labor from agriculture to manufacturing and services areas as workers migrated from rural to urban areas have not materialized in the LAC region (or at least not to the same extent as in today's developed countries). The following subsection examines whether there is evidence to substantiate this hypothesis.

The LAC Region Has Mediocre Productivity Gains from Structural Transformation

The reallocation of labor between "rural" and "urban" sectors has important implications for overall productivity and economic growth (Kuznets 1973; Alvarez-Cuadrado and Poschke 2011; Herrendorf, Rogerson, and Valentinyi 2013)[24] and is posited to lie, at least in part, behind the global correlation

between GDP per capita and urbanization levels.

To examine structural transformation trends in the LAC region against those in the rest of the world, we relied on data from the Groningen Growth and Development Center (GGDC).[25] These data have been widely used in economic literature for analyzing long-term trends in the reallocation of labor and in output, and include data for 9 of the 33 LAC countries (including its four largest economies) and for subsets of countries around the world.[26] For simplicity, we refer to the nine-country LAC subset as *LAC-9*. We also use *Asia* and *North America* for the subsets of countries from those two regions.

For LAC-9, we find that the reallocation of people from rural to urban areas was accompanied by a reallocation of labor from agriculture to manufacturing and services (figure 1.7, panel b), which tend to cluster in or around cities. For example, between 1960 and 2009 the share of the labor force in LAC-9 in agriculture fell from 47 to 15 percent. Simultaneously, the share of the labor force in services roughly doubled from 32 to 64 percent. Few such dramatic changes were seen in industry, which on average absorbed 23 percent of the labor force over the period. A similar trend to that in LAC-9 is seen in Asia, which was also urbanizing in this period (see figure 1.7, panel a).

The large reallocation of labor in LAC-9 was, however, not coupled with a large shift in the composition of output, as measured by national value added (figure 1.7, panel e). Although the share of people working in services in LAC-9 went up by 32 percentage points between 1960 and 2009, the value added share of services in total output increased only by 5 percentage points over the same period, passing from 51 to 56 percent. Over the same period, the share of output coming from industry declined marginally from 38 to 37 percent.

These results suggest that the reallocation of labor from agriculture to industry and services in LAC-9 has not produced the expected labor productivity gains. According to our

FIGURE 1.7 **Change in the Structural Composition of the Economy, 1960–2009**

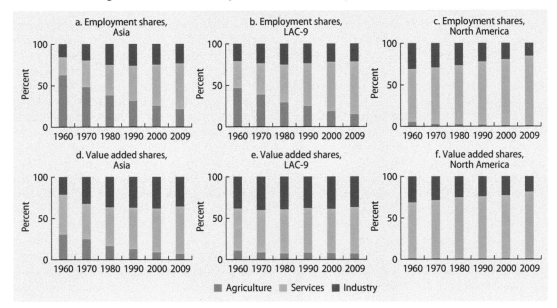

Source: Calculations using the Groningen Growth and Development Center database.
Note: LAC-9 = Argentina, Bolivia, Brazil, Chile, Colombia, Costa Rica, Mexico, Peru, and República Bolivariana de Venezuela.

estimates, a 1 percent increase in the services share of employment is linked to a 3.8 percent increase in overall labor productivity in the rest of the world but only a 0.7 percent increase in LAC-9.[27] A similar difference is found in industry, with an increase of 0.9 percent in productivity in LAC-9 against a 2.2 percent gain in the rest of the world. These findings, although they should be treated with caution because of data limitations, reflect previous findings from Timmer, de Vries, and de Vries (2015) and Pages (2010) who used the same data set,[28] and recent findings from Francis, Saliola, and Seker (2013) based on firm-level data for a shorter time-span.[29]

The lower than expected productivity gains obtained in LAC countries have widened the labor–productivity gap with the productivity frontier (North America). Timmer, de Vries, and de Vries (2015) argue that this widening comes from below-average productivity growth of services and manufacturing in the LAC region, and from the premature movement of workers in the LAC region from manufacturing to lower-productivity services such as retailing, wholesaling, construction, and

government.[30] Although this "premature deindustrialization" is attributed to external global forces, such as globalization and technological progress (Rodrik 2015), cities and governments can take steps to counteract the productivity consequences of deindustrialization. Cities can, for example, address the congestion forces that may inhibit firms from reaping the productivity gains linked to agglomeration (chapter 2).[31] They might also be able to help develop higher-value-added tradable services by addressing structural problems (such as local institutional and regulatory constraints) that stifle them.[32]

Conclusions

Among the multiple factors that shaped the emergence and persistence of LAC cities, first, location fundamentals seemed to have played less of a role in influencing the location of population and economic activities than in the rest of the world; and, second, agriculture fundamentals played a larger role than trade fundamentals in putting cities where they are today. These patterns likely stem from a mix of historical "accidents" and the fact that countries in the region urbanized before the fall of transport costs.

On the links between urbanization and productivity, comparing LAC with the rest of the world, we find that, using consistent measures of urbanization, the region's productivity is within global expectations for its urban share. Yet we also see substantial room for improvement because the region's gap with the global productivity frontier is widening.

Chapter 2 shifts the focus to LAC cities (and other regions) as the unit of analysis, examining dimensions of urbanization (the density of urban areas, the prevalence of multicity agglomerations, and urban primacy) beyond those captured by a country's urban population share; the relationship between these dimensions and national productivity performance; and productivity performance at the individual urban area level. These first two chapters provide a macrolevel foundation for the remaining chapters, which use microlevel data to analyze how the factors and trends they discuss affect workers and industries, transport infrastructures, human capital, and the spatial form of cities.

Notes

1. Henderson et al. (2016) classify three natural geographic endowments or location fundamentals: (i) base fundamentals (which include the presence of malaria and terrain ruggedness), (ii) agriculture fundamentals (which include a set of 14 biome indicators, among others), and (iii) trade fundamentals (which include five trade variables that focus on access to water transport). These three are expected to capture natural advantages that are spatially concentrated and could favor the concentration of population.

2. The cluster algorithm defines urban areas as dense, spatially contiguous clusters of population. For details, see box 1.2.

3. There were two waves of falling global transport cost. The first wave was from about 1840 to World War I. The second wave occurred right after 1950. Here we refer to the second wave (1950). See World Bank (2008), Krugman (1991a, 1991b, and 2007).

4. Around 1800 BCE, the growth of farming settlements—coupled with technological progress in modern-day Bolivia, Mexico, and Peru—sustained the critical mass for later development of cities in Latin America (Haas, Pozorski, and Pozorski 1987).

5. The R^2 goes up to 72 percent if one introduces country fixed effects, although it is not clear what these "fixed effects" might be capturing because the countries were not yet formed. They might be capturing differences in population density across the areas in the continent because some were sparsely populated and others were not, or the differences could be due to specific characteristics of indigenous civilizations that settled in the different areas of what became the LAC region.

6. According to legend, Huitzilopochtli, the god of war, the sun, and human sacrifice, directed the Mexican people to settle on the island in the middle of lake Texcoco. He "ordered his priests to look for the prickly pear cactus and build a temple in his honor. They followed the order and found the place on an island in the middle of the lake" (de Rojas 2012).

7. For example, when Hernán Cortés arrived in 1519 searching for gold in what is now Mexico, he landed in what he named Villa Rica de la Vera Cruz (modern-day Veracruz). He eventually declared the site a city to establish his legitimacy and use it as a point from which to stage attacks against Montezuma, the leader of Tenochtitlan (Saavedra-Chanduvi and Sennehauser 2009, 37; *The Economist* 2014).

8. The capital of Brazil, Brasilia, was founded in 1960 to serve as the nation's capital, replacing Rio de Janeiro, because Brasilia is in a more central location.

9. For example, being near the coast in precolonial times meant having nearby sources of food (fisheries) that could sustain settlements. In more recent times, a coastal location can also be an advantage for trade.

10. The persistence of subnational population density is not observed across all countries. Colombia and Mexico, for example, show higher than average persistence, whereas Argentina and Uruguay, for example, show a reversal of density (because the areas that are densely populated today were sparsely populated in precolonial times). Historical features lie behind many divergences in persistence, as covered by Maloney and Caicedo (2016).

11. WUP is compiled (from national sources) and maintained by the Population Division of the United Nation's Department of Economic and Social Affairs. We rely on data from the 2014 revision of WUP (https://esa.un.org/unpd/wup/).

12. The literature adopting subregional classifications of LAC presents no consensus on how to group the countries. We elected to include Mexico as part of South America, given its similarities (such as population, area, and density) with other countries in this subregion.

13. Calculations based on WUP, July 2017. Growth is calculated as the compound annual growth rate between year x and year $x+5$ for urban population (WUP estimates are available at five-year intervals). Over the same period, growth in the rural population passed from 1.18 percent per year between 1960 and 1961 to a contraction of 0.26 percent per year between 2014 and 2015. The rural population in the region has been shrinking since 1994.

14. We find that across the world there is a negative and statistically significant relationship ($p<0.01$) between the urban share and the urban population growth rate.

15. For all countries (except Austria), urban criteria fall into at least one of these four broadly defined categories. However, every country's definition is slightly different and may include particularities that are not fully reflected among these four. For example, the definition for Honduras was counted in the "population size" and "urban services or characteristics" categories, but it also has elements that do not fit neatly in either (such as "communication by land [road or train] or regular air or maritime service"). Austria's definition, according to the definition in the WUP, is based on commuting patterns into an urban core and does not fall into any of these categories.

16. The mean difference between Latin America and the Caribbean and the rest of the world is also statistically significant at the 10 percent level in a simple one-sided, two-sample, t-test where the alternative hypothesis is that the mean difference is negative (that is, the mean for LAC countries is less than that for non-LAC countries). Likewise, a Mann–Whitney U test—which may be more appropriate given the large size difference between the LAC and non-LAC samples and the absence of normality— rejects the null hypothesis that the LAC and non-LAC samples come from the same underlying population (Roberts et al. 2017).

17. Namely, LandScan 2012, GHS Pop, and WorldPop gridded population data.

18. Our analysis here is limited to urban shares as opposed to trends because only one cross-section (2012) of urban shares has been estimated using both the cluster method and the AI.

19. These results correspond to the use of the cluster method in combination with LandScan gridded population data for 2012.

20. This finding is consistent with results reported by Uchida and Nelson (2010) and the World Bank (2008), using the original version of the AI.

21. The estimated elasticity between GDP per capita and the urban share is 4.2 for 2012. The complete set of mechanisms linking urbanization to economic development is not entirely understood. We are grateful to Gilles Duranton for this observation.

22. We used the cluster algorithm and LandScan 2012 population grid. As shown by Roberts et al. (2017), similar results are found using the AI.

23. We conducted a similar analysis to the one in table 1.1, but with dummies for Sub-Saharan Africa countries, and found that they are systematically underperforming on official and consistent measures.

24. On the one hand are static productivity gains (gains in the level of productivity) when people move from traditionally less-productive sectors, such as agriculture, to more modern productive sectors, such as manufacturing and other industrial sectors. On the other hand are dynamic productivity gains (gains in the growth of productivity) resulting from changes in technology within each sector.

25. GGDC has data for 1950–2010, but our analysis covers 1960–2009 to ensure a balanced panel.

26. The GGDC dataset has been used by Timmer, de Vries, and de Vries (2015) and Rodrik (2015). Data from the World Development Indicators do not cover such a long period, nor are they consistent across years. *LAC-9* consists of Argentina, Bolivia, Brazil, Chile, Colombia, Costa Rica, Mexico, Peru, and República Bolivariana de Venezuela. *Asia* consists of India; Indonesia; Japan; Republic of Korea; Malaysia; Philippines; Singapore; Taiwan, China; and Thailand. *North America* consists of the United States. *Africa* consists of Botswana, Ethiopia, Ghana, Kenya, Malawi,

Mauritius, Nigeria, Senegal, South Africa, Tanzania, and Zambia. *Europe* consists of Denmark, Germany, France, Great Britain, Italy, Netherlands, Spain, and Sweden. *Middle East and North Africa* consists of the Arab Republic of Egypt and Morocco.

27. We conducted a regression analysis to test the relationship between the share of people employed in services and industry on the one hand and aggregate labor productivity (gross value added per employee) on the other. We found a significant and positive relationship between the shares of employment absorbed by the services and industrial sectors and a country's labor productivity. We also found that the Latin America and the Caribbean region is delivering significantly lower productivity gains—because of labor reallocation (from agriculture) to services and industry—than that observed in the rest of the world.

28. The primary limitation is that this data set covers only a small subset of countries in the world. In addition, the statistical foundations of GDP and employment estimates in many (developing) countries are subject to substantial measurement error (see, for example, Devarajan 2013; Jerven 2013), which can skew productivity estimates.

29. Using the World Bank Enterprise Surveys, Francis, Saliola, and Seker (2013) estimate performance using comparable firm-level data for 31 countries in the region. Their study finds that the annual growth rate in real labor productivity is declining in the manufacturing and services sectors in Latin America and the Caribbean, while concurrently those sectors add jobs. These trends show that LAC region's businesses are expanding their workforce but that revenue gains are lagging.

30. There is some growing evidence (Kim and Zangerling 2016) that lower productivity gains in the service sector in Latin America and the Caribbean might be linked to the concentration of labor in nontradable and low-value-added services, which appear to have limited productivity gains from agglomeration. A paper by Bonomi Barufi, Haddad, and Nijkamp (2016) finds that high- and low-tech manufacturing benefit the most from agglomeration economies in Brazil, followed by services associated with higher knowledge intensity. Low-skilled services and medium-tech manufacturing have the lowest coefficients of agglomeration economies.

31. A recent paper by Gaubert (2017), which studies the location choices of firms in a range of sectors across cities, also suggests that, in a general equilibrium model, there are productivity benefits from reducing congestion costs (increasing housing supply) because they allow for more efficient spatial organization of production in differentiated goods sectors.

32. As outlined in a recent World Bank book, *Africa Cities: Opening the Doors to the World* (Henderson, Venables, and Lall 2017), institutional and regulatory constraints can lead to a misallocation of land and labor, fragmented physical development, and limited productivity gains. All these can hold down the emergence of the tradable sector and trap cities into producing only locally traded goods and services.

References

Ades, Alberto, and Edward Glaeser. 1994. "Trade and Circuses: Explaining Urban Giants." *Quarterly Journal of Economics* 110 (1): 195–227.

Alvarez-Cuadrado, Francisco, and Markus Poschke. 2011. "Structural Change Out of Agriculture: Labor Push versus Labor Pull." *American Economic Journal: Macroeconomics* 3 (3): 127–58.

Arthur, W. Brian. 1994. *Increasing Returns and Path Dependence in the Economy.* Ann Arbor: University of Michigan Press.

Bairoch, Paul, and Christopher Braider. 1988. *Cities and Economic Development from the Dawn of History to the Present.* Chicago: University of Chicago.

Bonomi Barufi, Ana Maria, Eduardo A. Haddad, and Peter Nijkamp. 2016. "Industrial Scope of Agglomeration Economies in Brazil." *Annals of Regional Science* 56 (3): 707–55.

Chen, M., H. Zhang, W. Liu, and W. Zhang. 2014. "The Global Pattern of Urbanization and Economic Growth: Evidence from the Last Three Decades." *PLOS One* 9 (8): e103799.

Chenery, Hollis B., and Lance Taylor. 1968. "Development Patterns: Among Countries and over Time." *Review of Economics and Statistics* 50 (4): 391–416.

Comin, Diego, William Easterly, and Erick Gong. 2010. "Was the Wealth of Nations Determined in 1000 BC?" *American Economic Journal: Macroeconomics* 2 (3): 65–97.

Davis, Donald R., and David E. Weinstein. 2002. "Bones, Bombs, and Break Points: The Geography of Economic Activity." *American Economic Review* 92 (5): 1269–89.

Davis, James C., and J. V. Henderson. 2003. "Evidence on the Political Economy of the Urbanization Process." *Journal of Urban Economics* 53 (1): 98–125.

de Rojas, Jose Luis. 2012. *Tenochtitlán: Capital of the Aztec Empire.* Gainesville, FL: University of Florida Press.

Devarajan, Shantayanan. 2013. "Africa's Statistical Tragedy." *Review of Income and Wealth* 59 (2): 1–7.

Diamond, Jared M. 1997. *Guns, Germs and Steel: The Fate of Human Societies.* New York: W. W. Norton.

Dijkstra, L., and H. Poelman. 2014. "A Harmonised Definition of Cities and Rural Areas: The New Degree of Urbanization." Regional and Urban Policy Working Paper 01/2014, European Commission, Brussels.

Duranton, Gilles. 2015. "A Proposal to Delineate Metropolitan Areas in Colombia." *Desarrollo y Sociedad* 15: 223–64.

The Economist. 2014. "The Conquest of Mexico: On the Trail of Hernán Cortés." December 17.

Ellis, P., and M. Roberts. 2015. *Leveraging Urbanization in South Asia: Managing Spatial Transformation for Prosperity and Livability.* Washington, DC: World Bank.

Francis, David C., Federica Saliola, and Murat Seker. 2013. "Measuring Firm Performance in Latin America and the Caribbean." Brief, World Bank, Washington, DC.

Gaubert, Cecile. 2017. "Firm Sorting and Agglomeration." Working Paper, University of California, Berkeley.

Haas, Jonathan, Shelia Pozorski, and Thomas Pozorski, eds. 1987. *The Origins and Development of the Andean State.* Cambridge: Cambridge University Press.

Henderson, J. V. 2003. "The Urbanization Process and Economic Growth: The So-What Question." *Journal of Economic Growth* 8 (1): 47–71.

Henderson, J. V., Adam Storeygard, Tim L. Squires, and David N. Weil. 2016. "The Global Spatial Distribution of Economic Activity: Nature, History, and the Role of Trade." NBER Working Paper 22145, National Bureau of Economic Research, Cambridge, MA.

Henderson, J. V., Anthony J. Venables, and Somik Vinay Lall. 2017. *Africa's Cities: Opening Doors to the World.* Washington, DC: World Bank.

Herrendorf, Berthold, Richard Rogerson, and Akos Valentinyi. 2013. "Growth and Structural Transformation." NBER Working Paper 18996, National Bureau of Economic Research, Cambridge, MA.

Jerven, M. 2013. *Poor Numbers: How We Are Misled by African Development Statistics and What to Do about It.* Ithaca, NY: Cornell University Press.

Kim, Yoonhee, and Bontje Zangerling. 2016. *Mexico Urbanization Review: Managing Spatial Growth for Productive and Livable Cities in Mexico.* Washington, DC: World Bank.

Krugman, Paul. 1991a. *Geography and Trade,* Cambridge, Mass: MIT Press.

———. 1991b. "Increasing Returns and Economic Geography." *Journal of Political Economy* 99 (3): 483–99.

———. 2007. "The 'New' Economic Geography: Where Are We?" In *Regional Integration in East Asia,* edited by Masahisa Fujita, 23–34. New York: Palgrave Macmillan.

Krugman, Paul, and Raul Livas Elizondo. 1996. "Trade Policy and the Third World Metropolis." *Journal of Development Economics* 49 (1): 137–150.

Kuznets, Simon. 1973. "Modern Economic Growth: Findings and Reflections." *American Economic Review* 63 (3): 247–58.

Maloney, William F., and Felipe Valencia Caicedo. 2016. "The Persistence of (Subnational) Fortune." *The Economic Journal* 126 (598): 2363–2401.

Michaels, Guy, and Ferdinand Rauch. 2013. "Resetting the Urban Network: 117–2012." Economic Series Working Paper 684, University of Oxford, UK.

Olsson, Ola, and Douglas A. Hibbs Jr. 2005. "Biogeography and Long-Run Economic Development." *European Economic Review* 49: 909–38.

Organisation for Economic Co-operation and Development. 2012. *Redefining "Urban": A New Way to Measure Metropolitan Areas.* Paris: OECD Publishing.

Pages, Carmen, ed. 2010. *The Age of Productivity.* Washington, DC: Inter-American Development Bank.

Roberts, Mark, Brian Blankespoor, Chandan Deuskar, and Benjamin Stewart. 2017. "Urbanization and Development: Is Latin America and the Caribbean Different from the Rest of the World?" Policy Research Working Paper 8019, World Bank, Washington, DC.

Rodrik, Dani. 2015. "Premature Deindustrialization." *Journal of Economic Growth* 21 (1): 1–33.

Rozenfeld, Hernán D., Diego Rybski, Xavier Gabaix, and Hernan A. Makse. 2011. "The Area and Population of Cities: New Insights from a Different Perspective on Cities." *American Economic Review* 101 (5): 2205–25.

Saavedra-Chanduvi, Jaime, and Ethel Sennehauser. 2009. *Reshaping Economic Geography in Latin America and the Caribbean: A Companion Volume to the 2009 World Development Report.* Washington, DC: World Bank.

Spence, Michael, Patricia Clarke Annez, and Robert M. Buckley. 2009. *Urbanization and Growth: Commission on Growth and Development.* Washington, DC: World Bank.

Spolaore, Enrico, and Romain Wacziarg. 2013. "How Deep Are the Roots of Economic Development?" *Journal of Economic Literature* 51 (2): 325–69.

Timmer, M. P., G. J. de Vries, and K. de Vries. 2015. "Patterns of Structural Change in Developing Countries." In *Routledge Handbook of Industry and Development,* edited by J. Weiss and M. Tribe, 65–83. Abingdon, UK: Routledge.

Uchida, Hirotsugu, and Andrew Nelson. 2008. *Agglomeration Index: Towards a New Measure of Urban Concentration.* Washington, DC: World Bank.

Wahl, Fabian. 2016. "Does Medieval Trade Still Matter? Historical Trade Centers, Agglomeration and Contemporary Economic Development." *Regional Science and Urban Economics* 60 (C): 50–60.

World Bank. 2008. *World Development Report, 2009: Reshaping Economic Geography.* Washington, DC: World Bank.

The Many Dimensions of Urbanization and the Productivity of Cities in Latin America and the Caribbean

2

Mark Roberts

Introduction

The urban share of a country's population, as measured in chapter 1, is a useful indicator, but it captures only one aspect of a country's urbanization process. The character of urbanization may thus differ fundamentally among countries despite similar shares. Compare, for example, the notoriously "sprawling" nature of urbanization in the United States, complete with its sometimes seemingly never-ending suburbs, with the more "compact" urban development more typical of Western European countries.

This chapter aims to go beyond the previous chapter's analysis and provide a more in-depth examination of patterns of urbanization in the Latin America and the Caribbean (LAC) region and to see how these compare with those in the rest of the world along several dimensions of urbanization: density of urban areas, prevalence of agglomerations that consist of multiple "cities," and rates of urban primacy.[1] We also analyze whether these dimensions are related to

cross-country differences in gross domestic product (GDP) per capita.

In addition, this chapter examines productivity outcomes in individual LAC urban areas, benchmarking these against urban areas elsewhere in the world.[2] Because no settlement exists in isolation, we analyze the productivity dispersion across urban areas in LAC countries, again comparing them with those in non-LAC countries and regions. The better integrated are a country's urban areas through flows of goods, services, labor, capital, and ideas, the more productivity at the margin might be equalized between them, and the greater their contribution to productivity and growth at national level.[3]

To facilitate the comparison of urbanization patterns in the LAC region with those elsewhere, we build on the methods for the globally consistent definition of urban areas introduced in chapter 1, using the cluster algorithm of Dijkstra and Poelman (2014) to construct a global dataset of almost 64,000 urban areas in 192 countries for 2012. With this

The author thanks Angelica Maria Sanchez Diaz and Jane Park for excellent research assistance for this chapter, as well as Benjamin Stewart for invaluable Geographic Information System inputs.

dataset, we analyze differences in population size and density across urban areas. We also identify the presence of multicity agglomerations (MCAs), urban areas that consist of two or more cities. We analyze differences in the prevalence and characteristics of these MCAs between LAC and the rest of the world. By combining these data with high-resolution nighttime lights data, we also construct a measure of productivity at the individual urban area level. This facilitates analysis of the productivity performances of urban areas in the LAC region against those in the rest of the world, as well as of productivity dispersion across urban areas in LAC countries.

The main findings of the chapter are as follows:

- Urban areas in the LAC region stand out internationally for their high population densities, particularly in comparison with urban areas in Europe and Central Asia (ECA) and North America, where urban areas, on average, have similar populations but cover larger geographic areas. Most individual LAC countries also exhibit significantly higher urban densities than comparator countries.[4]

- The high urban densities in LAC countries may be exerting a negative effect on national levels of GDP per capita. This suggests that LAC cities may lack the "enabling environment" in both policy choices and infrastructure levels, required to mitigate productivity-sapping congestion costs and prevent them from overpowering the productivity benefits of agglomeration economies.

- Among world regions, Latin America and the Caribbean has the most MCAs in the world. A large share of the LAC region's urban population lives in these agglomerations and, as economic development continues, we can expect this share to increase further.

- There is no positive significant relationship, for the subregions of the Caribbean or Central America, between the share of a country's population living in MCAs and its GDP per capita, unlike North America and Western Europe but in common with the rest of the world. For South America, there is some evidence of a positive relationship, but this is far weaker than that for North America and Western Europe. Although alternative explanations exist, these results are consistent with the hypothesis that the difficulties associated with governing large metropolitan areas, which arise from the "fragmentation" of infrastructure and basic service provision across multiple local governments, can stifle the contribution that such areas make to national productivity unless effective coordination mechanisms are in place. Whereas North American and Western European countries have succeeded in this, LAC countries are less advanced.

- A significant number of LAC countries exhibit unusually high urban primacy, benchmarked against comparator countries in the rest of the world. These countries include Barbados and Dominica in the Caribbean, Costa Rica and Panama in Central America, and Argentina, Paraguay, and Uruguay in South America. However, despite concerns frequently expressed about the negative repercussions of high primacy on national economies, we find no evidence of a negative relationship with GDP per capita.

- Urban areas in South America and Mexico have relatively high productivity, globally benchmarked. However, they lag the global frontier of productivity performance. Urban areas in the rest of LAC tend to exhibit average productivity given their population sizes.

- LAC countries show relatively high productivity dispersion across urban areas, higher than in more developed countries. This high dispersion is associated with relatively low average national road density. This is consistent with relatively poorly integrated internal markets, and is suggestive of a spatial misallocation of resources across urban areas that may be undermining their aggregate contribution to national productivity.

Defining a Global Data Set of Urban Areas

A byproduct of the application of the cluster algorithm introduced in chapter 1 (in the "Urbanization in the LAC Region and the Rest of the World" section) is a global data set, for 2012, of 63,629 urban areas in 192 countries, including 7,197 urban areas in 34 LAC countries.[5] Each of these areas meets the criteria for an urban area specified by the algorithm, a spatially contiguous area for which population density (measured at a resolution of 1 km^2) is at least 300 people per square kilometer throughout the entire area and the overall population is at least 5,000. It is important to note that urban areas thus defined do not necessarily conform to official administrative boundaries of towns and cities. Rather, they correspond to a wide array of places, ranging from settlements that just meet the criteria[6] to extended urban agglomerations that cover hundreds of square kilometers and include tens of millions of people. At the extreme upper end of the distribution are nine urban areas—Delhi in India; Dhaka and Rajshahi in Bangladesh; Jakarta and Surabaya in Indonesia; Lahore in Pakistan; and Beijing, Chongqing, and Shanghai in China—all of which have implausibly large estimated populations of more than 45 million and which we, therefore, drop from further analysis, leaving us with a final global sample of 63,620 urban areas.[7]

In this global sample, we would also ideally like to quantify the number of local government units in each area, which would allow us to compare local government fragmentation in urban areas in the LAC region with the equivalent in the rest of the world. Whether such fragmentation is good or bad for infrastructure and service delivery, and thus productivity, is open to debate. By drawing an analogy with competitive markets for private goods, Tiebout (1956) hypothesized that competition between different political jurisdictions within an urban area may lead to efficiency in the local public sector. This is because residents will vote with their feet and move from jurisdictions where local service provision is less efficient to jurisdictions where it is more efficient. Against this, however, many analysts argue that, because of interjurisdictional spillovers, local government fragmentation—absent effective mechanisms for coordination between local governments—undermines the efficient provision of infrastructure and basic services in the wider urban area. Given that governance challenges often increase as the size of an urban area rises, discussion tends to focus on large metropolitan areas (Muzzini et al. 2016, for Argentina; Kim and Zangerling 2016, for Mexico).[8]

Unfortunately, there is no global data set of local government administrative boundaries that would allow us to quantify the number of local government units within each urban area.[9] We are, however, able to identify urban areas that consist of multiple "cities," where a "city" in this context is defined by its administrative boundaries. In some cases, such a "city" may represent a distinct center or subcenter of an urban area, but, in others, it may amount to little more than a suburb of another "city" in the same area, even though it is administratively distinct. Following CIESIN (2013); Zhou, Hubacek, and Roberts (2015); and Ellis and Roberts (2016); we refer to such urban areas as *multicity agglomerations* (MCAs).

We identify "cities" in urban areas, and thus MCAs, by using Geographic Information System (GIS) techniques to overlay a global layer of individual settlement points on a global map of our urban areas.[10] The results that we report in the main text focus on MCAs defined based on cities that have a minimum population of 100,000 each. This is because the global layer of settlement points more reliably identifies such cities. Importantly, however, our main regression results (reported in the "Implications for National Productivity" section later in this chapter) are robust to redefining an MCA as an urban area containing two or more settlements, as taken from the global settlement point layer, of any population size.[11]

In total, the number of MCAs with two or more cities, each with a minimum population of 100,000, identified is small—only 295 globally, including 54 in the LAC region (0.46 percent of all urban areas worldwide).

Urban Areas in the LAC Region Are More Densely Populated Than Those Elsewhere

Using our global sample of urban areas, we compare patterns of urbanization in the LAC region with those in the rest of the world along dimensions that go beyond the simple comparison of urban shares. The feature of LAC urbanization that most stands out from such a comparison is the higher average population density in its urban areas. As table 2.1 shows, at 2,360 people per square kilometer, the mean population density for LAC urban areas is 1.54 times the global figure. Similarly, the median population density for

TABLE 2.1   **Summary Statistics for Global Sample of Urban Areas**

	Mean	25th percentile	Median	75th percentile	99th percentile	Maximum
World (N = 63,620; total urban population ≈ 3.73 billion)						
Population	58,642	6,632	10,154	22,417	732,556	43,790,629
Area (km²)	36.8	5.5	10.9	22.8	389.4	22,321
Population density (per km²)	1,529	723	1,181	1,901	6,488	36,186
No. of cities in urban area	0.057	0	0	0	1	66
Latin America and the Caribbean (N = 7,197; total urban population ≈ 432.9 million)						
Population	60,151	7,259	11,762	24,928	832,365	20,588,698
Area (km²)	18.4	4.4	7.2	13.1	209.6	3,404
Population density (per km²)	2,360	1,304	1,961	2,948	8,180	19,232
No. of cities in urban area	0.080	0	0	0	1	30
Caribbean (N = 473; total urban population ≈ 23.6 million)						
Population	49,826	6,790	11,419	23,001	668,129	3,431,292
Area (km²)	18.3	4.7	8.3	14.7	176.9	569
Population density (per km²)	2,007	1,045	1,568	2,495	6,944	9,956
No. of cities in urban area	0.101	0	0	0	1	20
Central America (N = 1,778; total urban population ≈ 110 million)						
Population	61,860	6,941	11,043	24,047	916,871	19,782,701
Area (km²)	20.3	5.4	8.3	14.1	212.4	2,651
Population density (per km²)	1,930	1,052	1,542	2,383	6,778	10,232
No. of cities in urban area	0.069	0	0	0	1	16
South America (N = 4,946; total urban population ≈ 299.4 million)						
Population	60,524	7,427	12,182	25,368	819,726	20,588,698
Area (km²)	17.7	3.7	6.6	12.5	207.0	3,404
Population density (per km²)	2,549	1,479	2,152	3,117	8,757	19,232
No. of cities in urban area	0.082	0	0	0	1	30

Source: Calculations based on analysis of urban areas defined using the cluster algorithm of Dijkstra and Poelman (2014), as applied to LandScan 2012 gridded population data.
Note: "No. of cities in urban area" refers to the number of cities with a population exceeding 100,000 whose settlement points intersect with an urban area. An urban area that intersects with two or more such settlement points is defined as a multicity agglomeration.

FIGURE 2.1   **Percentage of Urban Areas with Population Densities Higher Than the Global Median, by Region**

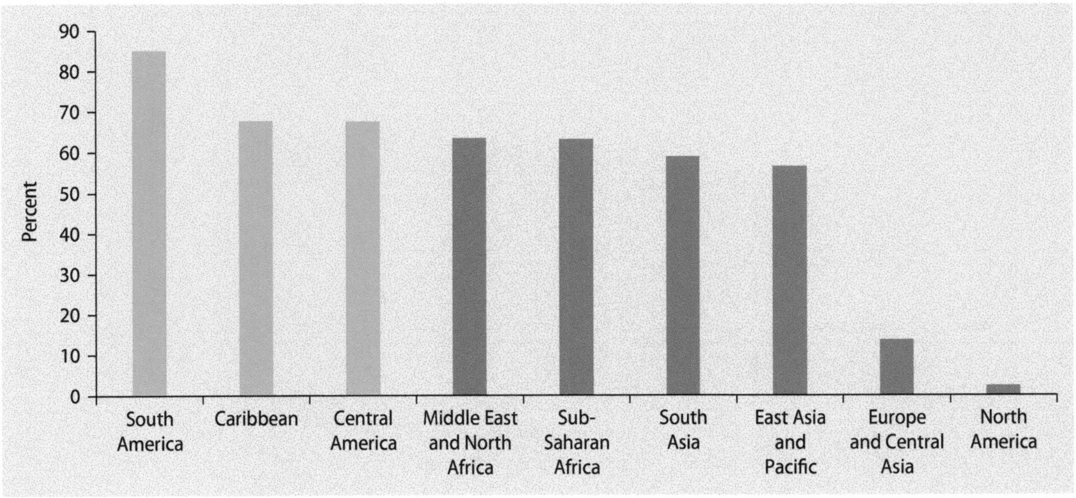

Source: Calculations based on analysis of urban areas defined using the cluster algorithm of Dijkstra and Poelman (2014), as applied to LandScan 2012 gridded population data.
Note: An urban area is classified as dense if its mean population density exceeds the global median of 1,180 people per square kilometer.

LAC urban areas, which is almost 2,000 people per square kilometer, exceeds the median for all urban areas globally by 66 percent.

Likewise, if we define urban areas as either "dense" or "not dense" depending on whether their mean population densities exceed or fall below the median of almost 1,200 people per square kilometer for all areas globally, South America, Central America, and the Caribbean lead the way globally on the relative prevalence of dense urban areas (figure 2.1). The contrast is particularly marked against the more developed regions of ECA and North America. Whereas the proportion of urban areas classified as dense exceeds 65 percent in each of the three LAC subregions, in ECA the figure is just less than 14 percent and in North America a little over 2 percent. The higher urban densities in the LAC region are the result not so much of differences in the populations of urban areas but in the land areas that they cover (figure 2.2). LAC urban areas tend to be geographically much smaller than those in ECA and North America.[12]

High population densities across LAC urban areas are, moreover, attributable not just to a few large countries: the proportion of urban areas classified as "dense" is at least 50 percent for all but four of the 34 LAC countries in the global sample (figure 2.3). In six of these countries—Aruba, Belize, Brazil, Dominica, Peru, and República Bolivariana de Venezuela—that proportion exceeds 90 percent and in a further seven is 80–90 percent. Three countries that break the pattern are Argentina, Grenada, and Barbados, with dense proportions of roughly 36 percent, 25 percent, and 20 percent respectively. In several, mainly Caribbean, countries (Antigua and Barbuda, the Bahamas, Guyana, Jamaica, and St. Kitts and Nevis) the split between "dense" and "not dense" is roughly 50:50, which, by construction, mirrors the global distribution.

The finding of high urban population densities in most LAC countries also carries over when, instead of comparing them with the rest of the world, we compare each LAC country with a corresponding set of three comparator countries selected using the methodology set out in box 2.1. As annex 2B shows, 20 LAC countries exhibit mean urban population densities significantly greater than those in the corresponding comparators.[13]

FIGURE 2.2   Distribution of Area Size and Population across Urban Areas, Selected Regions

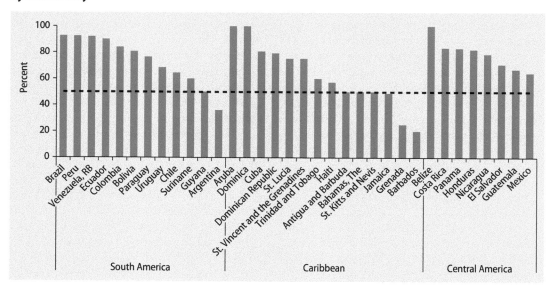

Source: Calculations based on analysis of urban areas defined using the cluster algorithm of Dijkstra and Poelman (2014), as applied to LandScan 2012 gridded population data.
Note: Panels a and b show, for different regions, the distribution of area (in square kilometers) and population (in natural logs), respectively, of urban areas using an Epanechnikov kernel. For expositional purposes, the distributions of area are trimmed at 100 km².

FIGURE 2.3   Percentage of Urban Areas with Population Densities Higher Than the Global Median, by LAC Country

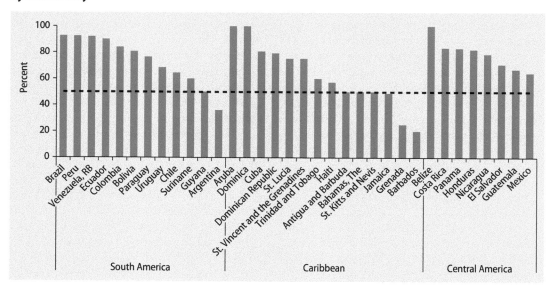

Source: Calculations based on analysis of urban areas defined using the cluster algorithm of Dijkstra and Poelman (2014), as applied to LandScan 2012 gridded population data.
Note: Countries are sorted in descending order within each of three subregions (South America, Caribbean, and Central America). The black dashed line is included to facilitate comparison of the distribution of "dense" versus "not dense" urban areas in any given LAC country to the distribution of such areas globally (by definition, 50 percent of urban areas globally are classified as "dense"). LAC = Latin America and the Caribbean.

BOX 2.1   Comparing Apples with Apples: Selecting Comparators for LAC Countries

Throughout this chapter, we benchmark individual Latin American and Caribbean countries against a corresponding matched set of comparator countries drawn from the rest of the world. These comparisons complement the more straightforward regional comparisons, that is, the comparisons of Latin America and the Caribbean (LAC) against other World Bank–defined regions, presented in this chapter. Such regional comparisons suffer from the problem that the differences they reveal may be driven by differences in the composition of the "types" of countries, for example, in the proportion of small island nations that make up each region. The individual-country benchmarking is intended to provide a cleaner comparison, because a LAC country can, in key respects, be considered more like its corresponding set of comparator countries than countries outside that set.

In selecting comparator countries for a given LAC country, there is a temptation to use the development level (gross domestic product per capita) as one of the criteria. It would seem natural to compare a middle-income LAC country against middle-income countries in the rest of the world. However, we avoid this temptation because gross domestic product per capita is too closely related to the outcome of productivity.

Instead, we adopted a two-stage procedure for selecting comparator countries. In the first stage, we classified all countries globally as island, landlocked, or the rest and, for each LAC country, searched for countries in the rest of the world falling into the same category. For each LAC country, this gives a long list of potential comparators. In the second stage, we then whittled down the list to a final set of three comparators by selecting the "nearest neighbors" on population, land area, and overall mean population density. In doing so, we imposed the restriction that the set of comparators must include at least one country from each of the East Asia and Pacific and Europe and Central Asia regions, which are commonly used comparator regions for the LAC region (Ferreyra et al. 2017). We selected the third comparator country unrestrictedly from the rest of the world. This helps to avoid all comparator countries being drawn from, for example, Sub-Saharan Africa, and helps to ensure geographic diversity among the comparators.

One might ask, "Why restrict the number of comparators for each LAC country to three?" The choice was based on experimentation with the data. For any given LAC country, it was found that, as the number of countries in its comparison set was expanded, the quality of the "match" with the added marginal country decreased, undermining the quality of the comparison. Three was found to be the optimal average size of the comparison group.

High urban densities represent a double-edged sword. On the one hand, they can help to stimulate powerful agglomeration economies that spur productivity through a variety of mechanisms, including through the spillover of knowledge between firms and workers, the growth of a large local base of intermediate input suppliers, and better matching of workers with jobs (Marshall 1890; Duranton and Puga 2004). However, high densities also give rise to adverse congestion forces, which can undermine productivity within cities. These include not only traffic congestion externalities but also costs that arise more generally from the pressure of urban population on the supply of basic urban services and infrastructure, land and housing markets, and the environment (Ellis and Roberts 2016). High urban densities can also work to propagate infectious disease vectors and act as a stimulus for crime and violence.

Glaeser (2011) has dubbed these congestion forces the "demons of density," and there can come a tipping point for any urban area where the positive externalities and spillovers of density come to be outweighed by the negative effects of congestion, such that the effects of increased density on productivity are negative. The exact urban density of this "tipping point" is dependent on the "enabling environment" for positive net agglomeration effects that cities offer, where this enabling environment is itself a function of policy choices that affect the management of cities and levels of urban infrastructure development. For example, investments in urban infrastructure and increases in the supply of affordable housing will tend to alleviate congestion costs at any given urban density and push the "tipping point" further away. Technologies and the mix of industries that characterize an urban area may also exert an important influence on the "tipping point"—for example, improvements in the technology for fighting and deterring crime may also push the point farther away. Comprehensive data on the types of congestion forces and the costs in terms of productivity and welfare are lacking; box 2.2 discusses the limited information available.

BOX 2.2   Congestion Forces in LAC Urban Areas

How strong are congestion forces in Latin American and Caribbean urban areas, and how large are the costs that they impose on firms and workers? Unfortunately, because of the absence of comprehensive data, we can provide no direct answer to this quesion. More generally, within the field of urban economics, there is a surprising dearth of rigorous empirical research on the quantification of congestion costs, their relationship to urban density, and the influence that policy can have on mitigating their effects. There are, however, three areas where we can provide some basic descriptive information.

Congestion in Housing Markets
Absent a sufficiently elastic supply of formal housing, high urban densities can generate strong upward pressure on rents and house prices. The consequent pricing-out of households from the formal housing market can, in turn, cause the proliferation of informal housing (often, slums), which acts as the outward manifestation of "excessive" congestion forces in land and housing markets.

In the Latin America and the Caribbean (LAC) region, congestion in these markets is evident in the existence of the infamous *favelas* of Rio de Janeiro and the *villas* of Gran Buenos Aires. More generally, although countries such as Mexico have made inroads into expanding their housing stock and the access of low-income households to mortgage finance (Kim and Zangerling 2016), slums remain a notable feature of the region's urban landscape.[a] According to UN-Habitat data, one in every five urban residents in the LAC region was living in a slum in 2014, implying an overall urban slum population of 104 million, roughly equal to the entire population of the Philippines. Furthermore, it took the LAC region just under 25 years to reduce the share of its urban population in slums from about 35 percent in 1990 to its 2014 figure. If we extrapolate forward this pace of reduction, slums will remain a feature of LAC cities for decades to come.

Traffic Congestion
Although regional rates of motorization in the LAC region (about 100–300 vehicles per 1,000 people) are a fraction of existing rates in developed nations (roughly 500–700 vehicles in Europe and the United States), they are nonetheless associated with traffic congestion that is among the worst in the world (Barbero 2012; see also chapter 4). According to 2016 TomTom traffic index data, which cover 390 cities in 41 countries, Mexico City holds the dubious honor of being the world's most congested city because travel time in the city is, on average, 66 percent higher during the day than it would be in a free-flow traffic situation.[b]

A further eight LAC cities, out of the 12 LAC cities in the data, feature in TomTom's list of the 100 most congested cities. Even in the least congested of these cities, Belo Horizonte in Brazil, travel time within the city is, on average, 27 percent higher during the day than it would be if the roads were uncongested. To put these numbers into perspective, travel times in London are, on average, 44 percent higher than in the free-flow situation, and in New York 35 percent higher. More generally (figure B2.2.1), traffic congestion rises much more rapidly with population density for the LAC cities than for the non-LAC cities for which TomTom provides data.

(continued)

BOX 2.2   Congestion Forces in LAC Urban Areas *(continued)*

FIGURE B2.2.1   Relationship between Traffic Congestion and Population Density, LAC Cities versus Non-LAC Cities

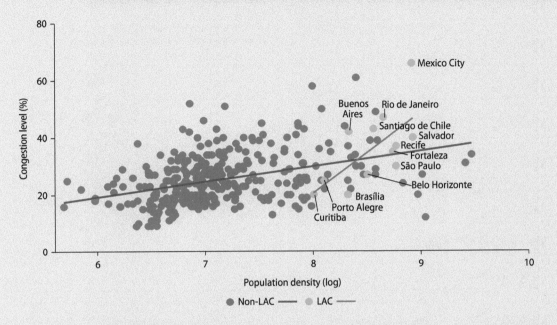

Source: Calculations based on TomTom traffic index data (https://www.tomtom.com/en_gb/ trafficindex/). Population density calculations based on urban areas defined using the cluster algorithm of Dijkstra and Poelman (2014), as applied to LandScan 2012 gridded population data.
Note: Congestion is measured as the percentage of extra travel time for trips by road in a city compared with the free-flow traffic situation. The data cover 390 cities globally, including 12 in three LAC countries (Brazil, Chile, and Mexico). LAC = Latin America and the Caribbean.

Air Pollution

This is an area where LAC cities perform much better, as seen in figure B2.2.2, panel a, which shows box plots of concentration in ambient air of fine particulate matter of 2.5 μm or less ($PM_{2.5}$) based on data covering about 3,000 cities globally, from the Global Urban Ambient Air Pollution database of the World Health Organization (WHO). Median air pollution across the 128 LAC cities in the database is notably less than that in other developing world regions. Panel b shows that, although for non-LAC developing country cities there is a significant positive correlation between a city's population density and its $PM_{2.5}$ concentration, no such correlation exists for LAC cities.

This is not to say, however, that the air in LAC cities is safe to breathe; it is far from it: Only 11 out of the 128 LAC cities in the WHO database have $PM_{2.5}$ levels less than what the WHO guidelines stipulate as representing a significant health threat.

(continued)

BOX 2.2   Congestion Forces in LAC Urban Areas *(continued)*

FIGURE B2.2.2   **Air Pollution in Cities in Latin America and the Caribbean and Other Regions**

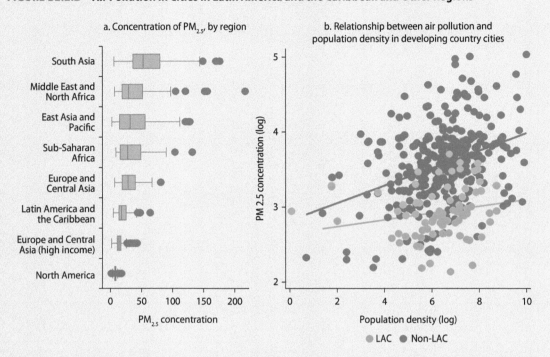

a. Concentration of PM$_{2.5}$, by region

b. Relationship between air pollution and population density in developing country cities

● LAC ● Non-LAC

Source: Calculations based on data on levels of PM$_{2.5}$ taken from the World Health Organization's Global Urban Ambient Air Pollution Database (http://www.who.int/phe/health_topics/outdoorair/databases/cities/en/).
Note: Panel a shows, for each region, a box plot of the mean annual PM$_{2.5}$ measured at the city level. Data cover measures of PM$_{2.5}$ mostly in 2013 and 2014, for almost 3,000 cities in 101 countries. Regions are sorted descending by the regional average. The left and right caps are the minimum and maximum value, excluding outliers. To identify outliers, we calculate the interquartile range; values outside the range defined by (25th Percentile − 1.5 × Interquartile Range, 75th Percentile + 1.5 × Interquartile Range) are considered outliers. Panel b shows a scatterplot for the relation between the natural log of a city's population density and its (natural log) PM$_{2.5}$ concentration. The sample for panel b covers 384 cities in 43 developing countries. LAC = Latin America and the Caribbean; PM$_{2.5}$ = annual concentration of fine particulate matter of 2.5 μm or less.

a. Although Mexico has made inroads into expanding its housing stock, the policies that have made this expansion possible have been criticized for, among other things, contributing to uncoordinated urban growth. Hence, much of the low-cost housing has been constructed on the outskirts of municipalities with poor access to employment opportunities and an absence of links with urban planning and infrastructure provision. This has contributed to much of the housing being left vacant. For a full discussion of these issues, see Kim and Zangerling (2016).
b. Although the TomTom data measure traffic congestion by comparing to the free-flow traffic situation, this does not provide an accurate measure of the true deadweight loss of congestion. The cost imposed on other road users by the marginal road user is given by the marginal cost of travel minus the average cost of travel. The deadweight loss of traffic congestion is then equal to the sum of these costs where the sum is over the road users who would not travel in the presence of optimal congestion pricing. See Akbar and Duranton (2017) for a further discussion and an attempt to empirically estimate the true deadweight loss of traffic congestion for Bogotá.

A Significant Share of Latin America and the Caribbean's Urban Population Lives in Large MCAs

Besides high population densities, another notable feature of LAC urbanization is the presence of MCAs. We define an MCA as an urban area that consists of two or more "cities," each of which is defined based on its administrative boundaries. While the number of these urban areas—295 globally—is very small set against the total number of urban areas (see the "Defining a Global Data Set of Urban Areas" section), their size and economic significance make them of special interest. Although MCAs represent only 0.46 percent of the urban areas in our global sample, they are home to an estimated 1.27 billion people—about one-third of the world's urban population. For a full list of the LAC region's MCAs, see annex 2C.

Such urban areas are also of interest because they tend to represent large metropolitan areas that are typically fragmented into multiple local government jurisdictions. In São Paulo, for example, the urban area, defined using the cluster algorithm, encompasses 34 municipalities; Mexico City, 57; and Santo Domingo in the Dominican Republic, 19 (map 2.1).[14] Although, as discussed earlier in this chapter, it has been argued, following Tiebout (1956), that the fragmentation of metropolitan areas into multiple jurisdictions can improve the efficiency of local service delivery by promoting competition between these jurisdictions, it can also create difficulties in coordinating infrastructure provision and service delivery at the level of the metropolitan area. Without mechanisms for metropolitan coordination, these difficulties can, in turn, have negative repercussions for the metro area's productivity (Ahrend et al. 2014; see also chapter 6).

With 54 MCAs, LAC is second only to East Asia and Pacific (EAP) in World Bank regions (table 2.2). Most of these MCAs (38) are in South America, with 12 in Central America and 4 in the Caribbean.[15] By population, the largest of these MCAs is São Paolo, with an estimated 20.6 million inhabitants. The urban area of Buenos Aires encompasses

more cities, however: 30 against São Paulo's 23. These MCAs exhibit high average population densities, exceeding the global median for all urban areas of just under 1,200 people per square kilometer. Again, this provides a major contrast with ECA, where 24 out of 40 MCAs are dense, and North America, where only 9 out of 33 MCAs are dense.

Except for EAP, agglomerations in the Caribbean and South America also generally consist of more cities than agglomerations in other regions do. The mean number of cities per agglomeration in the Caribbean is 6.75, and for South America, just less than 5. The mean number of cities per agglomeration in Central America is 4.42, which is less than in North America, but more than in ECA, Sub-Saharan Africa, the Middle East and North Africa, and South Asia. However, the distribution of the number of cities per agglomeration shows a heavy positive skew in all regions. The modal number of cities per agglomeration for all regions, including LAC and its subregions, is two.

The share of overall urban population living in MCAs ranges from just over 37 percent in Central America to 41 percent in South America, similar to EAP and South Asia (figure 2.4). Had we included the nine excluded large urban areas in the sample, this share would have been far higher in EAP and South Asia than in the LAC subregions.[16] At just under 45 percent, the share of North America's urban population living in MCAs is also higher than in the LAC subregions.

By distribution across countries, one half (27 out of 54) of the LAC region's MCAs are in only two countries: Brazil (19 MCAs) and Mexico (8 MCAs) (figure 2.5, panel a). Argentina, Chile, and Peru each has three, República Bolivariana de Venezuela and the Dominican Republic two each. A further nine countries in the region possess a single agglomeration, and the other 17 have no MCAs. Among LAC countries with at least one MCA, there is quite marked heterogeneity in the share of urban population living in those areas (figure 2.5, panel b). In Venezuela,

MAP 2.1   Examples of Multicity Agglomerations in Latin America and the Caribbean That Span Multiple Municipalities

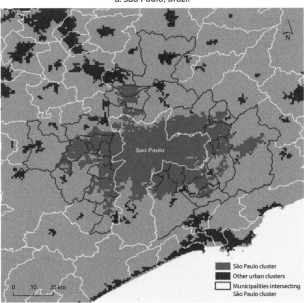

a. São Paulo, Brazil

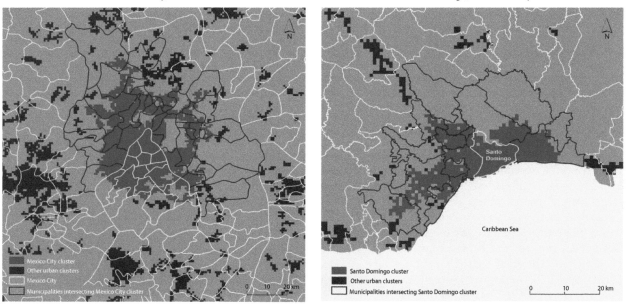

b. Mexico City, Mexico

c. Santo Domingo, Dominican Republic

Note: The red areas correspond to urban areas defined using the cluster algorithm of Dijkstra and Poelman (2014), as applied to LandScan 2012 gridded population data. The yellow lines represent subnational administrative boundaries at the Admin-2 (municipality) level that belong to a city as officially defined. The dark blue lines represent the boundaries of Admin-2 areas that intersect with the urban area but that do not belong to the officially defined city.

TABLE 2.2   **Number of Multicity Agglomerations, by Region**

	All multicity agglomerations			Dense multicity agglomerations		
	Total	% of global total	Mean no. of cities	Total	% of global total	Mean no. of cities
World Bank regions						
East Asia and Pacific	90	30.51	5.40	83	34.3	5.67
Latin America and the Caribbean	54	18.31	4.98	54	22.31	4.98
Europe and Central Asia	40	13.56	3.90	24	9.92	3.58
North America	33	11.19	4.45	9	3.72	7.67
South Asia	33	11.19	4.15	28	11.57	4.50
Sub-Saharan Africa	24	8.14	3.54	24	9.92	3.54
Middle East and North Africa	21	7.12	3.62	20	8.26	3.70
Total	295	100	4.59	242	100	4.88
LAC subregions						
South America	38	12.88	4.97	38	15.7	4.97
Central America	12	4.07	4.42	12	4.96	4.42
Caribbean	4	1.36	6.75	4	1.65	6.75

Source: Calculations based on analysis of urban areas defined using the cluster algorithm of Dijkstra and Poelman (2014), as applied to LandScan 2012 gridded population data.
Note: A multicity agglomeration is defined as an urban area with two or more cities, each of which has a population of at least 100,000; an agglomeration is classified as dense if its mean population density exceeds the sample median for all urban areas globally. "Mean no. of cities" refers to those with a population of at least 100,000 per multicity agglomeration.

FIGURE 2.4   **Percentage of Urban Population Living in Multicity Agglomerations, by Region**

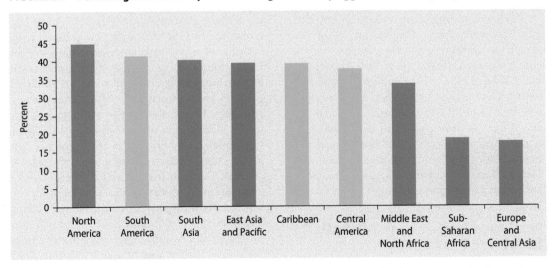

Source: Calculations based on analysis of urban areas defined using the cluster algorithm of Dijkstra and Poelman (2014), as applied to LandScan 2012 gridded population data.
Note: A multicity agglomeration is defined as an urban area with two or more cities, each of which has a population of at least 100,000.

FIGURE 2.5   **Multicity Agglomerations, by LAC Country**

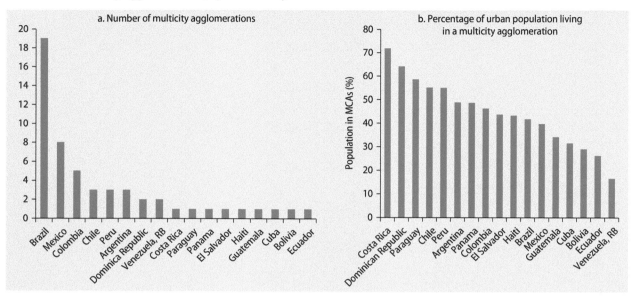

Source: Calculations based on analysis of urban areas defined using the cluster algorithm of Dijkstra and Poelman (2014), as applied to LandScan 2012 gridded population data.
Note: A multicity agglomeration is defined as an urban area with two or more cities, each of which has a population of at least 100,000.

the share is only some 17 percent, but in Costa Rica it is more than 70 percent (in the only agglomeration of San Jose). In Argentina, Brazil, Colombia, and Mexico, the shares are 40–50 percent.

There is a strong positive correlation, globally, between a country's urban share—as estimated using the cluster algorithm—and the share of its national population living in MCAs (figure 2.6). This implies that, as LAC countries continue to develop and urbanize, we can expect the potential governance challenges of having multiple jurisdictions within large metropolitan areas to mount, particularly for relatively populous LAC countries such as Ecuador, Guatemala, and Peru, which are still at an intermediate urban share.[17]

A Third of LAC Countries Analyzed Suffer from Potentially Excessive Primacy

One of the most debated characteristics of urbanization in the LAC region is excessive

primacy in many of the region's countries, where primacy refers to the share of a country's urban population residing in its largest city. Primacy is considered excessive when it acts as a drag on overall national productivity and on economic growth. It is caused by overcongestion in the largest city, which itself results from policy distortions that bias the allocation of resources toward that city at the expense of other cities or rural areas. High primacy rates in major Latin American countries have been linked to the widespread trade policy distortions of the import substitution industrialization era of the 1960s and 1970s, and to the concurrent high rates of political centralization in many LAC countries (Ades and Glaeser 1995; Davis and Henderson 2003; Krugman and Elizondo 1996).[18] Using a framework in which the effects of primacy on long-run economic growth can vary nonlinearly with a country's development level and its overall size, Henderson (2000) identifies 24 countries worldwide as suffering from

FIGURE 2.6   Cross-Country Relationship between Urban Share and Share of National Population Living in Multicity Agglomerations

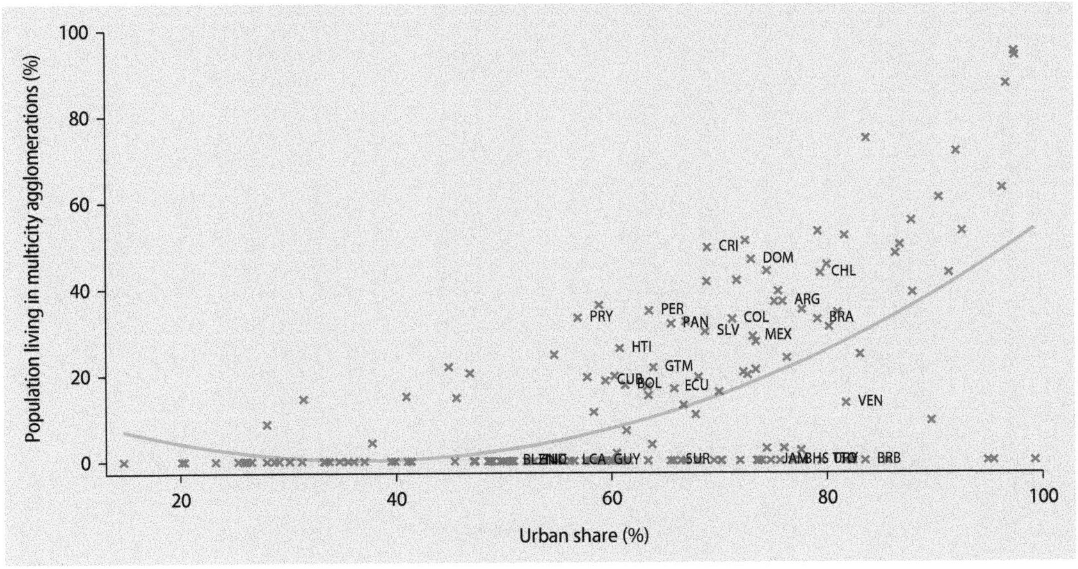

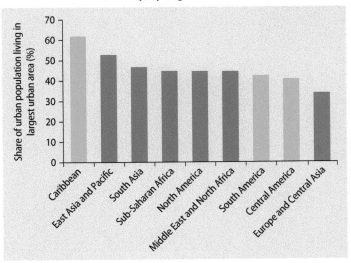

Source: Calculations based on analysis of urban areas defined using the cluster algorithm of Dijkstra and Poelman (2014), as applied to LandScan 2012 gridded population data.
Note: A multicity agglomeration is defined as an urban area with two or more cities, each of which has a population of at least 100,000; urban share is a country's urban share of the population as measured on the basis of the cluster algorithm. The figure illustrates 176 countries covered by the global data set of urban areas. We prefer to fit a nonlinear relationship in figure 2.6 rather than a linear relationship because this avoids a negative estimated intercept. Logically, the share of a country's population living in multicity agglomerations must be zero bound. For a list of country abbreviations, see annex 2A.

excessive primacy in 1990.[19] Out of these 24, 11 were in the LAC region.[20]

Yet, the strong persistence often inherent in urban systems still sees high urban primacy rates in the region even if the original factors have dissipated.[21] When we look at current rates of urban primacy (measured using our global data set of consistently defined urban areas), we see a marked difference between the Caribbean and Central and South America (figure 2.7).

The above simple comparisons may, however, be misleading. It is natural to expect that Caribbean countries, given their small sizes, will tend to exhibit higher primacy, and Henderson (2000) also reports that the "optimal" primacy, when the rate of long-run economic growth is maximized, is decreasing with a country's population size.[22] It is more relevant to compare Caribbean countries with their comparators. Figure 2.8, panel a, shows

FIGURE 2.7   Urban Primacy, by Region

Source: Calculations based on analysis of urban areas defined using the cluster algorithm of Dijkstra and Poelman (2014), as applied to LandScan 2012 gridded population data.
Note: For each region, the figure shows the unweighted mean urban primacy rate across countries. Urban primacy is defined as the share of a country's urban population living in its largest urban area. The figure is based on the nontrimmed global sample of urban areas. North America comprises Bermuda, Canada, and the United States.

FIGURE 2.8   **Urban Primacy, LAC Countries and Comparators**

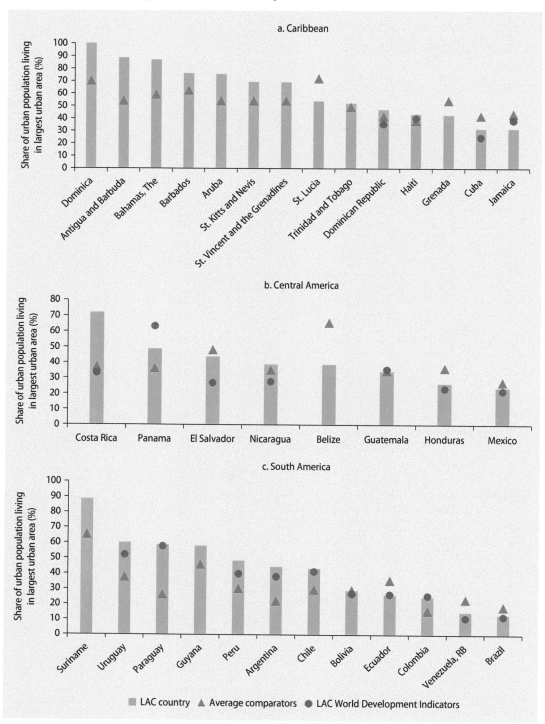

Source: Calculations based on analysis of urban areas defined using the cluster algorithm of Dijkstra and Poelman (2014), as applied to LandScan 2012 gridded population data, and World Development Indicators data (http://data.worldbank.org/data-catalog/world-development-indicators).
Note: The comparators for each LAC country were selected as described in box 2.1. "Average comparators" refers to the unweighted mean urban primacy rate in the comparator countries, and "LAC World Development Indicators" refers to a LAC country's urban primacy rate for 2012 as reported in the World Development Indicators. LAC = Latin America and the Caribbean.

that on such a comparison 7 out of 14 Caribbean countries exhibit urban primacy notably above the average for their corresponding sets of comparator countries. For the other seven, there is either no notable difference or the urban primacy rate is less than the average for the comparator countries.

Benchmarking urban primacy rates in LAC countries against those in their comparator countries also reveals that, although average urban primacy rates may not appear particularly high in either Central or South America, in some of the countries in these subregions high primacy may still be a potential problem for overall national productivity and economic growth (figure 2.8, panels b and c). In Central America, Costa Rica and Panama have urban primacy rates that notably exceed the averages for their comparator countries. In South America, Argentina, Chile, Paraguay, Peru, Suriname, and Uruguay all have urban primacy rates that appear high against their comparators. Several of these countries appear among the list that Henderson (2000) identifies as suffering from excessive primacy in 1990. More generally, relative to their comparison groups, 15 out of 35 LAC countries exhibit high, and potentially excessive, urban primacy.

For comparison, figure 2.8 also reports urban primacy rates for 2012 from the World Bank's World Development Indicators (WDI). Urbanization metrics reported in WDI, including urban primacy, are based on national definitions of urban areas.[23] As can be seen, levels of urban primacy calculated using our global data set conform well with those reported in WDI for both Caribbean and South American countries. Large differences are, however, apparent for Costa Rica, El Salvador, Nicaragua, and Panama.

Implications for National Productivity: Density and MCAs Matter, but Urban Primacy Does Not

In this section, we analyze whether, controlling for a country's overall urban share,

there is any relationship between the three key dimensions of urbanization examined—density, MCAs, and urban primacy—and national GDP per capita levels. For 2012, we examine the relationship between a country's (natural log) GDP per capita and (i) two alternative measures of urban density; (ii) the share of its overall population living in MCAs; and (iii) its urban primacy rate. On (i), the two measures of urban density that we explore are, first, the share of a country's overall population living in dense urban areas, and, second, the (natural log) mean density of a country's urban areas weighted by the share of each urban area in a country's overall urban population ("Log (Weighted Density)" in table 2.3).

Because the relationships presented are correlations, the following results, even if consistent with theories outlined previously,[24] cannot be regarded as providing causal evidence.[25]

Table 2.3 presents the results of several regressions, all estimated using a single global cross-section of 169 countries, of a country's (natural log) GDP per capita on dimensions of urbanization. Throughout columns 1–3 a country's GDP per capita continues to be positively and significantly correlated with the share of its overall population living in urban areas (its urban share), as measured using the cluster algorithm, even after accounting for other dimensions of urbanization.[26] The results in columns 1a and 1b show that, at any given urban share, a country's GDP per capita is negatively related with the two alternative measures of urban density. Although this negative relationship is insignificant when the measure of density is "Percentage of population in dense," it is highly significant when the measure is "Log (Weighted Density)"—compare column 1b with column 1a. In the latter case, a 10 percent increase in weighted urban density is associated with about a 5 percent drop in GDP per capita. In columns 1a and 1b, the share of a country's overall population living in MCAs bears no relationship to GDP per capita.

TABLE 2.3 Cross-Country Regression of Log(GDP per Capita) on Different Dimensions of Urbanization

	(1a)	(1b)	(2a)	(2b)	(3a)	(3b)
Urban share (%)	0.047***	0.036***	0.044***	0.036***	0.043***	0.034***
	(0.008)	(0.005)	(0.009)	(0.005)	(0.008)	(0.005)
Percentage of population in dense	−0.010		−0.006		−0.006	
	(0.007)		(0.008)		(0.008)	
Log(Weighted Density)		−0.477***		−0.415**		−0.432***
		(0.140)		(0.163)		(0.163)
Percentage of population in MCAs	−0.002	0.002	−0.004	−0.001	−0.003	0.001
	(0.006)	(0.006)	(0.006)	(0.007)	(0.006)	(0.007)
(North America) × (Percentage of Population in MCAs)			0.032***	0.025***	0.026**	0.019**
			(0.011)	(0.008)	(0.011)	(0.008)
(Western Europe) × (Percentage of Population in MCAs)			0.032***	0.024***	0.030***	0.022**
			(0.012)	(0.009)	(0.011)	(0.009)
(South America) × (Percentage of Population in MCAs)			0.006	0.010*	0.005	0.011*
			(0.005)	(0.006)	(0.005)	(0.006)
(Central America) × (Percentage of Population in MCAs)			0.006	0.008	0.007	0.009
			(0.006)	(0.007)	(0.006)	(0.007)
(Caribbean) × (Percentage of Population in MCAs)			−0.013	−0.011	−0.012	−0.009
			(0.017)	(0.017)	(0.017)	(0.016)
Urban primacy (%)					−0.014	−0.020
					(0.013)	(0.013)
[Urban primacy (%)]²					0.000	0.000
					(0.000)	(0.000)
Constant	6.716***	10.614***	6.738***	10.115***	7.123***	10.780***
	(0.256)	(1.165)	(0.257)	(1.339)	(0.416)	(1.264)
No. of countries	169	169	169	169	169	169
Adjusted R^2	0.341	0.388	0.349	0.389	0.346	0.388

Source: Calculations based on analysis of global data set of urban areas as constructed using the cluster algorithm of Dijkstra and Poelman (2014) and the World Development Indicators data (http://data.worldbank.org/data−catalog/world-development-indicators).
Note: The dependent variable is the natural log of GDP per capita in 2012 international dollars (purchasing power parity exchange rates); robust standard errors. "Urban share (%)" denotes the percentage share of a country's overall population living in urban areas; "Percentage of population in dense" denotes the percentage share of a country's overall population living in dense urban areas, where a dense urban area is one that has a mean population density that exceeds the global median for all urban areas; "weighted density" denotes the mean density of urban areas within a country weighted by the share of each urban area in a country's overall urban population; "Percentage of population in MCAs" denotes the percentage share of a country's overall population living in MCAs, where an MCA is defined as an urban area with two or more cities, each of which has a population of at least 100,000. GDP = gross domestic product; MCA = multicity agglomeration.
*p < 0.1. **p < 0.05. ***p < 0.01.

Columns 2a and 2b then introduce interactions between the share of a country's population living in MCAs and the country's region. The intention is to explore whether there are heterogeneous effects across regions. For example, we might expect that more developed regions have been more successful in designing and implementing institutions to overcome the coordination challenges associated with the governance of large metropolitan areas, in which case an increase in the share of the population living in such areas may be expected to lead to a net positive increase in GDP per capita.

Consistent with this hypothesis, we see that, for both North America and Western Europe, there are positive and statistically significant interaction effects with "Percentage of population in MCAs," and that this is the case irrespective of the measure of urban density used in the regression specification. Where the measure of density is "Log (Weighted Density)," a 1 percentage point increase in the share of the overall population living in MCAs is associated with a 2.5 percent increase in GDP per capita for North American countries and an almost identical 2.4 percent increase for Western European countries—see column 2b. This is consistent with the idea that countries in these regions have succeeded in developing and implementing institutions that, although perhaps not completely solving the governance challenges of large metropolitan areas, address them sufficiently to allow for a net positive effect on productivity. For South America, there is also a (marginally) significant positive interaction effect with "Percentage of population in MCAs" when the measure of density is "Log (Weighted Density)," but not when it is "Percentage of population in dense." For South America, a 1 percentage point increase in "Percentage of population in MCAs" is associated only with a 1.0 percent increase in GDP per capita. Finally, for both the Caribbean and Central America, there are no significant interactions with "Percentage of population in MCAs," regardless of the measure of density.

These results suggest that LAC countries have yet to reach the point of institutional maturity in the governance of large metropolitan areas where they can fully leverage these areas for net productivity gain.[27] This is especially true for Caribbean and Central American countries.[28]

Columns 3a and 3b of table 2.3 further investigate the effects of urban primacy on GDP per capita conditional on other dimensions of urbanization. In these columns, although the estimated coefficient on urban primacy is negative, it is statistically insignificant. Hence, unlike Henderson (2000), we find no evidence that a country's urban primacy has a significant negative effect on its GDP per capita.

The aforementioned results on MCAs are strengthened when we redefine an MCA as an urban area with two or more settlements, *irrespective of the populations of those*

settlements. Here, the estimated coefficient on "Percentage of population in MCAs" is not only negative but also statistically significant in several of the specifications (annex 2D). In North American and Western European countries, however, this negative effect is more than overturned. By contrast, for LAC countries, the effect of an increase in "Percentage of population in MCAs" on GDP per capita remains negative.

International Benchmarking of LAC Urban Areas' Productivity: Better Than Average, but Lagging the Global Frontier

Whereas the analysis in the chapter has focused thus far on different dimensions of urbanization and their relationship to GDP per capita at the national level, it now turns to an analysis of productivity measured at the level of individual urban areas, again benchmarking against the rest of the world. Ideally, we would like to be able to use subnational economic accounts data to construct measures of labor and total factor productivity (TFP) at the individual urban area level. However, most countries lack such data and, where they are available, as, for example, for Brazil, India, and the European Union, they relate to subnational administrative areas whose boundaries may only crudely approximate those of "true" urban areas (see chapters 1 and 6).

To overcome this challenge, we turn to nighttime lights data, which have the advantage of being globally available at a fine spatial resolution, and so allow for the construction of a consistent proxy measure of economic activity for our full global sample of urban areas. We proxy each urban area's economic activity by the total light emitted from the area at night—a measure that, following, for example, Addison and Stewart (2015), we refer to as the "sum of lights." This proxy measure, calculated for 2015 using data averaged over all cloud-free nights, then acts as the basis for constructing a measure of productivity (box 2.3).

BOX 2.3   VIIRS Nighttime Lights Data

The use of nighttime lights data to proxy for economic activity has, since the seminal work of Henderson, Storeygard, and Weil (2011, 2012), become a well-established practice. The 2015 annual composite product that we use in this chapter, however, differs from that used in most previous research.[a] Most previous research relied on nighttime lights data derived from sensors on board meteorological satellites that were part of a program that originated in the 1960s.[b] Instead, we use nighttime lights data from a new satellite instrument, the Visible Infrared Imaging Radiometer Suite (VIIRS), launched in 2011, which provides much higher resolution data. The new data also overcome several problems with the "old" data, such as "overglow" or "blooming," which cause light to spill over the geographic area from which it is emitted.[c,d]

Evidence of the suitability of the new VIIRS data to proxy for economic activity is provided in table B2.3.1. Column 1 reports the results, for 2015, from a regression of GDP levels on a measure of economic activity (the "sum of lights") derived from the VIIRS data for a global sample of 181 countries, whereas columns 2 and 3 report corresponding results for a sample of 31 LAC countries and Brazil's municipalities, respectively. In all three cases, the VIIRS data are very strongly positively correlated with GDP (R^2 values range from 0.77 to 0.96). And, as shown by columns 4 through 6, these correlations remain significant even after controlling for population, which suggests that the VIIRS data are picking up variation in productivity, in addition to variation in population.

TABLE B2.3.1   Regression of Log(GDP) on VIIRS Nighttime Lights Data, 2015

	(1) Global	(2) LAC	(3) Brazilian municipalities	(4) Global	(5) LAC	(6) Brazilian municipalities
Log(NTL)	0.780***	0.920***	0.837***	0.513***	0.549***	0.454***
	(0.032)	(0.032)	(0.006)	(0.040)	(0.060)	(0.009)
Log(Population)				0.447***	0.421***	0.584***
				(0.047)	(0.061)	(0.012)
Constant	15.75***	14.02***	7.25***	11.88***	11.87***	3.94***
	(0.384)	(0.381)	(0.037)	(0.428)	(0.370)	(0.078)
No. of observations	181	31	5,418	181	31	5,418
R^2	0.826	0.956	0.769	0.890	0.981	0.835

Source: Analysis based on nighttime lights data from the VIIRS 2015 annual composite product (https://ngdc.noaa.gov/eog/viirs/download_dnb_composites.html); World Bank World Development Indicators data (http://data.worldbank.org/data-catalog/world-development-indicators); and Instituto Brasileiro de Geografia e Estatística data.
Note: For the global and LAC country samples, GDP is measured in constant international dollars (2005 PPP exchange rates); for Brazilian municipalities, GDP is measured in current local currency units. log(NTL) denotes the natural logarithm of an area's "sum of lights" in 2015 as calculated using the VIIRS data; log(Pop) denotes the natural logarithm of an area's population in 2015. Robust standard errors are in parentheses. GDP = gross domestic product; LAC = Latin America and the Caribbean; NTL = nighttime lights; PPP = purchasing power parity; VIIRS = Visible Infrared Imaging Radiometer Suite.
*$p < 0.1$. **$p < 0.05$. ***$p < 0.01$.

a. All nighttime lights data products, including the 2015 annual composite product that we use in this chapter, are produced by the National Oceanic and Atmospheric Administration of the U.S. government (https://ngdc.noaa.gov/eog).
b. The satellites were part of the U.S. Department of Defense's Defense Meteorological Satellite Program.
c. For example, the Pacific Ocean can be lit up as far as 50 km from the coastline near Los Angeles (Pinkovskiy 2013).
d. Chapters 4 and 6 use an algorithm attributable to Abrahams, Lozano-Gracia, and Oram (2017) to address the problem of "overglow" in the old data. Despite the superiority of the new data, the old data are preferred in these chapters because they require time series data for their analysis.

TABLE 2.4   **The 15 Urban Areas in the LAC Region with the Highest Estimated Economic Activity, as Measured by Nighttime Lights Data, 2015**

Rank	Country	Urban area	Relative sum of lights	Population	Population density	No. of cities in urban area
1	Argentina	Buenos Aires	388.0	14,183,924	4,167	30
2	Brazil	São Paulo	284.7	20,588,698	6,455	23
3	Mexico	Mexico City	218.9	19,782,701	7,462	16
4	Brazil	Rio de Janeiro	161.9	9,932,480	5,730	7
5	Chile	Santiago	105.6	5,837,310	5,238	3
6	Peru	Lima	96.4	9,056,851	8,931	22
7	Brazil	Brasilia	71.5	2,019,961	4,126	1
8	Brazil	Porto Alegre	66.5	3,453,232	3,299	9
9	Brazil	Belo Horizonte	55.2	4,181,234	4,937	6
10	Mexico	Monterrey	53.3	3,870,579	4,373	8
11	Mexico	Guadalajara	50.7	4,219,190	5,822	4
12	Colombia	Bogotá	49.7	7,861,739	13,445	2
13	Brazil	Campinas	49.5	2,304,343	2,609	4
14	Brazil	Curitiba	49.0	2,773,894	3,003	4
15	Paraguay	Asuncion	48.7	2,172,047	2,886	5

Source: Analysis of nighttime lights data from the 2015 VIIRS annual composite product (https://ngdc.noaa.gov/eog/viirs/download_dnb_composites.html). *Note:* The relative sum of lights is the ratio of an urban area's sum of lights to the unweighted mean sum of lights for all urban areas in the LAC region; the relative sums of lights, population, and population density are for the urban areas as derived using the cluster algorithm of Dijkstra and Poelman (2014); both population and population density are calculated using LandScan 2012 gridded population data. "No. of cities in urban area" refers to the number of cities with a population of at least 100,000 whose settlement points intersect the urban area. LAC = Latin America and the Caribbean; VIIRS = Visible Infrared Imaging Radiometer Suite.

On the basis of the nighttime lights data, table 2.4 shows the 15 urban areas in the LAC region with the highest estimated absolute economic activity.[29] These areas correspond with some of the largest urban areas in the region with all but one, Brasilia, an MCA. However, an urban area's economic activity rank does not necessarily coincide with its population rank: Buenos Aires, with an estimated population of 14.2 million, beats both São Paolo and Mexico City, with estimated populations of about 20 million. This suggests that Buenos Aires is the more productive, at least from a labor productivity standpoint.

Notwithstanding this observation on Buenos Aires, column 1 in table 2.5 shows that, globally, there is a significant positive relationship between an urban area's population and its economic activity, as measured by its sum of lights, in 2015. There is, however,

a significant and positive mean difference in economic activity for urban areas in the LAC region against those in the rest of the world (column 2). LAC urban areas tend to have levels of economic activity significantly greater than that predicted by their populations—relative to the rest of the world they are, on average, more productive. Because we do not control for an urban area's capital stock given data limitations, this higher productivity may be attributable to a higher capital–labor ratio, higher TFP, or both—in other words, the higher level of productivity most accurately represents higher labor productivity.

As seen in column 3, and in figure 2.9, this better than average performance is driven by urban areas in South America and Mexico. However, it is also clear from figure 2.9 that even these areas fall short of the global "frontier" of productivity performance (marked by the outer envelope of data points in the figure).

TABLE 2.5   Relationship between Log(Nighttime Lights) and Log(Population), All Urban Areas Globally

	(1)	(2)	(3)
Log(Population)	1.281***	1.271***	1.270***
	(0.041)	(0.040)	(0.040)
Latin America and the Caribbean		1.164***	
		(0.361)	
South America (and Mexico)			1.411***
			(0.324)
Central America (except Mexico)			−0.123
			(0.401)
Caribbean			−0.307
			(0.940)
Constant	−7.637***	−7.674***	−7.660***
	(0.628)	(0.600)	(0.601)
No. of observations	63089	63089	63089
Adjusted R^2	0.351	0.375	0.382

Source: Calculations based on nighttime lights data from the 2015 VIIRS annual composite product (https://ngdc.noaa.gov/eog/viirs/download_dnb_composites.html).
Note: The dependent variable is the natural log of an urban area's sum of lights, where urban areas have been identified by applying the cluster algorithm of Dijkstra and Poelman (2014) to LandScan 2012 gridded population data; standard errors are clustered at the country level. VIIRS = Visible Infrared Imaging Radiometer Suite.
*$p < 0.1$. **$p < 0.05$. ***$p < 0.01$.

Compared with South America and Mexico, urban areas in the Caribbean and the rest of Central America are, on average, less productive. The relationships between population and estimated economic activity for these two subregions are statistically indistinguishable from the global relationship. Hence, from a global perspective, the productivity performance of urban areas in the Caribbean and Central America (excluding Mexico) may be judged "average."[30]

We can also use the residual from the regression in column 1 of table 2.5 as a measure of an urban area's productivity relative to its population-based predicted level, where a positive (negative) value implies higher (lower) than predicted productivity. Again, given that this regression does not control for an urban area's capital stock, this measure can best be thought of as a measure of (relative) labor productivity.

On the basis of this measure, figure 2.10 benchmarks, for each LAC country, the mean productivity in its urban areas against

FIGURE 2.9   Relationship between Log(Nighttime Lights) and Log(Population), All Urban Areas Globally

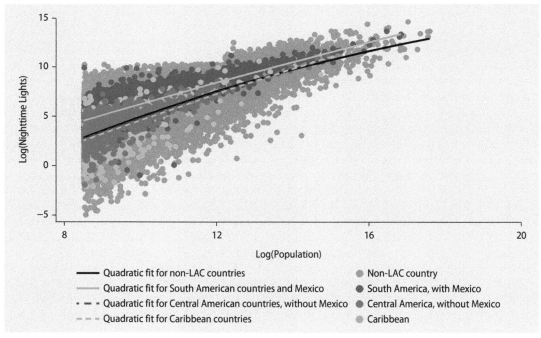

Source: Calculations based on nighttime lights data from the 2015 VIIRS annual composite product (https://ngdc.noaa.gov/eog/viirs/download_dnb _composites.html).
Note: Log(Nighttime Lights) denotes the natural logarithm of an urban area's sum of lights for 2015, where urban areas have been identified by applying the cluster algorithm of Dijkstra and Poelman (2014) to LandScan 2012 gridded population data. LAC = Latin America and the Caribbean; VIIRS = Visible Infrared Imaging Radiometer Suite.

FIGURE 2.10   Mean Urban Area Productivity in LAC Countries Benchmarked against International Comparators

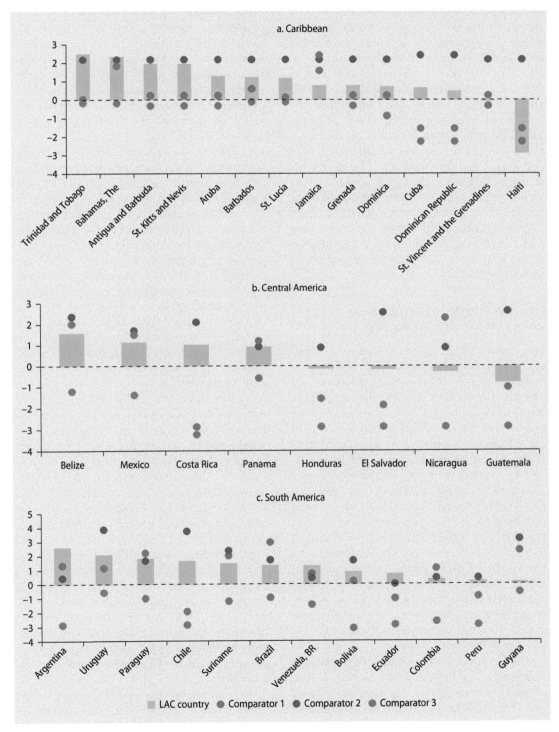

Source: Based on nighttime lights data from the 2015 VIIRS annual composite product (https://ngdc.noaa.gov/eog/viirs/download_dnb_composites.html).
Note: Productivity is measured using the residuals from the regression in column 1 of table 2.5. A country's mean urban area productivity is given by the mean of these residuals across its urban areas. LAC = Latin America and the Caribbean; VIIRS = Visible Infrared Imaging Radiometer Suite.

the corresponding means for each of its comparator countries, where the comparator countries are again selected following the methodology in box 2.1. In most cases, mean productivity in urban areas is lower than in at least one of the comparator countries, but in only two cases—Haiti and Jamaica—does mean productivity lag all three comparators. This matches the impression given by figure 2.9 that, although LAC urban areas are by no means the worst performers on productivity, they can certainly improve a lot. The only LAC countries for which mean productivity across urban areas is higher than in all three comparator countries are Trinidad and Tobago and the Bahamas in the Caribbean, and Argentina, Ecuador and, more surprisingly, República Bolivariana de Venezuela in South America.

Productivity is Highly Dispersed across LAC Urban Areas

Dispersion of productivity across a country's urban areas provides direct information on inequalities in performance and can yield indirect clues on their aggregate contribution to GDP and productivity nationally. This is because, in a world of perfect factor mobility, we expect productivity across urban areas to tend to equalize at the margin as people and firms gravitate to the places where they will earn the highest returns, which is where they will be most productive. To the extent that productivity differences persist under such conditions, we would expect these to be the result of differences in, for example, urban amenities that workers value and that, all else constant, may persuade them to accept a lower wage in one urban area than in another (Rosen 1979; Roback 1982).

An alternative explanation of persistent differences in productivity across urban areas at the margin is that they are due to barriers that prevent workers—and, more generally, factors—from moving to the urban areas in which they earn the highest returns, which is where they will be most productive. Hence, it may be expensive, in monetary or nonmonetary terms, for a worker to move between urban areas. One reason could be a lack of domestic market integration, which could include an inadequately developed national transport network, another could be that housing is much more expensive.

These two explanations of persistent differences in productivity both imply that the contribution of urban areas to aggregate GDP will fall below potential, but the two differ on their welfare implications: when persistent productivity differences are driven by differences in amenities across urban areas and there is perfect factor mobility, the only reason why a worker would choose not to relocate from a less to a more productive area is because he or she is already happy there. By contrast, when persistent productivity differences are driven by barriers to migration, workers may be "trapped," in which case a reduction in barriers would increase the aggregate contribution from urban areas to national GDP and productivity, and would be welfare enhancing. However, even where productivity differences are driven by amenities and everyone is happy where they are, the possibility of an improvement in both the aggregate contribution of urban areas to national GDP and to welfare remains. Hence, under free mobility, a worker may be "enticed" to move to a more productive urban area if the things that he or she values become more readily available in that area or, equivalently, the things that he or she dislikes become less prevalent. A reduction in pollution or crime in the more productive area might, for example, act as an enticement. In this case, relocation will benefit aggregate GDP *and* welfare.

Productivity dispersion across urban areas in each of the three LAC subregions is notably higher than in North America (figure 2.11).[31] The distributions of productivity in urban areas in the three LAC subregions contain notable overlaps with not only the corresponding distribution for North America but also the corresponding distribution for SSA. Whereas the most productive urban areas in the LAC region rival many North American urban areas, the least productive trail the best performers in SSA.[32]

Of course, the higher productivity dispersion across urban areas in the three LAC subregions could be largely attributable to between-country productivity differences rather than within-country productivity differences in each (sub)region. This would be consistent with, for example, a story of a relative lack of regional integration in the LAC region compared with North America. However, we also observe high productivity dispersion across urban areas within individual LAC countries against their comparator countries (figure 2.12). Dispersion within LAC countries is higher than in all three comparators in virtually all cases, Trinidad and Tobago and Uruguay aside. In this instance, we restrict the selection of comparator countries to high-income countries, without imposing any restrictions on the region from which the comparators are drawn, but otherwise follow the methodology for selecting comparators set out in box 2.1. The rationale is that we expect such countries to exhibit high domestic market integration. Therefore, if we observe high dispersion in LAC countries against their comparators, this suggests that the high dispersion may, at least in part, be driven by a relative lack of domestic market integration.

Further evidence that a lack of domestic market integration may be contributing to high productivity dispersion across LAC country urban areas is provided by figure 2.13, which shows, for a global sample of 112 countries, a highly statistically significant negative relationship between the

FIGURE 2.11   Distribution of Productivity across Urban Areas, Selected Regions

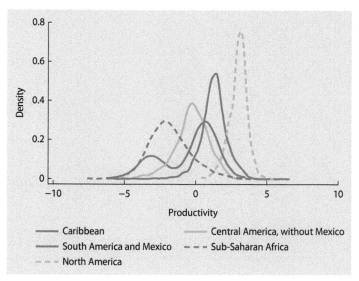

Source: Calculations based on nighttime lights data from the 2015 VIIRS annual composite product (https://ngdc.noaa.gov/eog/viirs/download_dnb_composites.html).
Note: The figure shows density plots of the residuals from the regression in column 1 of table 2.5. These residuals may be interpreted as measuring productivity across urban areas where urban areas have been identified by applying the cluster algorithm of Dijkstra and Poelman (2014) to LandScan 2012 gridded population data. VIIRS = Visible Infrared Imaging Radiometer Suite.

dispersion of productivity across urban areas within a country and the (natural) log of the country's density of roads (length of roads per 100 km² of land area), which we take as a proxy measure of domestic market integration.[33] As discussed in detail in chapter 4, national road densities in LAC countries lag those in the most developed countries.

The above evidence matches the idea that high dispersion of productivity across LAC urban areas is driven by barriers associated with weak domestic market integration that prevents workers from moving. Easing these barriers would have beneficial effects not only for aggregate GDP and productivity but also for aggregate welfare. Another, potentially complementary, explanation is grounded in persistent differences in amenities across urban areas (box 2.4).

FIGURE 2.12 **Productivity Dispersion (Measured by the Coefficient of Variation) across Urban Areas in LAC Countries Benchmarked against High-Income International Comparators**

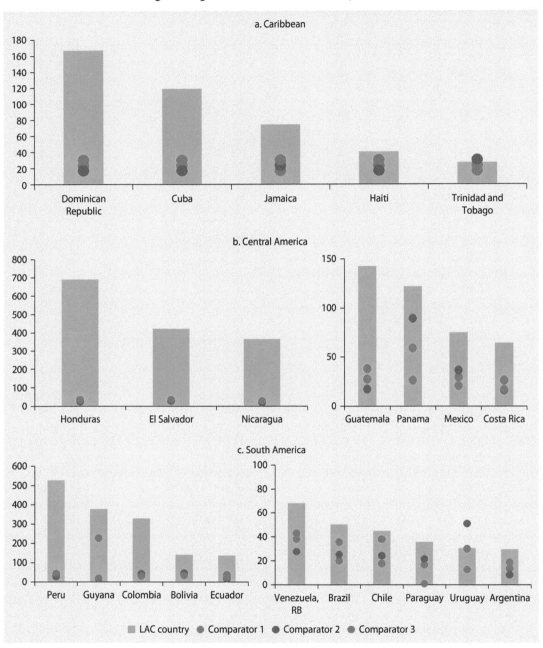

Source: Calculations based on nighttime lights data from the 2015 VIIRS annual composite product (https://ngdc.noaa.gov/eog/viirs/download_dnb _composites.html).
Note: Productivity is measured using the residuals from the regression in column 1 of table 2.5. Productivity dispersion across a country's urban areas is measured by the coefficient of variation. Comparators for each LAC country are restricted to high-income countries, but with no restrictions as to which regions the comparators are drawn from. The method for selecting comparators is as otherwise described in box 2.1. LAC = Latin America and the Caribbean; VIIRS = Visible Infrared Imaging Radiometer Suite.

Conclusions

Three main initial points emerge: urban areas in most LAC countries have high population density; the LAC region is home to many MCAs that present complicated governance challenges for delivering infrastructure and basic urban services;[34] and many countries still exhibit relatively high urban primacy, even though the era of import substitution industrialization has long passed and LAC countries have seen political and fiscal decentralization reforms over the last three decades.

On national GDP per capita, we have also seen evidence to suggest that, in the absence of an adequate enabling policy environment, the high density of the LAC region's urban areas may be having a negative effect, and that governance challenges associated with the region's MCAs may be constraining their contribution to it. By contrast, there is no evidence to suggest that high urban primacy rates are acting as such a drag.

Although urban areas in South America and Mexico are relatively productive by

FIGURE 2.13 Productivity Dispersion across Urban Areas in a Country Is Negatively Correlated with National Road Density, 112 Countries

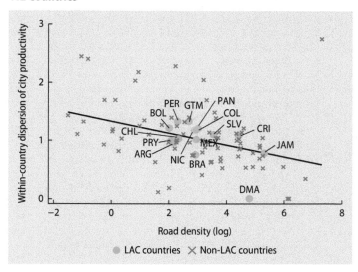

Source: Calculations based on nighttime lights data from the 2015 VIIRS annual composite product (https://ngdc.noaa.gov/eog/viirs/download_dnb_composites.html) and road density data from the World Development Indicators database (http://data.worldbank.org/data-catalog/world-development-indicators). *Note:* Productivity is measured using the residuals from the regression in column 1 of table 2.5. Productivity dispersion across a country's urban areas is measured by the interquartile range of the distribution of productivity. Road density is the ratio of the length of the country's total road network to the country's land area and is measured in kilometers per 100 km² of land area. LAC = Latin America and the Caribbean; VIIRS = Visible Infrared Imaging Radiometer Suite. For a list of country abbreviations, see annex 2A.

BOX 2.4   Cities and Aggregate Growth: United States and Brazil

In a recently published paper, Hsieh and Moretti (2017) present a model of spatial equilibrium that facilitates empirical analysis of the contribution that cities make to aggregate gross domestic product (GDP). In the model, aggregate GDP is increasing in the total factor productivity (TFP) of each city in a country, but decreasing in the dispersion of nominal wages across cities in a country. A high dispersion of nominal wages reflects large marginal productivity differences across cities—a sure sign that not all workers are living and working in the cities where they will be most productive. Policies that reduce the dispersion of nominal wages across cities by facilitating the movement of workers to cities in which they will be more productive—the high TFP cities—either

through reducing barriers to migration or making the productive cities relatively more attractive, will improve both aggregate GDP and aggregate welfare.

Applying their framework to the United States using data for 220 metropolitan areas, Hsieh and Moretti find that, after conditioning on observable worker characteristics, nominal wage dispersion increased by a factor of two across U.S. cities between 1964 and 2009, reflecting a worsening spatial distribution of workers. They calculate that, if it were not for this deteriorating distribution, U.S. GDP in 2009 would have been 13.5 percent higher than it was. They attribute most of the increased nominal wage dispersion across U.S. cities to constraints on housing supply, arising from, for example, tight land

(continued)

BOX 2.4   Cities and Aggregate Growth: United States and Brazil *(continued)*

use restrictions in high TFP cities such as New York; San Francisco; and San Jose, California. Hsieh and Moretti contend that, by contributing to a dearth of affordable housing, these restrictions have deterred workers from moving there. They calculate that, if land use restrictions in these three cities were brought into line with those in the median U.S. city, U.S. GDP would increase by nearly 10 percent.

In his background paper for this book, Bastos (2017) takes the Hsieh and Moretti framework and applies it to the Latin America and the Caribbean region's biggest economy and most populous country, Brazil. Unlike Hsieh and Moretti's findings for the United States, he finds that the dispersion of nominal wages (conditioned on worker characteristics) across 36 Brazilian metropolitan areas declined in 1999–2014. Employment and population growth over this period were fastest in the metro areas with the highest (conditional) nominal wages in 1999. This all points to an improving spatial allocation of workers across metro areas. Bastos presents evidence that this improved spatial allocation may be attributable to a relative improvement in living conditions in the most productive metro areas. For example, homicide rates

declined in the metro areas in the period, with the largest declines in the highest productivity cities.

Still, Brazil remains a long way from an efficient allocation of workers, and Bastos reports that wage dispersion across Brazilian metro areas remains higher than across their U.S. counterparts. This suggests that the potential contribution to aggregate GDP of Brazil's most productive metro areas has still to be fully leveraged. As with the United States, a shortage of affordable housing in the most productive metro areas is a culprit. High-wage metro areas in Brazil experienced a larger increase in their formal housing deficits between 2000 and 2010 than low-wage metro areas. Although informal housing presumably filled the gap for some migrants to high-wage metro areas (see box 2.2), the poor quality of such housing may have deterred would-be migrants, "trapping" them in less productive cities.

Despite the appeal of both the Hsieh and Moretti framework and Bastos' empirical application of it to Brazil, some caveats are in order. The most notable is, perhaps, that because of data availability Bastos' analysis is necessarily confined to the formal sector, which employs only a minority of workers in Brazil.

global standards, they lag the global frontier of productivity performance. By contrast, urban areas in the Caribbean and Central America (outside Mexico) appear average in global terms. The impression of untapped urban productivity gains continues to hold when we compare LAC countries against comparator countries that are similar both from a geographic viewpoint (whether an island, non-island, or landlocked), and in terms of their size and population density.

Behind the averages lies considerable productivity variation: whereas the most productive LAC urban areas are on a par with many in North America, the least productive are on a par with many in Africa. Productivity dispersion across urban areas

within LAC countries is also high relative to high-income comparator countries, and appears to be at least partly driven by weak internal market integration. Keeping workers "trapped" in relatively unproductive urban areas, this weakness may be constraining the aggregate contribution of urban areas to national productivity and welfare.

In part II we turn to a more rigorous empirical analysis that picks up on several of this chapter's themes as they relate to the determinants of cities' productivity: internal market integration (chapters 3 and 4), human capital (chapter 5), and fragmented urban governance in large metropolitan areas (chapter 6).

Annex 2A: List of Comparator Countries for Each LAC Country

Code	Country	Global comparators			High-income comparators		
		Comparator 1	Comparator 2	Comparator 3	Comparator 1	Comparator 2	Comparator 3
ATG	Antigua and Barbuda	Micronesia, Fed. Sts.	Cyprus	Seychelles	New Caledonia	Iceland	Bermuda
ARG	Argentina	Cambodia	Ukraine	Algeria	Saudi Arabia	Netherlands	Poland
ABW	Aruba	Micronesia, Fed. Sts.	Cyprus	Seychelles	Bermuda	New Caledonia	Iceland
BHS	Bahamas, The	New Caledonia	Cyprus	Cabo Verde	Iceland	New Caledonia	Cyprus
BRB	Barbados	Vanuatu	Cyprus	São Tomé and Príncipe	New Caledonia	Iceland	Malta
BLZ	Belize	Brunei Darussalam	Montenegro	Djibouti	Brunei Darussalam	Equatorial Guinea	Estonia
BOL	Bolivia	Moldova	Turkmenistan	Chad	Austria	Slovak Republic	Czech Republic
BRA	Brazil	China	Turkey	United States	United States	Canada	Saudi Arabia
CHL	Chile	Cambodia	Sweden	Cameroon	Greece	Portugal	Belgium
COL	Colombia	Myanmar	Ukraine	South Africa	Spain	Poland	France
CRI	Costa Rica	Cambodia	Croatia	Eritrea	Croatia	Finland	Norway
CUB	Cuba	Papua New Guinea	Ireland	Sri Lanka	New Zealand	Ireland	Cyprus
DMA	Dominica	Kiribati	Cyprus	Seychelles	New Caledonia	Iceland	Bermuda
DOM	Dominican Republic	Papua New Guinea	Ireland	Sri Lanka	New Zealand	Ireland	Cyprus
ECU	Ecuador	Cambodia	Romania	Senegal	Greece	Belgium	Portugal
SLV	El Salvador	Cambodia	Belgium	Togo	Denmark	Israel	United Arab Emirates
GRD	Grenada	Micronesia, Fed. Sts.	Cyprus	Seychelles	New Caledonia	Iceland	Bermuda
GTM	Guatemala	Cambodia	Portugal	Côte d'Ivoire	Netherlands	Belgium	Greece
GUY	Guyana	Timor-Leste	Estonia	Montenegro	Equatorial Guinea	Brunei Darussalam	Estonia
HTI	Haiti	Papua New Guinea	Cyprus	Sri Lanka	New Zealand	Ireland	Cyprus
HND	Honduras	Cambodia	Bulgaria	Benin	United Arab Emirates	Sweden	Israel
JAM	Jamaica	New Zealand	Cyprus	Ireland	Ireland	New Zealand	Cyprus
MEX	Mexico	Indonesia	Turkey	Iran, Islamic Rep.	France	Germany	Italy
NIC	Nicaragua	Cambodia	Bulgaria	Denmark	Denmark	Finland	Croatia
PAN	Panama	Timor-Leste	Georgia	Bosnia and Herzegovina	Kuwait	Lithuania	Croatia
PRY	Paraguay	Serbia	Turkmenistan	Lao PDR	Austria	Slovak Republic	Luxembourg
PER	Peru	Cambodia	Ukraine	Angola	Saudi Arabia	Netherlands	Poland

(continued)

ANNEX 2A   List of Comparator Countries for Each LAC Country *(continued)*

		Global comparators			High-income comparators		
Code	Country	Comparator 1	Comparator 2	Comparator 3	Comparator 1	Comparator 2	Comparator 3
KNA	St. Kitts and Nevis	Micronesia, Fed. Sts.	Cyprus	Seychelles	Bermuda	New Caledonia	Iceland
LCA	St. Lucia	Tonga	Cyprus	São Tomé and Príncipe	New Caledonia	Iceland	Malta
VCT	St. Vincent and the Grenadines	Micronesia, Fed. Sts.	Cyprus	Seychelles	New Caledonia	Iceland	Bermuda
SUR	Suriname	Brunei Darussalam	Montenegro	Djibouti	Brunei Darussalam	Equatorial Guinea	Estonia
TTO	Trinidad and Tobago	Fiji	Cyprus	Mauritius	New Zealand	Cyprus	Ireland
URY	Uruguay	Timor-Leste	Norway	Lithuania	Kuwait	Lithuania	Oman
VEN	Venezuela, RB	Malaysia	Ukraine	Mozambique	Poland	Netherlands	Spain

Annex 2B: Statistical Tests of Differences in Population, Area, and Population Density between LAC Countries and Their Comparators

	Log population (p values)			Log area (p values)			Log population density (p values)		
Country	> comp.[a]	t-test[b]	KS test[c]	> comp.[a]	t-test[b]	KS test[c]	> comp.[a]	t-test[b]	KS test[c]
Caribbean									
Cuba	+	0.621	0.913	−	0.000	0.000	+	0.000	0.000
Dominican Republic	+	0.304	0.233	−	0.000	0.000	+	0.000	0.000
Haiti	−	0.085	0.161	−	0.006	0.027	+	0.031	0.162
Jamaica	−	0.562	0.443	−	0.000	0.000	+	0.000	0.000
Central America									
Belize	−	0.325	0.662	−	0.093	0.079	+	0.397	0.007
Costa Rica	+	0.025	0.040	+	0.656	0.014	+	0.012	0.195
El Salvador	+	0.000	0.000	+	0.101	0.000	+	0.047	0.011
Guatemala	+	0.000	0.000	+	0.002	0.000	+	0.235	0.349
Honduras	+	0.453	0.421	−	0.562	0.014	+	0.018	0.056
Mexico	−	0.000	0.000	−	0.000	0.000	+	0.001	0.000
Nicaragua	+	0.001	0.004	−	0.853	0.216	+	0.000	0.000
Panama	+	0.688	0.049	−	0.000	0.000	+	0.000	0.000
South America									
Argentina	−	0.738	0.426	−	0.264	0.000	+	0.240	0.000
Bolivia	+	0.108	0.544	−	0.000	0.000	+	0.000	0.000
Brazil	+	0.000	0.000	−	0.000	0.000	+	0.000	0.000
Chile	+	0.000	0.000	+	0.085	0.000	+	0.000	0.000

(continued)

ANNEX 2B   Statistical Tests of Differences in Population, Area, and Population Density between LAC Countries and Their Comparators (continued)

Country	Log population (p values) > comp.[a]	t-test[b]	KS test[c]	Log area (p values) > comp.[a]	t-test[b]	KS test[c]	Log population density (p values) > comp.[a]	t-test[b]	KS test[c]
Colombia	+	0.007	0.003	−	0.000	0.000	+	0.000	0.000
Ecuador	+	0.000	0.000	+	0.001	0.000	+	0.000	0.000
Guyana	+	0.227	0.080	−	0.065	0.270	+	0.000	0.000
Paraguay	+	0.370	0.883	−	0.000	0.000	+	0.000	0.000
Peru	+	0.000	0.001	−	0.000	0.000	+	0.000	0.000
Uruguay	+	0.056	0.009	−	0.000	0.000	+	0.000	0.000
Venezuela, RB	+	0.000	0.000	−	0.000	0.000	+	0.000	0.000

Source: Calculations based on analysis of urban areas defined using the cluster algorithm of Dijkstra and Poelman (2014), as applied to LandScan 2012 gridded population data.
Note: The table shows results only for countries where one of the six hypothesis tests conducted shows a significant difference between a LAC country and its corresponding set of comparator countries. For a full list of comparator countries, see annex 2A. KS test = Kolmogorov-Smirnov test; LAC = Latin America and the Caribbean.
a. This column indicates whether the mean of each variable across urban areas is greater (+) or less (−) than that for the pooled set of comparator country urban areas.
b. This column represents a two-tailed and two-sample t-test of the difference in means between a country and its comparators.
c. This column compares a country's distribution with that of its comparators where the null hypothesis is that the distributions are identical.

Annex 2C: List of Multicity Agglomerations in the LAC Region

Rank	Country	Urban area	Relative sum of lights	Population	Population density	No. of cities in urban area
1	Brazil	São Paulo	285	20,588,698	6,455	23
2	Mexico	Mexico City	219	19,782,701	7,462	16
3	Argentina	Buenos Aires	388	14,183,924	4,167	30
4	Brazil	Rio de Janeiro	162	9,932,480	5,730	7
5	Peru	Lima	96	9,056,851	8,931	22
6	Colombia	Bogotá	50	7,861,739	13,445	2
7	Chile	Santiago	106	5,837,310	5,238	3
8	Mexico	Guadalajara	51	4,219,190	5,822	4
9	Brazil	Belo Horizonte	55	4,181,234	4,937	6
10	Mexico	Monterrey	53	3,870,579	4,373	8
11	Brazil	Recife	42	3,465,982	6,461	5
12	Brazil	Porto Alegre	67	3,453,232	3,299	9
13	Colombia	Medellín	16	3,450,578	15,399	3
14	Dominican Republic	Santo Domingo	25	3,431,292	6,027	2
15	Venezuela, RB	Caracas	29	3,325,327	8,862	4
16	Brazil	Fortaleza	40	3,272,611	6,260	3
17	Guatemala	Ciudad de Guatemala	30	3,061,338	4,992	4
18	Brazil	Salvador	32	2,797,798	7,551	2
19	Brazil	Curitiba	49	2,773,894	3,003	4
20	Ecuador	Guayaquil	17	2,600,395	10,200	2

(continued)

ANNEX 2C   List of Multicity Agglomerations in LAC *(continued)*

Rank	Country	Urban area	Relative sum of lights	Population	Population density	No. of cities in urban area
21	Haiti	Port-au-Prince	5	2,497,164	6,121	3
22	Brazil	Campinas	50	2,304,343	2,609	4
23	Costa Rica	San Jose	26	2,272,653	4,040	2
24	Paraguay	Asuncion	49	2,172,047	2,886	5
25	Cuba	La Habana	14	2,054,052	5,205	20
26	Mexico	Toluca	25	2,021,447	2,405	2
27	Brazil	Belem	21	2,005,080	8,325	2
28	Brazil	Goiania	34	1,867,097	3,057	3
29	Colombia	Barranquilla	21	1,859,324	8,875	2
30	El Salvador	San Salvador	10	1,825,864	4,435	6
31	Bolivia	La Paz	18	1,806,596	8,055	2
32	Brazil	São Goncalo	25	1,786,076	4,011	3
33	Brazil	Santos	34	1,465,472	4,120	5
34	Brazil	Itaquari	34	1,404,090	3,672	5
35	Dominican Republic	Santiago de los Caballeros	11	1,256,166	2,622	2
36	Brazil	Natal	16	1,138,317	4,381	3
37	Panama	Panama	13	1,111,798	5,499	2
38	Colombia	Bucaramanga	8	1,052,221	4,864	2
39	Mexico	San Luis Potosi	13	1,029,379	4,885	2
40	Brazil	Teresina	14	936,407	4,653	2
41	Mexico	Cuernavaca	12	934,042	2,480	2
42	Argentina	Greater Mendoza	37	927,595	2,316	4
43	Chile	Viña del Mar	17	832,365	3,350	3
44	Peru	Trujillo	6	821,578	8,326	2
45	Brazil	São José dos Campos	18	819,726	3,192	2
46	Brazil	Coxipo da Ponte	19	803,896	2,976	3
47	Chile	Talcahuano	16	759,765	3,269	2
48	Mexico	Tampico	14	715,843	3,221	2
49	Mexico	Heroica Veracruz	10	688,503	5,109	3
50	Colombia	Pereira	3	631,139	7,821	2
51	Argentina	San Juan	16	481,644	2,898	2
52	Brazil	Volta Redonda	9	475,645	2,809	2
53	Peru	El Tambo	2	431,053	12,497	2
54	Venezuela, RB	Guarenas	5	399,325	6,136	2

Source: Calculations based on analysis of urban areas defined using the cluster algorithm of Dijkstra and Poelman (2014), as applied to LandScan (2012) gridded population data, and nighttime lights data from the 2015 VIIRS annual composite product (https://ngdc.noaa.gov/eog/viirs/ download_dnb_composites.html).
Note: Multicity agglomerations are identified by using Geographic Information Systems techniques to overlay a global layer of individual settlement points on a global map of urban areas, as derived using the cluster algorithm. Each multicity agglomeration is named after the most populous settlement point that falls within its area. Where an urban area intersects with two or more settlement points, each of which had an estimated population of 100,000 or more in 2000, we identify this as an multicity agglomeration. The global settlement point layer that we use is the Center for International Earth Science Information Network's Global Rural-Urban Mapping Project Settlement Point Layer v 1.1 (http://sedac .ciesin.columbia.edu/data/set/grump-v1-settlement-points-rev01). Relative sum of lights is the ratio of an urban area's sum of lights to the unweighted mean sum of lights for all urban areas in Latin America and the Caribbean. Both population and population density are calculated using LandScan (2012) gridded population data. "No. of cities in urban area" refers to the number of cities with a population of at least 100,000 whose settlement points intersect the urban area. VIIRS = Visible Infrared Imaging Radiometer Suite.

Annex 2D: Cross-Country Regression of Log(GDP per Capita) on Different Dimensions of Urbanization: Alternative Definition for a Multicity Agglomeration

	(1a)	(1b)	(2a)	(2b)	(3a)	(3b)
Urban share	0.054*** (0.007)	0.044*** (0.004)	0.042*** (0.006)	0.048*** (0.004)	0.041*** (0.007)	0.046*** (0.004)
Percentage of population in dense	−0.011* (0.006)		0.007 (0.006)		0.007 (0.006)	
Log(Weighted Density)		−0.469*** (0.145)		−0.125 (0.173)		−0.151 (0.171)
Percentage of Population in MCAs	−0.008* (0.004)	−0.007 (0.004)	−0.017*** (0.005)	−0.016*** (0.005)	−0.017*** (0.005)	−0.017*** (0.005)
(North America) × (Percentage of Population in MCAs)			0.035*** (0.005)	0.028*** (0.005)	0.034*** (0.006)	0.027*** (0.005)
(Western Europe) × (Percentage of Population in MCAs)			0.041*** (0.006)	0.033*** (0.006)	0.042*** (0.006)	0.034*** (0.006)
(South America) × (Percentage of Population in MCAs)			0.008** (0.004)	0.011*** (0.004)	0.008** (0.003)	0.011*** (0.003)
(Central America) × (Percentage of Population in MCAs)			0.005 (0.005)	0.007 (0.006)	0.006 (0.005)	0.008 (0.005)
(Caribbean) × (Percentage of Population in MCAs)			0.005 (0.007)	0.005 (0.007)	0.006 (0.007)	0.006 (0.007)
Urban primacy (%)					−0.014 (0.012)	−0.012 (0.012)
[Urban primacy (%)]^2					0.000 (0.000)	0.000 (0.000)
Constant	6.539*** (0.235)	10.304*** (1.199)	6.434*** (0.210)	7.402*** (1.417)	6.754*** (0.400)	7.863*** (1.396)
No. of countries	169	169	169	169	169	169
Adjusted R^2	0.353	0.399	0.513	0.509	0.511	0.509

Source: Calculations based on analysis of global data set of urban areas as constructed using the cluster algorithm of Dijkstra and Poelman (2014) and World Development Indicators data (http://data.worldbank.org/data-catalog/world-development-indicators).

Note: The dependent variable is the natural log of GDP per capita in 2012 international dollars (PPP exchange rates); robust standard errors. "Urban share" denotes the percentage share of a country's overall population living in urban areas; "Percentage of population in dense" denotes the share of a country's overall population living in dense urban areas, where a dense urban area is one that has a mean population density that exceeds the global median for all urban areas; "weighted density" denotes the mean density of urban areas within a country weighted by the share of each urban area in a country's overall urban population; "Percentage of populations in MCAs" denotes the share of a country's overall population living in MCAs, where an MCA is defined as an urban area that contains two or more cities of any population size. GDP = gross domestic product; MCA = multicity agglomeration; PPP = purchasing power parity.

$p < 0.1$. **$p < 0.05$. ***$p < 0.01$.

Notes

1. Urban primacy is defined as the share of a country's urban population living in its most populous urban area.
2. The preference in this chapter is to refer to "urban areas." This is because "urban areas" provides a more apt description for small urban settlements that might usefully be referred to as towns (rather than cities).
3. In settings with high factor mobility, it has been traditional to argue that capital and labor will move until a spatial equilibrium is reached. In this equilibrium, utility levels across homogeneous agents will be equalized (Rosen 1979; Roback 1982). All else equal, this will tend to

make for the spatial equality of wages and profits, not to mention the spatial equality of productivity levels at the margin (Glaeser et al. 1992; Glaeser 2000). Even in spatial equilibrium, however, differences in productivity (and in wages) at the margin will remain, to the extent that there are differences in amenities (for example, differences in climate) that households value across areas. See the "Productivity Is Highly Dispersed across LAC Urban Areas" section in this chapter.

4. A LAC country's comparators are its "nearest neighbors" on population, land area, and average population density. Comparator countries are also countries that are similarly geographically located, that is, an island or non–island nation, and landlocked or nonlandlocked.

5. This is based on the application of the cluster algorithm to LandScan 2012 globally gridded population data. In their background paper, Roberts et al. (2017) also apply the cluster algorithm to GHS-Pop and WorldPop gridded population data. They find that the resultant maps of urban areas for LAC show a high level of agreement with the map produced using LandScan 2012 data.

6. These settlements may be more aptly described as towns rather than cities.

7. These nine urban areas represent less than 0.23 percent of the original sample of 63,629 urban areas.

8. The final section in chapter 6, "Institutional Fragmentation, Metropolitan Coordination, and Productivity," identifies three main lines of thought regarding whether fragmentation is good or bad for the economic performance of an urban area. Like Tiebout, the "polycentrist" school argues that fragmentation is good, whereas the "centrist" school argues that it is bad. In between these two extremes, the "regionalist" view recognizes the benefits of having multiple local governments while highlighting the importance of metropolitan coordination, defined as the efforts of governmental institutions to manage and solve problems in common between jurisdictions.

9. Chapter 6 develops such a data set, but only for a subsample of LAC metropolitan areas.

10. The global settlement point layer that we use is the Center for International Earth Science Information Network's Global Rural–Urban Mapping Project (GRUMP) Settlement Point Layer v 1.1 (http://sedac.ciesin.columbia.edu /data/set/grump-v1-settlement-points-rev01). This data set provides geographic coordinates for 70,629 individual settlements, as well as associated estimates of population for 1990, 1995, and 2000. For a complete description, see CIESIN (2017). Throughout the chapter, we follow the convention of naming an urban area after the largest settlement point that it intersects with.

11. See annex 2D. Settlements in this case can include places that are officially classified as rural even though they intersect with an urban area as defined by the cluster algorithm.

12. As table 2.1 shows, LAC urban areas have a median area of 7.2 km², compared with those in ECA (22.0 km²) and North America (21.4 km²). The corresponding mean areas are 18.4 km² (LAC), 51.2 km² (ECA), and 91 km² (North America). Our findings on the high density of LAC urban areas relative to those in North America echo earlier research findings by Ingram and Carroll (1981) who, for a small sample of 24 large Latin American cities, found that average population densities in the 1950s–1970s resembled those of "old" North American cities such as New York, Chicago, Philadelphia, Washington, DC, and Boston in the north and east, but were considerably higher than those of newer North American cities such as Houston, San Diego, San Jose, and Phoenix in the south and west.

13. This assessment is based on a series of simple two-sample t-tests. In performing these t-tests, we pool urban areas in the three comparator countries and test whether the mean across urban areas for the LAC country is significantly different from the corresponding mean for this pooled set of urban areas. Alternative results based on performing t-tests against each individual comparator country are, overall, consistent with those based on the pooling of urban areas in the comparator countries, especially when comparing levels of urban population density. We prefer to report results based on pooling primarily for reasons of space. Similar comments apply to the results of the Kolmogorov-Smirnov test that are reported in annex 2B, as well as to all subsequent analysis in the chapter relating to the benchmarking of individual LAC countries against their comparators.

14. In Mexico City, only 16 of the 57 municipalities belong to the city as defined by its official administrative boundaries.

15. Out of the 12 MCAs in Central America, eight are in Mexico.

16. Including the nine largest urban areas in the global sample, the share of EAP's overall urban population living in MCAs rises to 56.4 percent, and the share for South Asia rises to 72.3 percent.

17. See the section in this chapter on "Implications for National Productivity" and chapter 6.

18. High urban primacy has also been linked to an absence of well-developed national transport networks (Ades and Glaeser 1995; Davis and Henderson 2003).

19. More specifically, Henderson (2000) uses an augmented Solow-Swan growth framework, a neoclassical growth model in which capital accumulation is subject to diminishing marginal returns and growth is ultimately driven by exogenous technological progress. For an overview of this model see, for example, Barro and Sala-i-Martin (2003).

20. The 11 LAC countries that Henderson (2000) identifies as suffering from excessive primacy in 1990 are Argentina, Chile, Costa Rica, Dominican Republic, El Salvador, Guatemala, Nicaragua, Panama, Paraguay, Peru, and Uruguay. However, Henderson calculates urban primacy using official national definitions of urban areas.

21. By the late 2000s, all but two LAC countries had directly elected local mayors, and the average share of subnational spending in total expenditures had reached 31.4 percent. This contrasts with the early 1980s, when only six LAC countries had directly elected mayors and the equivalent share was 13.1 percent (Chona, n.d.).

22. In table A2 of his paper, Henderson (2000) reports that, for a country with a GDP per capita of $17,200 (1987 constant international dollars), the estimated "optimal" primacy rate declines from 23 percent at a national population of 8 million to 18 percent at 22 million. At a population of 100 million, the optimal rate is 10 percent. A similar rate of decline in the optimal rate is reported at lower GDP per capita.

23. WDI follows the United Nations' World Urbanization Prospects database in adopting national definitions of urban areas.

24. These theories are that high levels of urban density may have a negative effect on national GDP per capita if they give rise to excessive congestion forces ("demons of density") that overwhelm agglomeration economies; high urban primacy may negatively affect national GDP per capita for similar reasons; and a large share of a country's population living in MCAs may also adversely affect national GDP per capita if the costs of fragmentation outweigh the benefits, and there is a lack of metropolitan coordination.

25. Potential sources of bias that would need to be investigated before drawing causal inferences include both omitted variables and reverse causality. For example, in the relationship between GDP per capita and urban primacy, both could be partly driven by the level of development of national transport networks and a country's openness to international trade.

26. In table 2.3, "urban share (%)," "Percentage of population in dense," and "Percentage of population in MCAs" are all measured as shares of a country's population; all measures are on a scale of 0–100.

27. Consistent with this, CAF (2017) reports that, against Organisation for Economic Co-operation and Development countries, Latin America has a low prevalence of metropolitan governance bodies, informal or formal. Half of Latin American metropolitan areas have no coordination mechanisms whatsoever, and only one in five cities has some form of formal framework.

28. In Mexico, for example, Kim and Zangerling (2016) document how comprehensive national efforts to designate and coordinate metropolitan areas have only begun in the past decade, particularly box 3.3 (pp. 50–51).

29. In the analysis that follows, we drop from our global sample urban areas that either (i) have a zero or negative sum of lights or (ii) fall in the top percentile of urban areas on the global distribution of sum of lights, but that have a population of less than 200,000. On (ii), this leads to the exclusion of, for example, small urban areas centered on oil refining that appear very bright at night because of flaring. Excluding areas on the basis of (i) and (ii) leads to a final sample of 63,089 urban areas for the analysis in this section.

30. The finding that LAC urban areas are, on average, more productive than those in the rest of the world may seem to contradict the finding in table 1.2 of chapter 1 that LAC countries have levels of GDP per capita that fall close to the fitted line for the global relationship between a country's development level

and its urban share (as measured on the basis of the cluster algorithm). However, the units of analysis that underpin these two findings are very different, individual urban areas in this chapter versus countries in chapter 1.

31. Figure 2.11 groups Mexico with South America rather than Central America, because Mexico's productivity distribution more closely resembles those of South American countries than of other Central American countries.

32. For the Caribbean, productivity levels across urban areas exhibit an interesting bi-modal distribution, driven by the three largest countries in the subregion, Haiti, Cuba, and Dominican Republic, which are home to 387 of the Caribbean's 473 urban areas. Hence, the lower mode corresponds to urban areas in Haiti and the upper mode to urban areas in Cuba and the Dominican Republic.

33. Although based on a smaller sample of 91 countries, a similarly strong negative correlation is evident between the dispersion of productivity across urban areas within a country and the (natural) log level of the country's density of *paved* roads.

34. For detailed descriptions of these challenges in the cases of Argentina, Central America, and Mexico see Muzzini et al. (2016), World Bank (2016), and Kim and Zangerling (2016) respectively.

References

Abrahams, A., N. Lozano-Gracia, and C. Oram. 2017. "Deblurring DMSP Nighttime Lights: A New Method Using Gaussian Filters and Frequencies of Illumination." Unpublished manuscript.

Addison, D., and B. Stewart. 2015. "Nighttime Lights Revisited: The Use of Nighttime Lights Data as a Proxy for Economic Variables." Policy Research Working Paper 7496, World Bank, Washington, DC.

Ades, A. F., and E. L. Glaeser. 1995. "Trade and Circuses: Explaining Urban Giants." *Quarterly Journal of Economics* 110 (1): 195–227.

Ahrend, R., E. Farchy, I. Kaplanis, and A. C. Lembcke. 2014. "What Makes Cities More Productive? Evidence on the Role of Urban Governance from Five OECD Countries." Regional Development Working Paper 2014/05, Organisation for Economic Co-operation and Development, Paris.

Akbar, P. A., and G. Duranton. 2017. "Measuring the Cost of Congestion in a Highly Congested City: Bogotá." Working Paper 04/2017, Development Bank of Latin America, Caracas.

Barbero, J. 2012. *Infrastructure in the Development of Latin America*. Caracas: Development Bank of Latin America.

Barro, R. J., and X. Sala-i-Martin. 2003. *Economic Growth*. Cambridge, MA: MIT Press.

Bastos, P. 2017. "Spatial Misallocation of Labor in Brazil." Background paper for this book, World Bank, Washington, DC.

CAF (Development Bank of Latin America). 2017. *Urban Growth and Access to Opportunities: A Challenge for Latin America*. 2017 Report on Economic Development (RED). Caracas.

CIESIN (Center for International Earth Science Information Network). 2013. "Report for Phase I: Mapping, Quantification and Analysis of Evolution of Patterns of Urban Physical Extent and Morphology in South Asian Cities, 1999–2010." Background paper for *Leveraging Urbanization in South Asia: Managing Spatial Transformation for Prosperity and Livability*, World Bank, Washington, DC.

———. 2017. Documentation for the Global Rural-Urban Mapping Project, Version 1 (GRUMPv1): Settlement Points, Revision 01. New York.

Chona, G. n.d. *Intergovernmental Fiscal Relations and Decentralization in Latin America and the Caribbean: Challenges and Policy Questions*. New York: Inter-American Development Bank. http://decentralisatie.org/?wpfb_dl=385.

Davis, J., and J. V. Henderson. 2003. "Evidence on the Political Economy of the Urbanization Process." *Journal of Urban Economics* 53 (1): 98–125.

Dijkstra, L., and H. Poelman. 2014. "A Harmonised Definition of Cities and Rural Areas: The New Degree of Urbanization." Regional Working Paper, Directorate-General for Regional and Urban Policy, European Commission, Brussels.

Duranton, G., and D. Puga. 2004. "Micro-Foundations of Urban Agglomeration Economies." In *Handbook of Regional and Urban Economics*, Volume 4: Cities and Geography, edited by J. V. Henderson and J.-F. Thisse, 2063–2117. Amsterdam: Elsevier.

Ellis, P., and M. Roberts. 2016. *Leveraging Urbanization in South Asia: Managing Spatial Transformation for Prosperity and Livability.* Washington, DC: World Bank.

Ferreyra, M. M., C. Avitabile, J. Botero Álvarez, F. Haimovich Paz, and S. Urzúa. 2017. *At a Crossroads: Higher Education in Latin America and the Caribbean.* Washington, DC: World Bank.

Glaeser, E. 2000. "New Economics of Urban and Regional Growth." In *The Oxford Handbook of Economic Geography*, edited by G. L. Clark, M. S. Gertler, M. P. Feldman, and K. Williams, 83–98. New York: Oxford University Press.

———. 2011. *Triumph of the City: How Our Greatest Invention Makes Us Richer, Smarter, Greener, Healthier, and Happier.* New York: Penguin Press.

Glaeser, E., H. D. Kallal, J. Scheinkman, and A. Shleifer. 1992. "Growth in Cities." *Journal of Political Economy* 100 (6): 1126–52.

Henderson, J. V. 2000. "The Effects of Urban Concentration on Economic Growth." Working Paper 7503, National Bureau of Economic Research, Cambridge, MA.

Henderson, J. V., A. Storeygard, and D. N. Weil. 2011. "A Bright Idea for Measuring Economic Growth." *American Economic Review* 101 (3): 194–99.

———. 2012. "Measuring Economic Growth from Outer Space." *American Economic Review* 102 (2): 994–1028.

Hsieh, C. T., and E. Moretti. 2017. "Housing Constraints and Spatial Misallocation." Working Paper 21154, National Bureau of Economic Research, Cambridge, MA.

Ingram, G. K., and A. Carroll. 1981. "Symposium on Urbanisation and Development: The Spatial Structure of Latin American Cities." *Journal of Urban Economics* 9 (2): 257–73.

Kim, Y., and B. Zangerling. 2016. *Mexico Urbanization Review: Managing Spatial Growth for Productive and Livable Cities in Mexico.* Washington, DC: World Bank.

Krugman, P., and R. L. Elizondo. 1996. "Trade Policy and the Third World Metropolis." *Journal of Development Economics* 49 (1): 137–50.

Marshall, A. 1890. *Principles of Economics.* London: Macmillan and Co.

Muzzini, E., B. Eraso Puig, S. Anapolsky, T. Lonnberg, and V. Mora. 2016. *Leveraging the Potential of Argentine Cities: A Framework for Policy Action.* Washington, DC: World Bank.

Pinkovskiy, M. L. 2013. "Economic Discontinuities at Borders: Evidence from Satellite Data on Lights at Night." Working paper, MIT Economics, Cambridge, MA.

Roback, J. 1982. "Wages, Rents, and the Quality of Life." *Journal of Political Economy* 90: 1257–78.

Roberts, M., B. Blankespoor, C. Deuskar, and B. Stewart. 2017. "Urbanization and Development. Is Latin America and the Caribbean Different from the Rest of the World?" Policy Research Working Paper 8019, World Bank, Washington, DC.

Rosen, S. 1979. "Wages-based Indexes of Urban Quality of Life." In *Current Issues in Urban Economics*, edited by P. Mieszkowski and M. Straszheim, 74–104. Baltimore: John Hopkins University Press

Tiebout, C. M. 1956. "A Pure Theory of Local Expenditures." *Journal of Political Economy* 64 (5): 416–24.

World Bank. 2016. *Central America Urbanization Review. Making Cities Work for Central America.* Washington, DC: World Bank.

Zhou, N., K. Hubacek, and M. Roberts. 2015. "Analysis of Spatial Patterns of Urban Growth across South Asia Using DMSP-OLS Nighttime Lights Data." *Applied Geography* 63: 292–303.

The Determinants of City Productivity in Latin America and the Caribbean

Cities in Latin America and the Caribbean (LAC) need to raise the bar to reach the global "frontier" of productivity performance and further contribute to the region's economic development. To help understand what is required to achieve this, part II of the book takes a more in-depth and rigorous look at the key determinants of city productivity in the region. Chapter 3 takes a relatively broad look at these determinants using a rich data set of household surveys for 16 LAC countries, focusing on market access, skill, and density. Although skill is a strong predictor of productivity differences across cities, market access and, especially, density have somewhat weaker roles. This suggests an absence of wider positive agglomeration effects beyond those associated with skill, which may be linked to the lack of an adequate "enabling environment" for generating these effects. Chapters 4 and 5 then provide deeper analysis of the roles of market access and skill, respectively. Chapter 6 goes beyond the concept of density to analyze the role of a city's spatial form more generally in determining its productivity, as well as the role of a city's fragmentation into different administrative jurisdictions and the mechanisms for metropolitan coordination.

The Empirical Determinants of City Productivity | 3

Mark Roberts

Introduction

One city may be more productive than another for two basic reasons. First, a city may be home to workers and firms whose characteristics make them more productive: it may have an unusually talented workforce, whose members would be equally productive no matter where they lived.[1] From a productivity viewpoint, such a city is *the sum of its parts*. Second, a city may have attributes associated with its environment that, because of positive externalities and spillovers, enhance the productivity of workers and firms beyond that expected on the basis of their individual characteristics. Such a city becomes *more than the sum of its parts*.

The first implies that, at least from a productivity perspective, there is nothing special about cities and the concentrations of people and firms that are their defining characteristic. Differences in productivity across cities are entirely attributable to compositional differences associated with the "sorting" of workers and firms into different cities (for example, the tendency of more skilled and able workers to move to certain cities or for more inherently productive firms to gravitate toward certain cities). The second

implies that cities are indeed "special places," which, through their environment, can help workers and firms become more productive than they might otherwise be. Aligned with this second explanation, urban economics has identified three closely interrelated, and, to a significant degree, overlapping, theories of "urban success." These theories, all of which focus on different types of positive agglomeration effects, aim to explain differences in productivity across cities beyond those associated with sorting.

Agglomeration economies. The first theory is that cities can generate higher productivity than rural areas because of the positive externalities, known as agglomeration economies, that their large population sizes or densities create. Agglomeration economies can arise through several mechanisms.[2] The "thick" labor markets that characterize cities can help generate better matches between workers and firms, so that each person is more likely to find his or her "perfect" job. Cities can also provide the conditions for the growth of a large and diversified array of specialized suppliers of goods and services, which provide the intermediate inputs that help fuel the growth of the local economy.

The work discussed in this chapter is based primarily on background papers by Quintero and Roberts (2017) and Reyes, Roberts, and Xu (2017). The author thanks Jane Park for her excellent research assistance with the chapter.

The geographic proximity of people and firms in cities can give rise to the, often unintended, spillover of ideas as workers learn from each other through observation and interaction.[3]

Human capital externalities (HCEs). The second theory is that cities can generate higher productivity not so much because of their size or density but because they tend to have higher overall human capital or skill, which helps generate positive HCEs. In many ways, this theory can be considered a special case of the first theory. Whereas the first theory emphasizes several channels through which agglomeration impacts positively on a city's productivity, HCE theory focuses on just one of these channels—namely, the spillover of ideas between people. Furthermore, in doing so, it also hypothesizes that the spillover of ideas is more likely to come from higher- than lower-skilled workers, leading to the prediction that a worker's individual productivity will be increasing with the average human capital of the city in which she or he lives (Rauch 1993; Moretti 2004).[4]

Market access. The third theory is that cities can generate higher productivity because they also tend to benefit from higher levels of access to large consumer markets and to supplier markets of intermediate inputs. This superior access stems from both a city's own "internal" market and its connectivity to other surrounding areas and cities. Higher consumer and supplier market access make it easier for firms to cover the fixed costs of setting up a new plant, which helps stimulate increases in profits and productivity (Krugman 1991a, 1991b; Krugman and Venables 1995; Fujita, Krugman, and Venables 1999). Again, this theory is closely related to the first theory insofar as it focuses attention on a specific (sub)set of mechanisms through which positive agglomeration effects may arise. It shares with agglomeration economies theory the hypothesis that a larger "internal" market aids city productivity by stimulating the growth of a large and diversified array of specialized suppliers of intermediate goods. But it then goes beyond this by also emphasizing connectivity to the markets of other surrounding areas and cities.[5]

Although the three theories have been well studied for developed countries and a handful of developing countries, little rigorous empirical evidence exists on their relevance for most developing countries, including for countries in Latin America and the Caribbean (LAC) (Overman and Venables 2005; Henderson 2010; Duranton 2015).[6] The main aim of this chapter, therefore, is to shed empirical light on the relative importance of these three theories or, to put it another way, the channels through which positive agglomeration effects arise. It also distinguishes the extent to which variations in productivity across cities, and between urban and rural areas, are attributable to compositional differences in the workforce—"sorting"—versus the underlying environment. The chapter draws on a data set of harmonized household survey and sample census microdata for 16 LAC countries. These data have been matched with data that describe differences in cities' environments.

Complementing this analysis, which views productivity through the lens of workers, the chapter also reports analysis based on firm-level World Bank Enterprise Survey (WBES) data for a global sample of cities. This global perspective allows for a comparison on whether LAC differs from the rest of the world on its strength of city-level determinants of firm productivity, controlling for the characteristics of individual firms. It goes beyond the three theories of urban success to highlight the characteristics of a city's business environment that are important for determining productivity.

The chapter's main findings are as follows:

- Nominal wages are, on average, higher in urban than rural areas throughout LAC, reflecting higher average productivity. Higher productivity is also typically seen in and around larger and more densely populated cities.
- Much of this productivity variation stems from observable workforce compositional differences associated with the sorting of workers between cities and areas. Notably, more productive

areas tend to be populated by better educated workers.

- An important component of subnational productivity remains, whose variation cannot be explained by workforce compositional differences. This suggests that, from a productivity viewpoint, sorting is not the entire story and that cities are more than the sum of their parts. This is consistent with the three theories of urban success.
- Positive agglomeration effects are present in LAC countries. These effects are driven, however, mainly by HCEs with a lesser role for market access. Once an area's average level of human capital (or skill level) and its market access have been controlled for, population density exerts no positive influence on productivity. This suggests that other channels for positive agglomeration effects—for example, positive externalities associated with labor market pooling or spillovers of knowledge beyond those emphasized by HCE theory—may not be operative.
- One potential explanation is that the enabling environment for these other types of positive agglomeration effects may not be present in LAC cities. Current levels of infrastructure and existing policies may not be adequate to support the high population densities that characterize LAC cities, resulting in excessively strong congestion forces that offset these other positive effects.
- The finding of a lack of significant agglomeration effects beyond HCEs and market access is confirmed when one analyzes global WBES data. These data also highlight obstacles to hiring skilled labor (which are worse in the LAC region than elsewhere) as a major constraint on firm productivity in cities. Other elements of a city's business—and, therefore, also wider enabling environment, including modern infrastructure, basic protection from crime, and access to formal banking finance—are also critical for productivity.

Cities Are More Productive Than Rural Areas

Average Productivity in Cities Exceeds That in Rural Areas

Cities (and, more generally, urban areas) offer potential productivity advantages over rural areas, largely explained by the three theories of urban success. In line with these theories, countries worldwide have higher average nominal urban than rural wages. Urban firms can generally afford to pay higher wages than rural firms because their employees are more productive.[7]

Figure 3.1 shows the presence of large urban–rural wage ratios in a sample of 15 LAC countries for which we have data for both types of area (seven each South American and Central American, and one Caribbean).[8] The figure's data sources underlie much of the rest of the analysis in the "Large Subnational Variations in Productivity" and "Explaining Underlying Variations in Productivity" sections (box 3.1).

Compositional Differences Associated with Sorting Explain a Lot, but Not Everything

Given the large urban–rural productivity disparities, it might be thought that, despite the already high urbanization rates in the region, there might be large unexploited productivity gains to be had from rural–urban migration. However, it is also possible that the differences in average wages between urban and rural areas are attributable to compositional differences in the workforce between the two types of area, rather than to anything special about cities. These compositional differences can arise from the "sorting" of workers into different areas based on observable characteristics (such as educational attainment) and not so easily observable characteristics (such as ability and motivation) (Combes and Gobillon 2015).

Table 3.1 shows important differences in key observable characteristics of workers between urban and rural areas in the 15-country data set. Most important, in all 15 countries, workers who live in cities are,

FIGURE 3.1 **Ratio of Nominal Mean Urban to Nominal Mean Rural Wage in 15 LAC Countries, 2000–14**

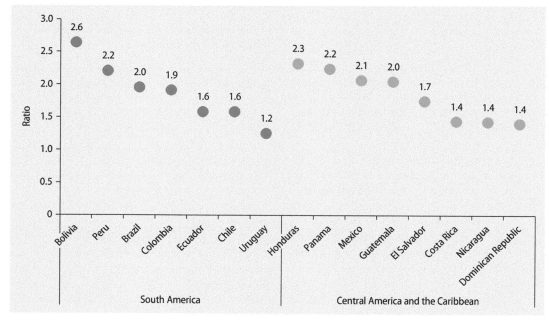

Source: Calculations based on household survey microdata from SEDLAC (http://sedlac. econo.unlp.edu.ar/eng/) for all countries except Brazil. For Brazil, the calculation is based on IPUMS International (https://international.ipums.org/international/) population census sample microdata.
Note: The ratio is the mean hourly nominal wage for urban relative to rural residents in each country calculated using pooled data for 2000–2014, where the mean hourly wage has been detrended using survey-year fixed effects. The figure is organized in descending order of urban–rural nominal wage ratio in each subregion. Argentina is excluded because its household survey (the *Encuesta Permanente de Hogares*) covers urban areas only. LAC = Latin America and the Caribbean; SEDLAC = Socio-Economic Database for Latin America and the Caribbean.

BOX 3.1   **SEDLAC: A Treasure Trove of Harmonized Data**

Our analysis in this chapter draws on successive rounds of household survey microdata for 16 LAC countries that, apart from Brazil, come from the Socio-Economic Database for Latin America and the Caribbean (SEDLAC).[a] This database has been constructed by the Center for Distributive, Labor and Social Studies (CEDLAS) at the *Universidad National de La Plata* and the World Bank's Poverty Group for the LAC region. The raw microdata from household surveys are not uniform across LAC countries, but the beauty of SEDLAC is that it also provides harmonized survey microdata. Hence, the team behind SEDLAC makes strenuous efforts to ensure that the data are comparable across countries and over time "by using similar definitions of variables in each country/year, and by applying consistent methods of processing the data" (CEDLAS and World Bank 2014).

The version of SEDLAC used for this book covers different survey years for different countries— for example, 1974–2014 for Argentina, 1987–2013 for Chile, and 2001–14 for Colombia. To ensure consistency across the LAC countries of analysis, we use SEDLAC data only from 2000 onward. To allay potential concerns over a lack of representativeness of the survey data at the level at which we analyze it, we pool successive cross-sections of data.[b] This has the effect of greatly increasing sample sizes for subnational areas, and therefore also increasing the statistical precision of our estimates.

SEDLAC provides microdata on household members working in the formal and informal sectors. To avoid potential selection bias, our analysis focuses on a broad sample of workers covering formal and informal sectors irrespective

(continued)

BOX 3.1   SEDLAC: A Treasure Trove of Harmonized Data *(continued)*

of job characteristics. However, we chose to restrict our samples only to wage workers, excluding self-employed workers whose reported income levels may not be comparable across countries (Duranton 2016). Likewise, our samples exclude workers who report zero income (mostly family helpers in agriculture and retail trade). Our final samples comprise all employed wage workers age 14–65 years. A worker's wage is taken to be the nominal hourly wage earned in the primary occupation.[c]

For our empirical investigation of agglomeration effects, in the "Explaining Underlying Variations in Productivity" section, we further match the harmonized survey data from SEDLAC with data from a LAC geospatial database that was constructed for this book in collaboration with the University of Southampton's GeoData Center (Branson et al. 2016).[d] This database aligns with the identifiers for subnational areas in SEDLAC. It is this matching that also enables the mapping of subnational variations in mean hourly wages shown in maps 3.1 and 3.2.

a. The "Cities Are More Productive Than Rural Areas" section focuses on only 15 of the 16 countries because Argentina's household survey covers only urban areas. For Brazil, we instead take microdata on workers from the population census sample for 2000 provided by IPUMS International (https://international.ipums.org/international/). We perform our own harmonization of the IPUMS Harmonized data for Brazil with the SEDLAC data for the other 15 countries in our sample. SEDLAC covers 24 countries. However, besides Brazil, eight countries were dropped either because changes in administrative units and their coding over time prevented SEDLAC from providing reliable geographic identifiers or because technical difficulties prevented the loading of the microdata from SEDLAC. The eight dropped countries are Paraguay, Suriname, and República Bolivariana de Venezuela in South America, and the Bahamas, Belize, Guyana, Haiti, and Jamaica in the Caribbean.
b. To account for this, all regressions in the first four sections of this chapter include survey-year fixed effects.
c. Wages are measured at 2005 purchasing power parity exchange rates. In SEDLAC, rural wages are also increased by 15 percent to capture differences in rural–urban prices (CEDLAS and World Bank 2014, 23). In our analysis, we undo this by multiplying the mean hourly wage of a rural worker by a factor of 0.8695. Although the results are not reported in this chapter, to test the robustness of results based on the broad sample, our background work also considered a narrower sample of workers that is restricted to "prime age" men, age 20–55 years, working in the private sector. We generally find very similar results for our broad and narrow samples (see Quintero and Roberts 2017).
d. For more information, visit http://www.geodata.soton.ac.uk/geodata/.

TABLE 3.1   Differences in Characteristics between Urban and Rural Workers in 15 LAC Countries

Region	Country	Area	Age in years (mean)	Years of schooling (mean)	Workers with higher education (%)	Male (%)	Married (%)
South America	Bolivia	Urban	36.5	10.4	17.6	57.6	65.1
		Rural	40.3	6.0	4.7	72.9	75.5
	Brazil	Urban	33.0	8.1	9.0	56.3	56.0
		Rural	32.4	4.5	1.2	70.9	61.4
	Chile	Urban	39.5	11.6	20.5	60.0	61.4
		Rural	39.9	8.5	5.8	73.9	63.0
	Colombia	Urban	37.2	9.6	16.1	56.6	57.3
		Rural	37.3	5.2	2.1	74.9	64.3
	Ecuador	Urban	38.4	10.6	17.3	60.5	53.0
		Rural	38.7	6.5	3.4	70.7	56.2
	Peru	Urban	37.4	10.6	24.4	56.2	56.5
		Rural	38.3	6.3	4.5	68.6	66.2
	Uruguay	Urban	39.6	10.1	11.2	55.7	62.2
		Rural	41.2	7.5	3.9	67.6	68.8
	Seven countries	**Urban**	**37.2**	**10.1**	**18.5**	**57.0**	**57.6**
		Rural	**38.1**	**6.0**	**3.5**	**71.7**	**64.9**

(continued)

TABLE 3.1   Differences in Characteristics between Urban and Rural Workers in 15 LAC Countries (continued)

Region	Country	Area	Age in years (mean)	Years of schooling (mean)	Workers with higher education (%)	Male (%)	Married (%)
Central America and the Caribbean	Costa Rica	Urban	37.0	9.9	17.5	60.0	54.6
		Rural	36.0	7.2	6.4	71.4	61.4
	Dominican Republic	Urban	36.5	9.8	16.6	61.0	56.7
		Rural	37.3	6.6	4.7	73.4	59.6
	El Salvador	Urban	36.9	8.9	11.2	53.3	57.1
		Rural	35.4	4.9	1.3	66.7	58.4
	Guatemala	Urban	34.6	7.4	6.7	58.9	59.9
		Rural	34.2	3.6	0.5	71.9	67.4
	Honduras	Urban	35.3	8.1	7.9	56.5	56.1
		Rural	35.7	4.3	0.7	72.6	62.4
	Mexico	Urban	36.6	9.8	15.2	61.2	61.4
		Rural	37.1	6.2	3.1	69.6	68.6
	Nicaragua	Urban	35.7	8.3	13.1	56.2	57.7
		Rural	35.2	4.3	1.7	74.1	64.4
	Panama	Urban	37.7	11.6	16.1	58.6	60.5
		Rural	38.2	7.5	4.1	73.7	64.9
	Eight countries	**Urban**	**36.5**	**9.6**	**14.5**	**60.1**	**60.0**
		Rural	**36.4**	**5.7**	**2.8**	**70.8**	**65.0**
LAC	**Fifteen countries**	**Urban**	**36.9**	**9.9**	**16.7**	**58.4**	**58.7**
		Rural	**37.2**	**5.8**	**3.2**	**71.2**	**65.0**

Source: Calculations based on household survey microdata from SEDLAC (http://sedlac.econo.unlp.edu.ar/eng/), for all countries except Brazil. For Brazil, the calculation is based on IPUMS International (https://international.ipums.org/international/) population census sample microdata.
Note: The table is sorted alphabetically by country name in each subregion. Descriptive statistics are based on wage/salary employees age 14–65 years. The values reported for LAC overall, and for the subregions (South America, and Central America and the Caribbean), are for the pooled sample of workers across all component countries. All differences in means and in proportions between urban and rural areas are statistically significant at the 1 percent level in a two-tailed test. IPUMS = Integrated Public Use Microdata Series; LAC = Latin America and the Caribbean; SEDLAC = Socio-Economic Database for Latin America and the Caribbean.

on average, significantly better educated than their rural counterparts. This is the case regardless of whether we measure education by number of years of schooling or by completion of higher education. Apart from Brazil, Costa Rica, El Salvador, Guatemala, and Nicaragua, urban workers are also, on average, slightly younger than rural workers. Workers in urban areas are also more likely to be female—which could be taken as an indication that urbanization promotes female labor force participation—and less likely to be married.

Given the differences in worker characteristics, the question arises of whether there remains a significant difference between average nominal wages between urban and rural areas once we control for these differences and, hence, sorting. In other words, does a city-dwelling worker earn significantly more than an "equivalent" worker who lives in the countryside? If so, this would suggest the existence of an urban productivity premium that may, at least partly, be explained by the three theories of urban success.

To disentangle the degree to which differences in nominal wages, and hence productivity, between urban and rural areas are attributable to observable compositional differences in the workforce versus other factors associated with cities, we ran a series of augmented Mincerian wage regressions using microdata for workers (Mincer 1974), where these data are again taken from the Socio-Economic Database for Latin America and the Caribbean (SEDLAC) or IPUMS. In these regressions, we include number of years of schooling, age and its square, and a worker's gender and marital status as key observable characteristics.[9] We also include a dummy variable that takes the value one if a worker lives in an urban area and zero otherwise. If the estimated coefficient on this urban dummy is positive and significant, then this suggests a positive urban productivity premium that allows an urban worker to earn more, in nominal terms, than an observationally equivalent rural worker. From these regressions, we can also calculate the percentage difference in the average nominal wage between urban and rural areas that can be

explained by the differences in the observed characteristics of workers between the type of area. We term this quantity the "worker premium" to distinguish it from the estimated coefficient on the urban dummy in our regressions, which reflects the existence of an "urban premium."

Figure 3.2 shows the results of this exercise. For all 15 LAC countries, differences in observable worker characteristics are important in explaining why nominal wages, and thus productivity, tend to be higher in cities than rural areas. On average across the countries, the average rural nominal wage would be 38 percent higher if the characteristics of rural workers were changed to be the same as those of urban workers—57 percent higher in the most

FIGURE 3.2   Urban and Worker Premiums in 15 LAC Countries

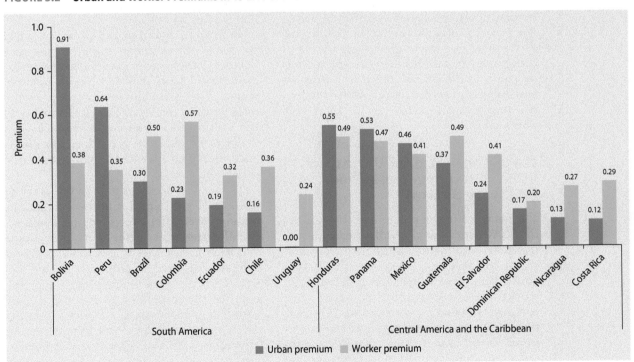

Source: Calculations based on household survey microdata from SEDLAC (http://sedlac.econo.unlp.edu.ar/eng/) for all countries except Brazil. For Brazil, the calculation is based on IPUMS International (https://international.ipums.org/international/) population census sample microdata.
Note: Urban premium is calculated as [exp(â)−1], where â is the estimated coefficient on a dummy variable, D_U, which takes the value one (zero) when a worker lives in an urban (rural) area from a regression of the (natural) log of the nominal wage on D_U and a set of observable worker characteristics (age, age squared, number of years of schooling, gender, and marital status). Worker premium is calculated as [exp(δ̂)−1], where δ̂ is the difference in the fitted natural log wage between urban and rural areas based on the difference in mean values of each of the worker characteristics between these areas. When multiplied by 100, the values of both the urban and worker premiums in the chart give, all else equal, the percentage difference in the mean hourly wage between urban and rural areas. The figure is sorted in descending order of urban premium in each subregion. LAC = Latin America and the Caribbean; SEDLAC = Socio-Economic Database for Latin America and the Caribbean.

extreme case, Colombia. But we also observe that, in 14 of the 15 countries, there remains a statistically significant urban productivity premium even after controlling for the differences in worker characteristics. The size of this premium ranges from 12 percent in Costa Rica to 91 percent in Bolivia, with an average of 36 percent. Uruguay is the exception: the small difference in average wages between urban and rural areas (figure 3.1) can be attributed to compositional differences in worker characteristics (sorting) rather than to urban success.

Although the significant urban productivity premium in all but one LAC country is consistent with the three theories, differences in the unobservable characteristics of workers could also explain that premium—for example, more able or motivated people (characteristics that are not easily captured by data) may be sorting into urban areas. Even then, it is likely that these unobserved differences are correlated with observed differences in number of years of schooling; and, to the degree that this is true, we can expect our estimates of the urban productivity premium to be relatively unbiased.[10]

Large Subnational Variations in Productivity, Explained Partly by Sorting

The evidence in the previous section shows that LAC cities are generally more productive than rural areas and that this productivity difference remains even after controlling for observable differences in workforce composition associated with sorting. However, it provides no information on the wider geographic variations in productivity in countries, which, as again reflected by variations in average nominal wages, are large—maps 3.1 and 3.2, panel a. The subnational areas depicted in the figures typically correspond to level 2 administrative units or *municipios*, in the 16 countries for which we have data.[11] The highest nominal wages—and so

productivity—tend to be seen in subnational areas that correspond to major cities.[12] As with our analysis of urban–rural wage ratios, the question arises as to the extent to which these differences are the product of sorting (that is, differences in workforce composition) versus differences in the underlying productivity of areas.

To answer this question, we again estimate a series of augmented Mincerian wage regressions, one for each LAC country, that control for key observable characteristics of workers.[13] This time, instead of just including a simple binary urban dummy, we include a dummy variable for each subnational area in a country.[14] The estimated coefficient on the dummy for a given subnational area can be interpreted as an estimate of its (natural) log of underlying productivity (or "location premium"), having controlled for the characteristics of its workforce and, hence, sorting.

As map 3.1b and map 3.2b show, when we map these estimates of underlying productivity, we see much less variation across subnational areas than for average nominal wages. This indicates that compositional differences in the workforce associated with the sorting of workers across places is a major factor that drives productivity differences between cities and, more generally, subnational areas.

But sorting does not tell the full story of productivity differences between locations because, even after controlling for compositional differences in the workforce, some variation in nominal wages remains across subnational areas in countries (figure 3.3 shows box plots of estimated location premiums for the sample of 16 countries). The variation in underlying productivity is particularly pronounced in Costa Rica, Ecuador, Honduras, and Peru. There are also important differences in the size of the median location premium across countries in, for example, Costa Rica and Ecuador, indicating that more of a residual effect of location is left over after controlling for sorting in these two countries than for, say, Honduras and Uruguay.

MAP 3.1 Subnational Variations in Nominal Wages in South America

a. Without controlling for differences in worker characteristics

b. Controlling for differences in worker characteristics

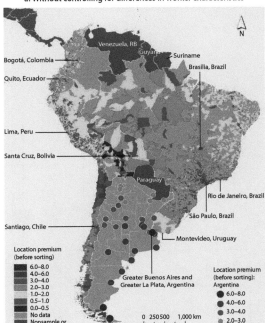
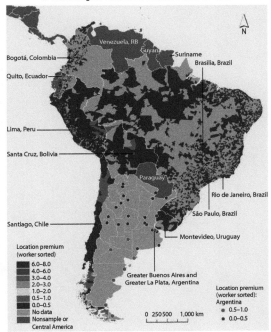

Source: Quintero and Roberts 2017.
Note: We use a separate point layer for Argentina to retain all locations for which SEDLAC allows us to estimate location premiums. Unlike other countries in our sample, these correspond to major cities/urban agglomerations, such as City of Buenos Aires and Greater La Plata, for which we lack a Geographic Information System shapefile of administrative boundaries. Location premium in the maps is calculated as exp(â) and expressed in 2005 purchasing power parity exchange rates, where, â is the estimated coefficient from a series of country-specific regressions on a location dummy, $L_{i,l(i),t}$, which takes the value one when a worker i lives in a location l in the year t and zero otherwise. These regressions also include survey-year fixed effects. In panel a, the location premium is estimated without controlling for observable worker characteristics. In panel b, the location premium is estimated controlling for observable worker characteristics (age, age squared, number of years of schooling, gender, marital status) SEDLAC = Socio-Economic Database for Latin America and the Caribbean.

MAP 3.2 Subnational Variations in Nominal Wages in Central America and the Caribbean

a. Without controlling for differences in worker characteristics

b. Controlling for differences in worker characteristics

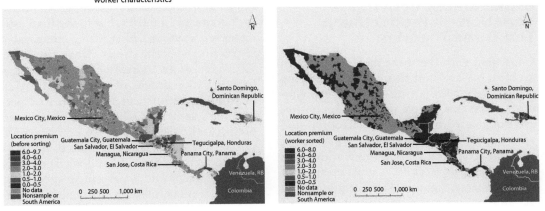

Source: Quintero and Roberts 2017.
Note: Location premium in the maps is calculated as exp(â) and expressed in 2005 purchasing power parity exchange rates, where â is the estimated coefficient from a series of country-specific regressions on a location dummy, $L_{i,l(i),t}$, which takes the value one when a worker i lives in a location l in the year t and zero otherwise. These regressions also include survey-year fixed effects. In panel a, the location premium is estimated without controlling for observable worker characteristics. In panel b, the location premium is estimated controlling for observable worker characteristics (age, age squared, number of years of schooling, gender, marital status).

FIGURE 3.3   **Subnational Variations in Underlying Productivity in 16 LAC Countries**

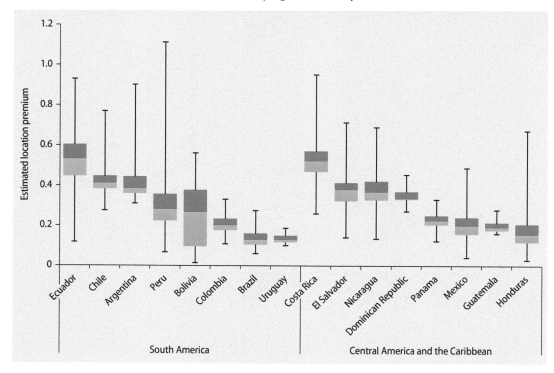

Source: Calculations based on household survey microdata from SEDLAC (http://sedlac.econo.unlp.edu.ar/eng/) for all countries except Brazil. For Brazil, the calculation is based on IPUMS International (https://international.ipums.org/international/) population census sample microdata.
Note: This figure is organized in descending order of the median estimated location premium in each subregion. Estimated location premiums measure subnational variations in underlying productivity after controlling for observable worker characteristics within the broad sample (all wage/salary employees age 14–65 years) and survey-year fixed effects. The upper and lower caps, respectively, indicate the maximum and the minimum estimated location premiums for each country. The bottom of the box, the border of two colors, and the top of the box, respectively, depict the first quartile, the median, and the third quartile of the estimated location premiums in each country. IPUMS = Integrated Public Use Microdata Series; LAC = Latin America and the Caribbean; SEDLAC = Socio-Economic Database for Latin America and the Caribbean.

Explaining Underlying Variations in Productivity: The Three Theories

Consistent with the three theories of urban success, we see that estimated underlying productivity levels (estimated location premiums) across our sample of 16 LAC countries are positively and significantly correlated with population density, average number of years of schooling among the working-age population (that is, skill),[15] and a measure of market access (figure 3.4).[16] For population density, which provides our measure of agglomeration, the estimated elasticity of underlying productivity is 9 percent.[17] This is higher than corresponding estimates

reported in the urban economics literature for developed countries, but lower than estimates reported for China. Using comparable regression specifications, Chauvin et al. (2017) report an elasticity of nominal wages for population density of 4.6 percent for U.S. metropolitan statistical areas, and 19.2 percent for a sample of Chinese provincial and prefectural cities. For our 16-country LAC sample, the estimated elasticities of underlying productivity for skill and market access are 62 percent and 4 percent, respectively. Using a similar, but not identical specification, Hering and Poncet (2010) report an estimated elasticity of underlying productivity with respect to market access of 8 percent for Chinese cities. So, as with the estimated

THE EMPIRICAL DETERMINANTS OF CITY PRODUCTIVITY

FIGURE 3.4 **Correlation between Underlying Productivity and Population Density, Average Number of Years of Schooling, and Market Access**

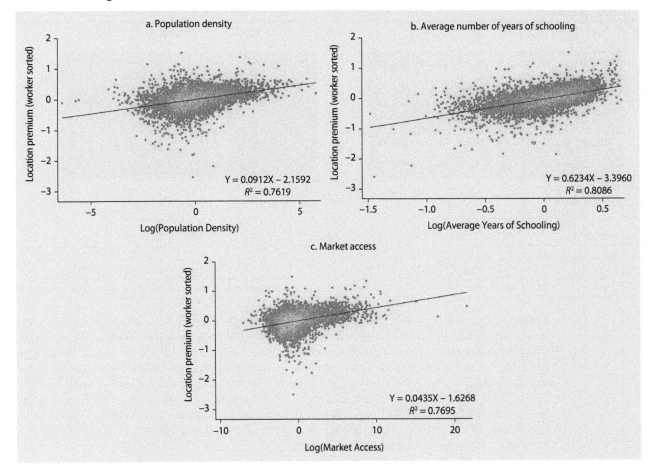

Source: Calculations based on Quintero and Roberts 2017.
Note: Scatterplots show the correlation between the estimated location premiums (expressed in natural logs) from Quintero and Roberts (2017) and the natural logs of population density, average number of years of schooling, and market access controlling for country fixed effects. Hence, subnational administrative areas are the units of observation and the correlations are estimated on the basis of the within-country variation in the data. Market access is measured as $MA_i = \sum_{i \neq j}(P_j/t_{ij}^2)$ where MA_i is subnational area i's market access, P_j is the population of subnational area j, and t_{ij} is the estimated travel time (by road) between subnational areas i and j.

elasticity for population density, this is lower in the LAC region than what has been found for China.[18]

Yet it is also true that population density, skill, and market access are all positively correlated with one another:[19] more densely populated areas tend to exhibit higher skill and greater market access. To disentangle the relative importance of the three variables, columns 1 through 3 of table 3.2 report regression results, where we also control for physical geographic conditions that could be correlated

with our measure of underlying productivity and our main explanatory variables.

Strong Human Capital Externalities, Some Role for Market Access, but Little Evidence of Wider Positive Agglomeration Effects

In column 1, we see that the estimated elasticity of underlying productivity with respect to population density declines to 4.9 percent once we control for geographic conditions.

TABLE 3.2   **Results of Regressions on the Determinants of Underlying Productivity Variations across Subnational Areas**

Dependent variable: Location premium (ln)	(1)	(2)	(3)	(4)	(5)
Population density (ln)	0.049***	0.013*	0.005	0.023*	0.002
Average number of years of schooling (ln)		0.576***	0.574***		
Percentage of working-age population with higher education				0.021***	0.020***
Market access (ln)			0.015***		0.027***
Mean air temperature (ln)	0.030	0.044	0.051	0.036	0.045
Terrain ruggedness (ln)	−0.031**	−0.024***	−0.017	−0.026*	−0.024
Total precipitation (ln)	−0.028	−0.008	−0.010	−0.003	−0.001
Constant	−0.99***	−2.37***	−2.70***	−1.28***	−1.82***
No. of observations	5,750	5,750	5,050	5,750	5,050
R^2	0.757	0.814	0.831	0.785	0.804
Adjusted R^2	0.756	0.813	0.830	0.785	0.803

Sources: Quintero and Roberts 2017; population data: Gridded Population of the World, v4.
Note: In all columns, country effects have been controlled for and standard errors have been clustered by country. In all columns, the dependent variable is the estimated location premium (measured in natural logs) from a series of country-level first-stage regressions after controlling for observable worker characteristics in the broad sample (all wage/salary employees age 14–65 years) and survey-year fixed effects. Worker characteristics include age, age squared, marital status, gender, and number of years of schooling.
***$p < 0.01$. **$p < 0.05$. *$p < 0.1$.

Although this estimate remains statistically significant, it is less than the estimated elasticity of 9 percent that we reported above when not controlling for geography. Once we also introduce skill, as measured by average number of years of schooling, in column 2, however, both the estimated size and statistical significance of the elasticity of underlying productivity with respect to population density fall dramatically. Including market access in column 3, then leads population density to lose its significance completely. Although skill and market access are significant, the former has a larger effect on underlying productivity. Although an increase in the average number of years of schooling from the 25th to the 75th percentile in our sample implies an estimated productivity increase of 23.4 percent, moving from the 25th to the 75th percentile for market access implies a productivity increase of only 4.1 percent.

It thus seems that, although LAC countries do experience positive agglomeration effects, these are not as strong, overall, as have been reported for China. Furthermore, these agglomeration effects are mainly those associated with the theories of HCEs and—to a much lesser, but still statistically significant extent—market access. By contrast, other types of positive agglomeration effects associated with the (more general) theory of agglomeration economies seem to be absent. This includes positive effects stemming from, for example, labor market pooling or more general spillovers of knowledge beyond those emphasized by HCE theory.

Absence of Wider Positive Agglomeration Effects May Be Linked to an Inadequate Enabling Environment

The absence of wider positive agglomeration effects could be linked to the high population densities of many LAC cities (see chapter 2). One hypothesis is that these high densities are leading to excessive congestion forces that are negating many of the positive externalities normally associated with urban density. In this context, it is not necessarily the high densities per se that matter, because LAC cities may lack the enabling environment to foster these wider positive agglomeration effects. Therefore, current policies and levels of infrastructure in LAC cities may not be sufficient to prevent these densities creating excessive congestion forces. Chapter 2 discussed issues of metropolitan coordination in the context of multicity agglomerations, a topic that chapter 6 looks at in more depth. It also mentioned the continued widespread existence of slums, which pose challenges for infrastructure provision—for two reasons. One, as highlighted by Fay et al. (2017), is the slums' location, which is often in flood-prone or environmentally protected areas. The other is that their dense and disorderly development hinders work on access roads or water, sewerage, and drainage. Fay et al. (2017) also highlight a lack of access to sanitation as a serious infrastructure issue, even for the middle classes, in Latin American cities.

However, further work is required to fully substantiate the above hypothesis. This is because it may be that, relative to our measures of human capital and market access, population density is a relatively poor measure of agglomeration, in which case its estimated coefficient may be biased downward.[20] Indeed, in previous chapters, we emphasized that the boundaries of subnational administrative units often conform only poorly with the "true" boundaries of cities. To the extent that agglomeration is more poorly measured, this could provide another explanation of why we find no evidence of positive agglomeration effects beyond those associated with HCEs and market access. It is also somewhat of a conundrum as to why excessive congestion forces associated with high densities combined with an inadequate enabling environment might be thwarting certain types of positive agglomeration effects, but not HCEs.[21]

In addition to reporting average number of years of schooling, table 3.2 also reports results using an alternative measure of skill: the share of the working-age population who have completed higher education—columns 4 and 5. This is closer to the measure of skill preferred in the academic literature on HCEs, much of which argues that raising the top of the human capital distribution will generate learning spillovers but that raising the bottom will not (Glaeser 1999). This amounts to arguing that workers experience significant learning only from highly educated colleagues. This alternative measure is also a highly statistically significant predictor of variations in underlying productivity across subnational areas. Comparing the results in columns 4–5 with those in columns 2–3, however, we can also see that our regressions fit better when using average number of years of schooling rather than the share of the working-age population with higher education.[22]

Effects Are Heterogeneous Across Countries

Beyond the above average results for all 16 LAC countries, we now investigate the considerable heterogeneity in estimated effects of population density, skill, and market access on underlying productivity across individual countries (figure 3.5).[23] Contrary to the overall average results, we find that the estimated elasticity of underlying productivity with respect to population density is positive and statistically significant for Brazil, Dominican Republic, Ecuador, and Peru: the estimated 95 percent confidence intervals, shown in panel a of the figure, do not encompass the value zero (indicated by the dashed line). By contrast, we estimate a significant negative elasticity for Chile and Nicaragua.

On market access, the overall positive average (and statistically significant) influence is driven mainly by four countries (Brazil, Costa Rica, Ecuador, and Nicaragua). For the remaining countries in the figure, the effect of market access is not significantly different from zero.[24]

With skill, the effect of average number of years of schooling is statistically significant for all countries. Even here, the estimated strength of HCEs varies dramatically across countries. We estimate extremely strong HCEs in Bolivia but comparatively weak externalities in the Dominican Republic, El Salvador, and Nicaragua.[25]

In addition to heterogeneity across countries, it is also fruitful to analyze, following the example of Duranton (2016) for Colombia, heterogeneity across different subgroups of workers (box 3.2).

FIGURE 3.5 **Cross-Country Heterogeneity in Estimated Elasticities of Underlying Productivity with Respect to Population Density, Average Number of Years of Schooling, and Market Access**

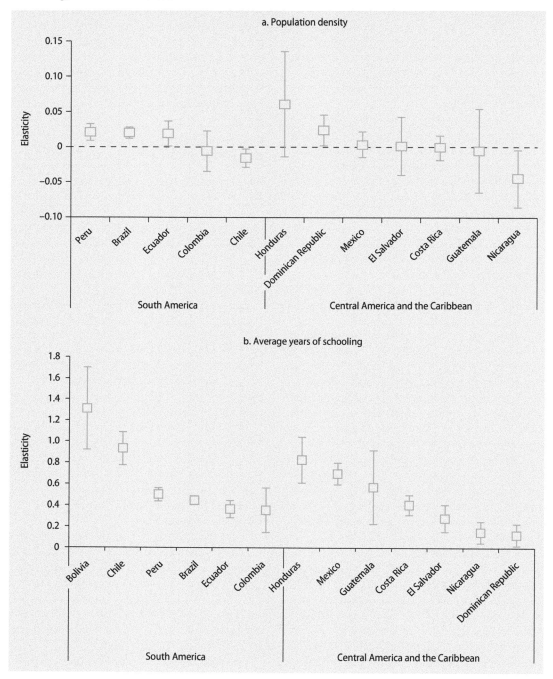

(continued)

FIGURE 3.5   Cross-Country Heterogeneity in Estimated Elasticities of Underlying Productivity with Respect to Population Density, Average Number of Years of Schooling, and Market Access (continued)

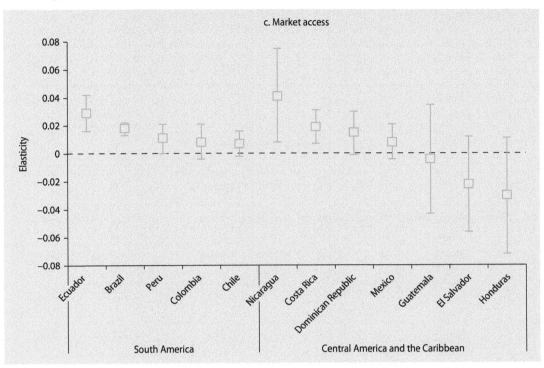

Source: Quintero and Roberts 2017.
Note: Figures show the estimated elasticities for each country derived from regressing—in individual country-level regressions—estimated subnational underlying productivity (measured in natural logs) on the variables shown in column 3 of table 3.2. The squares represent the point estimates, whereas the upper and lower caps indicate the upper and lower bounds of the 95 percent confidence intervals.

BOX 3.2   Which Groups of Workers Benefit More?

To explore heterogeneous effects of population density, skill as measured by average number of years of schooling, and market access on estimated underlying productivity variations across different types of workers, we performed a series of regressions for the following four dimensions, drawn from our broad sample, which consists of all employed wage workers age 14–65 years:

1. Young vs. old
2. Male vs. female
3. Private vs. public sector
4. Formal vs. informal

We used 35 years as the dividing line between young and old because this is roughly the mean

age of workers in all 16 countries. Given that our sample already excludes all self-employed workers and workers who report zero income (see box 3.1), we defined informal workers as those who work for firms with five or fewer employees.[a] All other workers are assumed to be formal. Our regressions for private vs. public sector and formal vs. informal workers exclude Brazil, because, for that country, no public sector workers were left in our original broad sample after data cleaning, and IPUMS International does not provide data that allow us to distinguish between formal and informal workers in a manner akin to that for other countries, for which the data instead come from SEDLAC.

(continued)

BOX 3.2   Which Groups of Workers Benefit More? *(continued)*

Table B3.2.1 summarizes the results. The most striking differences in estimated effects come in private vs. public sector workers and formal vs. informal workers. In both cases, the estimated elasticities of underlying productivity with respect to skill and market access are higher for private and formal workers than for public and informal workers. For market access, the estimated elasticities are close to zero for public and informal workers, and statistically insignificant.

Market access also has an insignificant effect for old and for female workers. However, the estimated elasticities in both cases are much closer to those

estimated for young and for male workers, respectively, which are statistically significant at the 10 percent level or better. Although they are smaller than for private vs. public sector and formal vs. informal workers, differences can also be observed in the estimated elasticity of underlying productivity with respect to skill for young vs. old and male vs. female workers. Old workers appear to benefit more from stronger HCEs than young workers, and male workers than female workers.

Population density exerts a negligible and statistically insignificant effect on underlying productivity for all subgroups.

TABLE B3.2.1   Heterogeneous Effects of Determinants on Underlying Productivity across Worker Subgroups

	(1a)	(1b)	(2a)	(2b)	(3a)		(4a)	(4b)
	Young	**Old**	**Male**	**Female**	**Private**	**Public**	**Formal**	**Informal**
Population density (ln)	-0.001	0.004	0.006	-0.001	0.002	0.012	0.004	-0.002
Average number of years of schooling (ln)	0.466***	0.580***	0.541***	0.495***	0.548***	0.172*	0.559***	0.401***
Market access (ln)	0.014***	0.010	0.011*	0.008	0.018***	-0.001	0.019***	0.004
Constant	-2.554***	-2.392***	-2.356***	-2.281***	-2.586***	-0.804***	-2.349***	-1.565***
No. of observations	3,756	3,757	3,758	3,754	3,758	3,440	3,758	3,732
Adjusted R^2	0.790	0.744	0.689	0.675	0.717	0.680	0.668	0.687

Source: Quintero and Roberts 2017; population data: Gridded Population of the World, v4.
Note: In all columns, country effects have been controlled for and standard errors have been clustered by country. In all columns, the dependent variable is the estimated location premium (measured in natural logs) from a series of country-level first-stage regressions after controlling for observable worker characteristics in the broad sample (all wage/salary employees age 14–65 years) and survey-year fixed effects. Worker characteristics include age, age squared, marital status, gender, and number of years of schooling.

a. The Socio-Economic Database for Latin America and the Caribbean provides two indicators for whether a worker is considered informal (CEDLAS and World Bank 2014). The first, based on a "productive" definition of informality, identifies a worker as informal if "(s)he belongs to any of the following categories: (i) unskilled self-employed, (ii) salaried worker in a small private firm, (iii) zero-income workers." The second, based on a "legalistic" or "social protection" notion of informality, identifies a salaried worker as informal if "s(he) does not have the right to a pension linked to employment when retired." We rely on the "productive" indicator because this suffers from fewer missing observations; however, because our sample already excludes both self-employed and zero-income workers, this amounts to equating informal employment with employment by small firms.
***p < 0.01. **p < 0.05. *p < 0.1.

What about Firms? Evidence from World Bank Enterprise Surveys

So far in the chapter, we have followed the dominant approach of the academic urban economics literature of using microdata on individual workers. It is also possible, however, to analyze productivity differences, and their determinants, from the perspective of firms, which can yield complementary

insights into the drivers of urban success. And analyzing firm data allows for a more direct measurement of productivity because it allows us to build measures of labor productivity and of total factor productivity (TFP).

Unfortunately, there are no equivalents of SECLAC or IPUMS for firm microdata. The background paper by Reyes, Roberts, and Xu (2017) for this book does, however, take advantage of what we suggest is the next best thing—harmonized WBES data for

FIGURE 3.6 **Different Dimensions of a City's Business Environment**

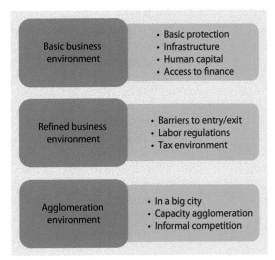

Basic business environment
- Basic protection
- Infrastructure
- Human capital
- Access to finance

Refined business environment
- Barriers to entry/exit
- Labor regulations
- Tax environment

Agglomeration environment
- In a big city
- Capacity agglomeration
- Informal competition

Source: Reyes, Roberts, and Xu 2017.

2006–2015. These data cover almost 49,000 firms in up to 529 cities, drawn from 110 countries globally. They include 66 cities in 23 LAC countries. The fact that LAC firms and cities form part of a much broader global sample means that the data can be used to compare the strength of city-level determinants of firm productivity, as measured by labor productivity and TFP, in the LAC region with those in the rest of the world.[26] The analysis conducted by Reyes, Roberts, and Xu (2017) focuses on the relationship between firm productivity and different elements of a city's business environment (BE), which itself can be considered part of a city's wider enabling environment for productivity enhancement. The BE in this context is broadly defined as comprising three main elements: basic BE, refined BE, and the agglomeration environment (figure 3.6).

Basic BE refers to those aspects of a city's BE that many analysts view as fundamental for development. It includes the basic functions of government protection, including containing corruption and providing basic protection from crime. It also encompasses a good supply of human capital and infrastructure, as well as access to finance—a key element for many researchers (Levine 1997; Demirgüç-Kunt and Maksimovic 1998; La

Porta et al. 1998; Beck, Demirgüç-Kunt, and Maksimovic 2005; Bloom et al. 2010). *Refined BE* includes the entry and exit barriers that exist for firms in a city, as well as a city's labor regulations and tax environment.

The *agglomeration environment* encapsulates (i) whether a firm is based in a large city, and therefore has the potential to benefit from agglomeration economies;[27] (ii) "capacity agglomeration," defined as the concentration of firms in a city that possess high capacity either in technology, management, or ability to adapt to a changing competitive environment; and (iii) informal competition in a city, measured by the share of firms in the city that self-report as competing with informal firms.[28]

Capacity agglomeration is proxied by the share of firms in a city that employ more than 50 workers. The use of this proxy is consistent with evidence that shows that large firms are more productive and export more than smaller firms (Bernard et al. 2007; Melitz and Ottaviano 2008); are more innovative (Cohen and Levin 1989); and conduct research and development (R&D) more efficiently (Cohen and Klepper 1996). Perhaps because the R&D centers of large firms provide key spillovers for small firms (Acs, Audretsch, and Feldman 1994), large firms are associated with higher industrial agglomeration (Barrios, Bertinelli, and Strobl 2006; Holmes and Stevens 2002). For the United States, the exogenous relocation of large firms has been found to positively affect incumbent firms' TFP (Greenstone, Hornbeck, and Moretti 2010), and firms are more likely to become large when colocated with other large firms (Li, Lu, and Wu 2012). Using the same proxy for capacity agglomeration, Li, Long, and Xu (2017) find that this measure helps explain China's productivity advantage over India in a quantitatively important way; Clarke, Qiang, and Xu (2015) find that it has predictive power for firm-level job growth using WBES data.

Like the analysis of worker data in previous sections, however, it is also possible that productivity differences across cities may be driven by compositional differences associated with the sorting of firms across cities. Different cities can be expected to be home to firms with different mixes of characteristics. To control for this, Reyes, Roberts, and Xu (2017) regress firm productivity not only on variables that capture the three different elements of a city's BE (basic and refined BE, and the agglomeration environment) but also on key characteristics of firms that can be observed in the WBES data.[29] Given that the regression analysis also includes country fixed effects, in effect it examines the determinants of firm productivity in countries at the city-industry level, assessing how much the strength of these determinants varies between LAC and the rest of the world.

Table 3.3 shows the main regression results for (natural log) labor productivity and TFP, where *LAC* is a dummy variable equal to one for LAC cities and zero for cities in the rest of the world. The regressions include only interactions for LAC where these were found to be statistically significant in one or more of the regressions estimated by Reyes, Roberts, and Xu (2017).[30] As seen, the number of these interactions is relatively small. It follows that the BE in LAC cities influences firm productivity in much the same way as it does in the rest of the world. Therefore, and perhaps somewhat surprisingly, the refined BE that cities offer is not a significant determinant of firm productivity, whether labor productivity or TFP, either in the LAC region or the rest of the world.[31]

TABLE 3.3   The Effects of a City's Business Environment on Firm Productivity

BE element	BE variable	(1) Log(Labor Productivity)		(2) Log(TFP)	
		Coefficient	SE	Coefficient	SE
Basic BE	Corruption obstacle	0.079	0.106	0.223	0.127
	Security cost	−2.903**	0.830	−3.540**	0.758
	Outage	0.049	0.114	0.014	0.102
	Web intensity	0.464**	0.119	0.333**	0.108
	Web intensity × LAC	−0.001	0.210	−0.016	0.194
	Skilled labor obstacle	−0.237*	0.095	−0.138	0.114
	Overdraft facility	0.327**	0.112	0.165	0.112
	Trade credit	0.285	0.149	−0.079	0.129
Refined BE	Land access obstacle	−0.076	0.108	−0.081	0.105
	Tax rate obstacle	0.197	0.104	−0.238*	0.111
	Labor regulation obstacle	0.091	0.121	0.181	0.119
Agglomeration environment	BigCity	0.102*	0.040	0.076	0.048
	BigCity × LAC	−0.205*	0.086	−0.019	0.072
	Capacity agglomeration	0.258	0.230	0.505*	0.199
	Inf competition	−0.043	0.114	0.002	0.102
	Inf competition × LAC	0.186	0.204	0.076	0.192
	No. of observations	48,614		19,603	
	Adjusted R^2	0.370		0.278	

Source: Calculations based on Reyes, Roberts, and Xu 2017.
Note: Labor productivity is measured as sales divided by the number of permanent employees. TFP (total factor productivity) is estimated as the residual from industry-specific production functions with log value added as the dependent variable and log capital and log labor as the independent variables. Capital is the replacement cost of land and machinery. Labor is the number of permanent employees plus 0.5 times the number of temporary employees. Regressions include a full set of country and industry fixed effects, as well the following controls: *Foreign* (share of foreign ownership of the firm), *OwnLargest* (ownership share of the largest owner), L_0 *20–100* (= 1 if firm's number of employees three years ago was 20–100; = 0 otherwise), L_0 *100+* (= 1 if firm's number of employees three years ago exceeded 100; = 0 otherwise), *Age 6–10* (= 1 if firm's age is between 6 and 10 years; = 0 otherwise), *Age 10+* (= 1 if firm's age is 10 years or greater; = 0 otherwise), and *exporter* (= 1 if firm exports; = 0 otherwise). BE = basic environment; SE = standard error.
**$p < 0.01$. *$p < 0.05$. Heteroscedasticity-corrected SEs were clustered at the city level.

By contrast, several different components of basic BE have significant effects on productivity in LAC and non-LAC cities alike. A lack of basic protection—as proxied by a high city-industry average spending by firms (as a proportion of sales) on security (by a high value of the variable "security cost")—has a large and significant negative effect on labor productivity and on TFP. The presence of modern infrastructure in a city (in fact, of the internet as captured by the variable "web intensity") has a significant positive effect on labor productivity and TFP. Access to formal finance, measured by the share of firms with an overdraft facility in a city ("overdraft facility"), likewise has a significant positive effect on firm productivity, although this effect is confined to labor productivity.[32] A shortage of skilled labor in a city ("skilled labor obstacle") has a significant negative effect on firm labor productivity, but not on TFP.

The findings that a lack of basic protection from crime in cities and the existence of skilled labor obstacles have significant negative effects on productivity are particularly important even if their effects are the same for LAC cities as for those in the rest of the world.

LAC cities have long been notorious for their high crime rates. According to data from the Brazilian think tank *Igarapé Institute*, LAC was, excluding war zones, home to 43 of the 50 most murderous cities in the world in 2016, with San Salvador, the capital city of El Salvador, holding the dubious distinction of being the global "murder capital" with 137 homicides per 100,000 inhabitants.[33] As figure 3.7 shows, average spending by firms on security across LAC cities (as a share of sales) also exceeds that in all other regions of the world (including average spending by firms in East Asia and Pacific cities), except for Europe and Central Asia and Sub-Saharan Africa. Our findings using the worker data (see "Explaining underlying variations in productivity"), highlight the central role of skill in determining urban success in the region. That skilled labor obstacles have significant negative effects on firm productivity corroborates this finding.

Although the effects of the basic BE and refined BE on firm productivity are similar in the LAC region to those in the rest of the world, the situation differs for the

FIGURE 3.7   Security Costs Incurred by Firms in Cities, Latin America and the Caribbean and Other Regions

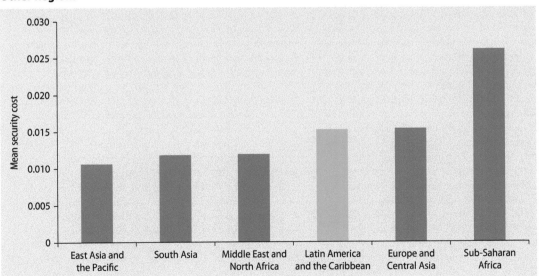

Source: Analysis of World Bank Enterprise Survey data from Reyes, Roberts, and Xu 2017.
Note: The y axis shows the mean spending by firms on security across cities (as a share of sales) in a region. For each city, security cost is the city-industry average of the share of a firm's sales paid for security. Europe and Central Asia covers 27 countries, only one of which (Sweden) is a Western European country. LAC = Latin America and the Caribbean.

agglomeration environment. Outside the LAC region, there is a "big city" labor productivity premium of 10 percent, which is statistically significant at the 5 percent level. For LAC, however, the premium is *negative*. Conditional on firm characteristics and other elements of the BE, labor productivity is some 10 percent lower for a LAC firm in a big city than for one in a smaller city. The existence of this negative effect is consistent and, therefore, serves to reinforce the finding of a lack of wider agglomeration effects, beyond HCEs, that was found using worker data. Although not statistically significant,

the results for TFP also suggest that the benefits of agglomeration might not be as strong in the LAC region as in the rest of the world. Besides being in a big city, capacity agglomeration is also found to be a statistically significant determinant of TFP, although, in this case its effect in the LAC region is not found to differ significantly from that in the rest of the world. The importance of a city's BE and agglomeration environment for the productivity of its firms is further investigated in box 3.3 for Colombian manufacturing firms, where particularly rich data exist for firms and cities.

BOX 3.3   The Determinants of Manufacturing Firm Productivity across Colombian Municipalities

With nearly 50 million inhabitants and an estimated urban population of 35 million, Colombia is one of the Latin America and the Caribbean (LAC) region's most populous and highly urbanized countries.[a] Although the areas east of the Andes account for nearly 60 percent of Colombia's total land area, most economic activity is concentrated in smaller areas to the west: the Andean region, with the capital city of Bogotá, and the Caribbean coast region.

In their background paper, Balat and Casas (2017), show that more than 70 percent of Colombian manufacturing firms are concentrated in seven major cities—Bogotá, Medellín, Cali, Bucaramanga, Manizales, Cartagena, and Barranquilla—in these two regions. Balat and Casas seek to explore whether this clustering benefits the productivity of Colombian manufacturing firms, while also analyzing the broader characteristics of Colombian municipalities that may either promote or hinder manufacturing firm productivity.

Balat and Casas use two distinct, and extremely rich, data sets. The first is a firm-level input-output panel that, for each firm, provides annual data on the revenue generated from each product sold, use of raw materials, investment, number of employees, overall wage bill, and, crucially, the municipality in which the firm is located.[b] The data set covers 2005–2013 and 22 manufacturing industries, for a total of almost 27,000 firm-year observations.[c] Using these

data, the authors estimate the total factor productivity (TFP) of each firm.[d] The second data set is a panel of municipal characteristics, which covers more than 1,300 variables for 1993–2014.[e] By joining these two data sets, Balat and Casas study the effect of a municipality's characteristics on the productivity of its firms. Key variables studied include those for the municipality relating to the nature of manufacturing agglomeration, fiscal performance, quality of education, and rates of conflict and violence.

Descriptive analysis shows that Bogotá not only forms the largest manufacturing cluster with the highest absolute concentration of firms in every industry but also exhibits the highest average manufacturing firm productivity. But Bogotá does not top productivity charts in every industry. Cali, for example, Colombia's third most populous municipality, is the most productive in apparel and metal products; Medellín in wood products and computing machinery; Barranquilla in textiles and printing; Manizales in machinery; Bucaramanga in rubber and plastic products; and Cartagena in food and paper products.

Further analysis reveals that an industry's localization in a municipality, as measured by its size relative to the size of the manufacturing sector there, is a significant and robust determinant of firm productivity.[f] By contrast, a diversified manufacturing base and a high level of competition within a municipality appear to be damaging for firm pro-

(continued)

BOX 3.3   The Determinants of Manufacturing Firm Productivity across Colombian Municipalities *(continued)*

ductivity, although these results are less robust. The overall scale of manufacturing activity within a municipality is likewise estimated to be unimportant for firm productivity.

Beyond the nature of the agglomeration environment, Balat and Casas also find other municipality-level characteristics (many of which have been highlighted as of more general importance in the main text of this chapter) to be important for firm TFP. Increased municipal expenditure on transport infrastructure is beneficial for TFP, whereas an undesirable business environment generated by increased taxes on firms adversely affects it. Firms

are also found to be more productive in municipalities that provide higher-quality schools, as reflected, for example, in lower student–teacher ratios and higher scores in mandatory high school exit exams.[g] High rates of crime and violence exert statistically and economically significant negative effects on TFP. Thus, a one-standard-deviation increase in the theft rate or in the number of terrorist attacks that occur in a municipality is associated with a decrease in firm TFP of up to 5 percent. Likewise, average productivity losses stemming from the presence of paramilitary and drug-trafficking groups in a municipality are estimated to be up to 3.2 percent.

Source: Based on Balat and Casas 2017.
a. For consistency with chapters 1 and 2, the estimate of Colombia's urban population is derived by applying the cluster algorithm of Dijkstra and Poelman (2014) to LandScan 2012 gridded population data.
b. The source of this panel data is the *Superintendencia de Sociedades* (Superintendence of Corporations) database.
c. Balat and Casas (2017) exclude firms engaged in the manufacture of coke, refined petroleum products, nuclear fuel, and basic metals (including metals such as gold, silver, platinum, and nickel) from their analysis. This is because these firms are commodity producers, and therefore their dynamics are different from those of other manufacturing firms.
d. Balat and Casas (2017) estimate firm-level TFP using an extended Cobb-Douglas production function with industry-specific coefficients. Their approach helps them to address major methodological challenges that arise from the inability to observe productivity shocks that might affect firms' input choices (endogeneity) and entry–exit decisions (selection).
e. This data set is maintained by the Center of Economic Development Studies at the Universidad de los Andes.
f. In constructing measures of localization and diversity, Balat and Casas (2017) experiment with several measures of the size of an industry, including number of firms in that industry, its employment, size of capital stock, and production.
g. Such as Saber 11, a standardized test similar to the SAT in the United States.

Conclusions

Although compositional differences in the workforce associated with the sorting of workers across locations have a major role in explaining productivity variations, urban success in the LAC region is also crucially dependent on the existence of a strong overall stock of human capital (that is, a high level of city skill) and, at least for certain countries, good access to large consumer and supplier markets through transport networks. By contrast, other types of positive agglomeration effects, such as those, for example, that we expect to arise from labor pooling or more general knowledge spillovers, seem to be weak to nonexistent in the region's cities. A possible hypothesis that may explain this is that, in the context of high urban population densities, LAC cities may not have an enabling environment

that is conducive to the fostering of wider positive agglomeration effects. Hence, current policies and levels of urban infrastructure may not be sufficient to prevent negative congestion effects offsetting more general positive agglomeration effects.

Results based on WBES firm-level data show that additional elements in a city's environment matter for productivity, such as prevention of crime and theft (which are notoriously high in LAC cities) targeted at firms, provision of modern infrastructure (Internet access), and access to formal banking finance. The findings on the importance of skill and crime are further reinforced by a case study of the determinants of firm productivity in Colombian municipalities.

Given the importance of the theories of market access and of HCEs in explaining urban success in the LAC region, the next two chapters examine them in more depth.

Annex 3A: Results of Regressions on the Determinants of Underlying Productivity Variations Based on the Single-Stage Approach

As an alternative to the two-stage approach to analyzing the determinants of productivity across subnational areas, many papers have followed a single-stage approach (Duranton 2016; Chauvin et al. 2017). Instead of first estimating location premiums and then regressing these premiums against potential area-level determinants of productivity, the single-stage approach simply includes the potential area-level determinants directly in a regression of a worker's (natural log) wage on her or his observable characteristics (directly in a Mincerian-style wage regression).[34]

As table 3A.1 shows, when we adopt this approach, we obtain higher estimated coefficients on population density than those reported in table 3.2 using the two-stage

approach. Nevertheless, the overall qualitative picture remains the same. Hence, the estimated elasticity of a worker's nominal wage with respect to the population density of the area in which she or he lives drops drastically as we introduce, first, an area's overall average number of years of schooling, then its market access—columns 2 and 3 of table 3A.1. Its statistical significance also declines. Whether the variable becomes statistically insignificant at all conventional levels (up to the 10 percent level) depends crucially on how we cluster the standard errors. When they are clustered at the area level, population density remains significant at the 5 percent level. It may be argued, however, that this is too restrictive because it rules out correlation between errors for workers who live in, for example, neighboring areas. When we instead cluster standard errors at national level, population density is insignificant even at the 10 percent level.[35]

TABLE 3A.1   Results of Regressions on the Determinants of Underlying Productivity Variations Based on the Single-Stage Approach

Dependent variable: Nominal hourly wage (ln)	(1)	(2)	(3)	(4)	(5)
Population density (ln)	0.057***	0.024***	0.012**	0.035***	0.017***
Average number of years of schooling (ln)		0.636***	0.605***		
Percentage of working-age population with higher education				0.015***	0.014***
Market access (ln)			0.013***		0.016***
Mean air temperature (ln)	0.013	0.018	0.020	0.018	0.022
Terrain ruggedness (ln)	−0.000	0.002	0.006	−0.005	−0.000
Total precipitation (ln)	−0.044***	−0.027***	−0.025***	−0.035***	−0.033***
Constant	−2.02***	−3.41***	−3.49***	−2.09***	−2.27***
No. of observations	4,000,142	4,000,142	3,766,690	4,000,142	3,766,690
R^2	0.337	0.346	0.349	0.343	0.346
Adjusted R^2	0.337	0.346	0.349	0.343	0.346

Source: Quintero and Roberts 2017; population data: Gridded Population of the World, v4.
Note: All estimations are based on the broad sample (all wage/salary employees age 14–65 years). In all columns, the dependent variable is the natural log of the nominal hourly wage in the main occupation. All regressions include country-year fixed effects and observable characteristics of individual workers (age, age squared, marital status, gender, and number of years of schooling), both individually and interacted with a full set of country dummies.
***$p < 0.01$. **$p < 0.05$. *$p < 0.1$. Standard errors are clustered at the area level.

Notes

1. The basic idea here is that through skill-selective migration workers with different characteristics "sort" into different cities. It is this sorting that leads to compositional differences in the workforce. But sorting is not necessarily independent of the three theories of urban success that we describe below. For example, the theory of human capital externalities (HCEs) could not explain productivity differences across cities without the compositional differences in the workforce that arise from sorting. Similarly, if the amenities that different cities offered were the same, there would be no incentive for more highly educated workers to sort into larger and more densely populated cities absent higher returns to human capital in those cities.

2. Agglomeration economies can also be separated into localization economies and urbanization economies. Localization economies are the positive externalities associated with the clustering together within a city of firms from the same industry (Marshall 1890). Urbanization economies are the positive externalities associated with the geographic concentration of a set of different industries within a given city (Jacobs 1969).

3. Duranton and Puga (2004) identify three mechanisms underpinning agglomeration economies, which they term "sharing, matching, and learning."

4. If unskilled and skilled workers are complementary inputs in the production processes within a city's firms, then this can also generate observationally similar effects to human capital externalities. This issue is explored in detail in chapter 5.

5. This chapter focuses on domestic market access—access to markets within the same country. However, as is discussed in chapter 4, access to international markets through both ports and airports is also likely to be an important determinant of a city's productivity. To help distinguish between agglomeration economies and market access, the measure of market access used in this chapter excludes from its calculation an area's own population. The exclusion of an area's own population also helps to mitigate reverse causality concerns.

6. Chauvin et al. (2017) examine empirically the roles of agglomeration economies and HCEs in driving urban productivity differences in Brazil, China, and India. Duranton (2016) examines these two theories for Colombia, in addition to investigating empirically the role of market access in driving productivity differences across cities. Authors who have studied the empirical relationship between subnational levels of productivity and market access without necessarily accounting for agglomeration economies and HCEs in a developing country context include Fally, Paillacar, and Terra (2010) for Brazil and Hering and Poncet (2010) and Roberts et al. (2012) for China.

7. For a detailed explanation of why nominal rather than real wages provide the appropriate measure of productivity, see Combes and Gobillon (2015).

8. Household survey microdata are available for Brazil from the Socio-Economic Database for Latin America and the Caribbean (SEDLAC). Although this data can be used to calculate the overall urban–rural wage ratio, it cannot be used for the more general analysis of subnational productivity variations that we perform in the "Large Subnational Variations in Productivity" and "Explaining Underlying Variations in Productivity" sections of this chapter. For consistency between sections, we therefore prefer to use IPUMS International data for Brazil throughout. Although SEDLAC does not classify areas as urban or rural, it identifies whether households are urban and rural. We follow the SEDLAC documentation (CEDLAS and World Bank 2014) in assuming that urban (rural) households live in urban (rural) areas.

9. In these regressions, age proxies a worker's experience.

10. Controlling for (time-invariant) unobservable characteristics of workers requires panel data (see, for example, Combes, Duranton, and Gobillon 2008; D'Costa and Overman, 2014), which are unavailable for a large sample of LAC countries.

11. We use Admin-2 level data for 9 of the 16 countries in our sample: Bolivia, Brazil, Colombia, Dominican Republic, El Salvador, Honduras, Mexico, Nicaragua, and Uruguay. For the other seven countries; we use Admin-1 level data for Argentina, Guatemala, and Panama; and Admin-3 level data for Chile, Costa Rica, Ecuador, and Peru. Admin-2 areas correspond to *municipios* in Brazil, Colombia, Dominican Republic, El Salvador, Honduras, Mexico, Nicaragua, and Uruguay, and to *provincias* in Bolivia.

12. Such as Bogotá, Buenos Aires, Lima, Mexico City, Panama City, Santa Cruz, Santiago, and São Paulo.

13. Again, the observable worker characteristics that we control for are number of years of schooling, age and its square, gender, and marital status.

14. As with the regressions in the previous section, we include survey-year fixed effects. We also estimate the regressions without a constant, allowing us to include a full set of subnational area dummies.

15. We use average number of years of schooling among the working-age population rather than only employed workers as our measure of skill because, in principle, there is no reason why knowledge may not spill over from an unemployed to an employed member of the workforce.

16. Our specification of market access follows a classic Harris-style formulation (Harris 1954), in which the market access of an area is the travel-time discounted sum of populations in all other subnational areas within the same country. In calculating market access, we exclude an area's own population, which helps distinguish the market access variable from population density, while mitigating endogeneity problems associated with reverse causation. We view market access as capturing the beneficial effects, for final goods producers, of access to consumer markets and access to suppliers of intermediate inputs. Although these two types of access (to consumers and suppliers) are, in principle, two separate concepts, empirical work has found it hard to separate them because of their extremely high correlation (see, for example, Redding and Venables 2004).

17. We prefer population density to overall population as our measure of agglomeration because the subnational administrative areas that we use in our analysis only provide approximations of "true" cities (see chapters 1 and 2).

18. Like the analysis in annex 3A, Hering and Poncet (2010) regress individual wages directly on market access controlling for individual observable characteristics. Rather than base their market access variable on population, they derive the variable through a two-step procedure that first involves the estimation of a gravity trade equation. We were unable to apply such a procedure owing to an absence of bilateral trade flow data for subnational areas.

19. The Pearson correlation coefficient for population density and average number of years of schooling is 0.30, whereas that for population density and market access is 0.67. For average number of years of schooling and market access, the correlation coefficient is 0.32. All estimated correlation coefficients are significant at the 5 percent level.

20. As noted, in our regressions we are able to control only for the sorting of workers based on their observable characteristics. However, sorting may also be taking place on the basis of such unobservable characteristics of workers as their ability and motivation. To the extent that these unobservable characteristics of workers are not correlated with their observable characteristics, our estimate of the coefficient on population density will be biased. If more able and motivated workers sort toward denser areas, then we would expect the direction of this bias to be upward, thereby strengthening our result of an estimated absence of agglomeration economies.

21. As an alternative to the two-stage approach to analyzing the determinants of subnational productivity that we have adopted in this chapter, many papers have followed a single-stage approach (Duranton 2016; Chauvin et al. 2017). Annex 3A shows that, when we apply this approach to our LAC sample, we obtain higher estimated coefficients on population density than those reported in table 3.2 using the two-stage approach. Nevertheless, the overall qualitative picture regarding weak positive agglomeration effects beyond HCEs remains the same. A further empirical concern with the regressions in table 3.2, and not discussed in the main text, is that there may be endogeneity stemming from either reverse causation from an area's location premium to its levels of population density, human capital, and market access or omitted variables that are correlated with both the left- and right-hand side variables. Addressing these endogeneity concerns would require the additional use of instrumental variables estimation. We would require a minimum of three instruments, one for each of our key independent variables. Finding plausible instruments is, however, tricky. Although data on precolonial population densities represent a possible instrument for population density, this would still leave us two instruments short.

22. The corresponding single-stage approach results are in columns 4 and 5 in table 3A.1, annex 3A. As can be seen, in this case, population density remains significantly positive at the 1 percent level, even after controlling for the share of working-age population who possess higher education and for market access.

23. Figure 3.5 does not show results for all 16 countries in our overall sample. Where results are not shown, this is either because of extremely wide confidence intervals due to small numbers of subnational areas or, as with Panama, a lack of sufficient observations to permit estimation.

24. In contrast to figure 3.5c, chapter 4 reports a significant positive effect of market access on productivity for Mexican subnational areas. The difference in results may be partly attributable to differences in data and partly due to differences in methods. For example, chapter 4 bases its measure of productivity on nighttime lights data rather than nominal wages, while it also merges some subnational areas to form larger metropolitan areas. Chapter 4 also relies on panel rather than cross-sectional data, but does not control for sorting based on the observable characteristics of individual workers. This does not rule out the importance for productivity of improving access to international markets—both through improved road and rail access to ports and airports and improvements in both port and airport infrastructure—even where the coefficient on market access is statistically insignificant.

25. Estimated variations in the strength of HCEs may also be attributable to differences in the quality of education across countries, such that one additional year of schooling in, for example, Nicaragua does not accomplish the same amount of learning as an additional year of schooling in Bolivia. The extent to which the estimated variations in the strength of HCEs are attributable to educational quality differences is an important area of future research.

26. Labor productivity is measured as sales divided by the number of permanent employees. TFP is estimated as the residual from industry-specific production functions with log value added as the dependent variable and log capital and log labor as the independent variables.

27. In this case, a large city is defined as either a national capital or a city with more than 1 million residents. Because it is a simple binary dummy variable for whether a firm is in a national capital or big city, the measure of agglomeration used by Reyes, Roberts, and Xu is somewhat cruder—given limitations of the WBES data—than the continuous measure of population density used in the earlier worker-based analysis.

28. This variable is denoted "Inf competition" in table 3.3. Informal firms tend to be relatively unproductive compared with formal firms, in part because they possess less managerial capital along with little organizational complexity and related know-how (La Porta and Shleifer 2014). Given this, Reyes, Roberts, and Xu hypothesize that firms that face higher informal competition are likely to benefit less from positive spillover effects within their industries.

29. This includes controlling for the industry that a firm belongs to, as well as the extent to which a firm is foreign owned, the ownership share of its largest owner, whether a firm is an exporter, a firm's size as measured by the number of workers it employs, and a firm's age.

30. Besides the results in table 3.3, Reyes, Roberts, and Xu also estimate regressions for three-year growth rates of labor productivity and TFP, and a firm's export share. We do not discuss these results because our focus is more on the long-run determinants of city productivity. Interactions for LAC with both "Web intensity" and "Inf competition" are included in table 3.3 because these interactions are significant in one or more of these supplemental regressions estimated by Reyes, Roberts, and Xu.

31. The exception is tax rate obstacle, which has a significant negative effect on TFP at the 5 percent level.

32. This suggests that access to finance boosts labor productivity through facilitating an increase in the capital–labor ratio rather than necessarily fostering innovation.

33. See https://www.economist.com/blogs/graphicdetail/2017/03/daily-chart-23. However, the LAC region's high homicide rates are primarily related to gang warfare associated with drug trafficking. It is not clear how much this violent crime affects firms.

34. Our preference for the two-stage approach is partly because, unlike the single-stage approach, it allows us to obtain estimates of

levels of underlying productivity for subnational areas. The main concern of the two-stage approach is that it might not provide reliable standard errors in the second stage, because the location premiums that act as the dependent variable in the second-stage regression are themselves estimates, and thus contain an estimation error that is likely greater for smaller subnational areas. However, given that the number of observations (about 4 million) that underlies our estimation of the location premiums is large, and that 99.4 percent of estimated location premiums from our first-stage regressions are significant at the 5 percent level (only 38 of 5,872 location premiums are insignificant at the 5 percent level), this concern seems to be relatively minor.

35. The "ideal" level of clustering for the standard errors likely lies between the area and national levels.

References

Acs, Z. J., D. B. Audretsch, and M. P. Feldman. 1994. "R&D Spillovers and Recipient Firm Size." *Review of Economics and Statistics* 76 (2): 336–40.

Balat, J., and C. Casas. 2017. "Firm Productivity and Cities: The Case of Colombia." Background paper for this book Washington, DC.

Barrios, S., L. Bertinelli, and E. Strobl. 2006. "Geographic Concentration and Establishment Scale: An Extension Using Panel Data." *Journal of Regional Science* 46 (4): 733–46.

Beck, T., A. Demirgüç-Kunt, and V. Maksimovic. 2005. "Financial and Legal Constraints to Growth: Does Firm Size Matter?" *Journal of Finance* 60 (1): 137–77.

Bernard, A. B., J. B. Jensen, S. J. Redding, and P. K. Schott. 2007. "Firms in International Trade." *Journal of Economic Perspectives* 21 (3): 105–30.

Bloom, N., A. Mahajan, D. McKenzie, and J. Roberts. 2010. "Why Do Firms in Developing Countries Have Low Productivity?" *American Economic Review* 100 (2): 619–23.

Branson, J., A. Campbell-Sutton, G. M. Hornby, D. D. Hornby, and C. Hill. 2016. "A Geospatial Database for Latin America and the Caribbean: Geodata." Southampton, U.K.: University of Southampton.

CEDLAS (Center for Distributive, Labor and Social Studies) and World Bank. 2014. *A Guide to SEDLAC—Socio-Economic Database for Latin America and the Caribbean.* Washington, DC: World Bank.

Chauvin, J. P., E. Glaeser, Y. Ma, and K. Tobio. 2017. "What Is Different about Urbanization in Rich and Poor Countries? Cities in Brazil, China, India and the United States." *Journal of Urban Economics* 98 (C): 17–49.

Clarke, G., C. Z. Qiang, and L. C. Xu. 2015. "The Internet as a General-Purpose Technology." *Economics Letters* 135 (C): 24–27.

Cohen, W. M., and R. C. Levin. 1989. "Empirical Studies of Innovation and Market Structure." In *Handbook of Industrial Organization, Volume 2,* edited by R. Schmalansee and R. D. Willing, 1059–1107. Amsterdam: Elsevier.

Cohen, W. M., and S. Klepper. 1996. "Firm Size and the Nature of Innovation within Industries: The Case of Process and Product R&D." *Review of Economics and Statistics* 78 (2): 232–43.

Combes, P., G. Duranton, and L. Gobillon. 2008. "Spatial Wage Disparities: Sorting Matters!" *Journal of Urban Economics* 63 (2): 723–42.

Combes, P., and L. Gobillon. 2015. "The Empirics of Agglomeration Economies." In *Handbook of Regional and Urban Economics, Volume 5,* edited by G. Duranton, J. V. Henderson, and W. Strange, 247–348. Amsterdam: Elsevier.

D'Costa, S., and H. G. Overman. 2014. "The Urban Wage Growth Premium: Sorting or Learning?" *Regional Science and Urban Economics* 48 (C): 168–79.

Demirgüç-Kunt, A., and V. Maksimovic. 1998. "Law, Finance, and Firm Growth." *Journal of Finance* 53 (6): 2107–37.

Dijkstra, L., and H. Poelman. 2014. "A Harmonised Definition of Cities and Rural Areas: The New Degree of Urbanization." Regional Working Paper, Directorate-General for Regional and Urban Policy, European Commission, Brussels.

Duranton, G. 2015. "Growing through Cities in Developing Countries." *World Bank Research Observer* 30(1): 39-73.

———. 2016. "Agglomeration Effects in Colombia." *Journal of Regional Science* 56 (2): 210–38.

Duranton, G., and D. Puga. 2004. "Micro-Foundations of Urban Agglomeration Economies." In *Handbook of Regional and Urban Economics, Volume 4: Cities and Geography,* edited by J. V. Henderson and J.-F. Thisse, 2063–2117. Amsterdam: Elsevier.

Fally, T., R. Paillacar, and C. Terra. 2010. "Economic Geography and Wages in Brazil: Evidence from Micro-data." *Journal of Development Economics* 91 (1): 155–68.

Fay, M., L. A. Andres, C. J. E. Fox, U. G. Narloch, S. Straub, and M. A. Slawson. 2017. *Rethinking Infrastructure in Latin America and the Caribbean; Spending Better to Achieve More.* Washington, DC: World Bank.

Fujita, M., P. Krugman, and A. J. Venables. 1999. *The Spatial Economy: Cities, Regions and International Trade.* Cambridge, MA: MIT Press.

Glaeser, E. 1999. "Learning in Cities." *Journal of Urban Economics* 46 (2): 254–77.

Greenstone, M., R. Hornbeck, and E. Moretti. 2010. "Identifying Agglomeration Spillovers: Evidence from Winners and Losers of Large Plant Openings." *Journal of Political Economy* 118 (3): 536–98.

Harris, C. D. 1954. "The Market as a Factor in the Localization of Industry in the United States." *Annals of the Association of American Geographers* 44 (4): 315–48.

Henderson, J. V. 2010. "Cities and Development." *Journal of Regional Science* 50 (1): 515–40.

Hering, L., and S. Poncet. 2010. "Market Access and Individual Wages: Evidence from China." *Review of Economics and Statistics* 92 (1): 145–59.

Holmes, T. J., and J. J. Stevens. 2002. "Geographic Concentration and Establishment Scale." *Review of Economics and Statistics* 84 (4): 682–90.

Jacobs, J. 1969. *The Economy of Cities.* New York: Random House.

Krugman, P. 1991a. *Geography and Trade.* Cambridge, MA: MIT Press.

———. 1991b. "Increasing Returns and Economic Geography." *Journal of Political Economy* 99 (3): 483–99.

Krugman, P., and A. J. Venables. 1995. "Globalization and the Inequality of Nations." *Quarterly Journal of Economics* 110 (4): 857–80.

La Porta, R., and A. Shleifer. 2014. "Informality and Development." *Journal of Economic Perspectives* 28 (3): 109–26.

La Porta, R., F. Lopez-de-Silanes, A. Shleifer, and R. Vishny. 1998. "Law and Finance." *Journal of Political Economy* 106 (6): 1113–55.

Levine, R. 1997. "Financial Development and Economic Growth: Views and Agenda." *Journal of Economic Literature* 35 (2): 688–726.

Li, D., Y. Lu, and M. Wu. 2012. "Industrial Agglomeration and Firm Size: Evidence from China." *Regional Science and Urban Economics* 42 (1–2): 135–43.

Li, W., X. C. Long, and L. C. Xu. 2017. "Regulation, Agglomeration, and the Reversal of Fortune between China and India." Working paper, World Bank, Washington, DC.

Marshall, A. 1890. *Principles of Economics.* London: Macmillan and Co.

Melitz, M. J., and G. Ottaviano. 2008. "Market Size, Trade and Productivity." *Review of Economic Studies* 75 (1): 295–316.

Mincer, J. 1974. *Schooling, Experience, and Earnings.* New York: National Bureau of Economic Research.

Moretti, E. 2004. "Human Capital Externalities in Cities." In *Handbook of Regional and Urban Economics, Volume* 4: Cities and Geography, edited by J. V. Henderson and J.-F. Thisse, 2243–91. Amsterdam: Elsevier.

Overman, H. G., and A. J. Venables. 2005. "Cities in the Developing World." Center for Economic Performance Discussion Paper 695, London School of Economics and Political Science, London.

Quintero, L., and M. Roberts. 2017. "Explaining Spatial Variations in Productivity: Evidence from 16 LAC Countries." Background paper for this book World Bank, Washington, DC.

Rauch, J. E. 1993. "Productivity Gains from Geographic Concentration of Human Capital: Evidence from the Cities." *Journal of Urban Economics* 34 (3): 380–400.

Redding, S., and A. J. Venables. 2004. "Economic Geography and International Inequality." *Journal of International Economics* 62 (1): 53–82.

Reyes, J., M. Roberts, and L. C. Xu. 2017. "The Heterogeneous Growth Effects of the Business Environment: Firm-Level Evidence for a Global Sample of Cities." Policy Research Working Paper 8114, World Bank, Washington, DC.

Roberts, M., U. Deichmann, B. Fingleton, and T. Shi. 2012. "Evaluating China's Road to Prosperity: A New Economic Geography Approach." *Regional Science and Urban Economics* 42 (4): 580–94.

Transport Infrastructure and Agglomeration in Cities | 4

Harris Selod and Souleymane Soumahoro

Introduction

Transport investment can contribute to cities' productivity. Improved transport systems, for example, may lower production costs in an industrial cluster and generate efficiency gains through *localization economies*. Similarly, they may generate, through *urbanization economies*, positive externalities to all firms in large urban centers.[1] There are also potentially wider economic benefits, which may themselves directly or indirectly induce sizable effects on productivity, including increased employment and market opportunities and enhanced human capital externalities (HCEs) in education and health due to improved access to transport.

Yet, despite increasing recognition of the importance of infrastructure for growth, the stock of physical capital in Latin America and the Caribbean (LAC) is thought to be low for the region's development level. Recent data suggest that paved road density in the LAC region is only marginally higher than in Sub-Saharan Africa (SSA) and about one-quarter that of the Middle East and North Africa (MENA), the next least-performing region (Dulac 2013).

This chapter explores the issue of low physical capital stock in the LAC region through the lens of investment in transport, and its implications for agglomeration effects in cities if such investment were increased—important issues for two main reasons. First, transport investment can be critical to make cities function more efficiently and become more sustainable. Second, there is ample empirical evidence suggesting that improved transport systems increase productivity in cities by facilitating the spatial concentration of firms (Ghani, Goswami, and Kerr 2016), by increasing firm birth (Holl 2004) and employment (Mesquita Moreira et al. 2013), and by improving firm efficiency (Datta 2012). (Similarly, chapter 3 documents that access to markets is a significant determinant of productivity for a sample of 16 LAC countries, even with cross-country heterogeneity in the estimated elasticities.)

The main findings are as follows:

- Despite recent years' growing policy enthusiasm for infrastructure investment, LAC continues to exhibit low road density and poor road quality, which likely translates into deficient access to transport infrastructure around cities as well as high congestion in cities.
- The prevalence of high physical and nonphysical transport costs in the LAC

region is a major constraint to domestic and international trade. It is also the source of negative externalities (congestion and pollution) that challenge the productivity and sustainability of LAC cities.

  o Physical investment can be accompanied by policy reforms that encourage competition in the transport industry and improve logistics and customs procedures.

  o Inefficient regulations to reduce congestion and related negative externalities could be complemented with, or replaced by, price incentives.[2]

• In Mexico (a case study), investment in roads is generally associated with local job growth, increased manufacturing specialization, and local economic development.

Transport, Agglomeration, and Productivity: A Brief Review

Transport investment can in theory have significant effects on productivity by exogenously lowering the costs of labor and intermediate goods for firms (Venables 2007; Graham 2007). However, in reviewing recent estimates of the relevant elasticities, the literature acknowledges nuanced findings (see Gramlich 1994; Deng 2013; Redding and Turner 2014; Straub 2011; Trebilcock and Rosenstock 2015; Berg et al. 2017). For example, from a macroeconomic perspective, several studies at the country or state level find positive returns to transport capital (Aschauer 1993; Calderón and Servén 2004a), whereas others identify insignificant effects (Holtz-Eakin 1994; Garcia-Mila, McGuire, and Porter 1996).[3] Holtz-Eakin (1994) argues, for example, that the impact of infrastructure capital on aggregate productivity is unlikely to be robust once the simultaneity bias linking the two is accounted for. Fernald (1999) challenges this view and provides evidence of the causal productivity gains associated with road investment in vehicle-intensive industries in the United States. The author

also shows that reduced congestion, rather than the increased stock of roads, is the relevant mechanism.

In terms of the productivity effects of transport capital in the urban space, various papers examine the role of transport investment in the movement of inputs within cities, especially labor, an issue that has been extensively investigated in the context of high- and middle-income countries. Evidence from U.S. cities suggests, for example, that roads enhance productivity in cities through their stimulating effects on employment (Duranton and Turner 2012) and on domestic trade flows (Duranton, Morrow, and Turner 2014). In Mexico, Gonzalez-Navarro and Quintana-Domeque (2016) exploit a random allocation of public funding to street paving to provide evidence of the beneficial effects of road upgrading. Their findings suggest that road paving increased household-level acquisition of durable goods (vehicles, appliances, and home improvements) through its positive effect on property values and access to credit.

Another effect associated with transport improvement includes the decentralization of production and population from core cities to peripheral areas (Baum-Snow 2007; Baum-Snow et al. 2012), where land is cheaper and the intercity transport network more easily accessible. There is also evidence from the United States (Duranton and Turner 2011) and Japan (Hsu and Zhang 2012) that additional roads may incentivize intracity (noncommercial) driving, therefore not relieving congestion.

The literature also examines the economic consequences of improved intercity transport infrastructure, in developed and developing countries. In the United States, for example, highway connection is found to increase earnings in services (Chandra and Thompson 2000), boost the wage of skilled relative to low-skilled workers (Michaels 2008), and stimulate city-level specialization in heavy goods through its effects on the weight of city exports (Duranton, Morrow, and Turner 2014). In Brazil, Bird and Straub (2014) exploit the creation of Brasilia and subsequent infrastructure investment as a "natural experiment," and find that access to roads reduced the inequality in the spatial distribution of economic activities among Brazilian regions. In India, Donaldson (forthcoming) examines the welfare effects of colonial railroads and finds that those railroads stimulated trade, reduced trade costs and interregional price gaps, and ultimately increased real agricultural income.

Similar positive productivity effects are found near the "Golden Quadrilateral," a major highway improvement project involving 5,846 km of roads in India (Ghani, Goswami, and Kerr 2016). In China, roads and railroads collectively contributed to an increase in county-level gross domestic product (GDP) per capita (Banerjee, Duflo, and Qian 2012). Still in China, the effects of the country's national expressway network exhibited significant subnational heterogeneity (Roberts et al. 2012), partially echoing the findings of Faber (2013) who documents a depressing effect of the highway network on the income of peripheral regions due to shrunk industrial output. In SSA, Storeygard (2016) identifies a causal link between low transport costs and city-level growth as measured by nighttime lights. In Ghana and Kenya, access to rail is found to stimulate local economic development in the short and long run (Jedwab, Kerby, and Moradi 2015; Jedwab and Moradi 2016).

Transport in Latin America and the Caribbean: History, Current State, and Challenges

History of Transport in the LAC Region

Most historians agree that the economic modernization of Latin America in the 19th century coincided with the development of physical infrastructure (Bulmer-Thomas et al. 2006). Innovations in transport helped many countries overcome the challenge of rugged terrain and hard-to-navigate waterways. The synergy of modern railroads with improved ports, and to a lesser extent roads, reduced transportation costs, facilitated the allocation of productive resources, and is believed to have spurred economic growth. By providing for low-cost national and international movement of agricultural products (cash crops, timber, and livestock), minerals (copper, silver, and coal), and people, the newly developed transport network accelerated market integration and created opportunities for specialization (Summerhill 2006).

Railroads as an engine of growth in the 19th and early 20th centuries. Railroads are described as the most attractive growth-enhancing infrastructure in 19th-century Latin America (Coatsworth 1979; Summerhill 2006). The financing opportunities brought by the first wave of globalization, coupled with improved political stability, generated more enthusiastic investment trends between 1870 and 1914.[4] In 1900, nearly 55,000 km of railroad track were in operation in the LAC region, 75 percent of which was in Argentina, Brazil, and Mexico. Between 1900 and 1930, rail networks continued to expand at an annual rate of 3.6 percent, before leveling off after World War I and the Great Depression. The development of the rail network in the LAC region appeared to be completed in the first half of the 20th century and only to have accompanied the early stages of urbanization. The share of the population living in urban areas, for example, increased from 27.6 percent in 1930 to 75.4 percent in 2000, but the aggregate length of railroads in service actually declined over the period (figure 4.1). This finding comes as no surprise given that the main function of railroads was to link primary resources (agricultural and mineral) to markets, including through ports, which became less important in subsequent phases of economic development.

The economic benefits of early investments in railroads are well documented and include increased social savings and improved export performance.[5] Social savings—or the potential output gains from the reduction of transport costs as a result of the more efficient allocation of labor and capital—increased substantially with investment in railroads. In Argentina and Brazil, for example, social savings generated from railroad freight were estimated to be about 26 and 22 percent of GDP in 1913, respectively (Summerhill 2006). In Mexico, investment in railroads

FIGURE 4.1   **Length of Railroad Track in Service and Urban Share in Latin America and the Caribbean, 1900–2007**

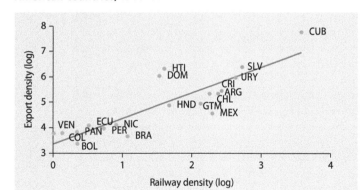

Source: Calculations based on the MOxLAD database (http://www.lac.ox.ac.uk/moxlad-database).
Note: The MOxLAD database groups sources, including Mitchell International Historical Statistics, World Development Indicators, Financial Statistics of the International Monetary Fund, and those of the Economic Commission for Latin America and the Caribbean.

FIGURE 4.2   **Export Density and Railroad Density in Selected Latin American Countries, 1900–30**

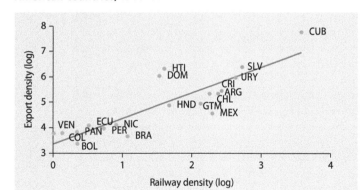

Source: Calculations based on the MOxLAD database (http://www.lac.ox.ac.uk/moxlad-database).
Note: Linear regression linking the natural log of export density (export value per square kilometer of land area) to the natural log of railroad density (kilometers of railroads per 1,000 km² of land area) in selected Latin American countries (using averages during 1900–30). For a list of country abbreviations, see annex 2A. y = 1.001x + 3.3568; R^2 = 0.7596.

engendered a social rate of return that exceeded 38 percent of GDP in 1910. To put these figures into perspective, social savings from railroad freight in the United States were below 9 percent of GDP in 1890. In the United Kingdom and Germany, they were respectively 11 percent and 5 percent in the 1890s.

Investments in railroads, combined with port improvements, also stimulated exports and so accelerated the integration of Latin American economies into the world market. Railroad coverage and export performance were highly correlated in 1900–1930 (figure 4.2). The cross-country elasticity of export density with respect to railroad density was about 1 in that period.[6] This suggests that investment in railroads boosted primary commodity exports or conversely that the profitability of exports was important during the first wave of globalization, leading to more investment in railroads. In both cases, higher spending on railroad infrastructure was key to the economic success of Latin America during the Belle Époque.[7]

The rise of roads from indigenous trails to modern motorways. Before the railroad revolution, early modern roads in Latin America were built upon precolonial indigenous routes. In the aftermath of World War I and the Great Recession, a period that coincided with stagnating railroad services, innovations in combustion engine technology accelerated the acquisition of motor vehicles in Latin America, generating new opportunities for profitable road investment. The bulk of such investment was, however, concentrated in a few countries. In 1930, for example, Argentina, Brazil, and Mexico—the three largest economies—collectively owned nearly 80 percent of passenger vehicles and about 74 percent of commercial vehicles in Latin America.[8] These statistics could reflect a bidirectional causal link between the growth in vehicle ownership and the development of roads. In Mexico, for example, the share of

public investments in roads exceeded 30 percent in 1937, up from 7.3 percent in 1925 (Cardenas 1987).

Box 4.1 presents, as an illustration, the history of road development in Mexico, which today has one of the most developed road networks in the LAC region.

Map 4.1 shows the growth of the road network over the past three decades, for which we have reconstructed panel georeferenced information on the road extent and road type (see Blankespoor, Bougna et al. 2017 for more detail). The maps show the relatively recent investments in larger capacity roads over the past two decades.

In contemporary LAC, roads have gradually emerged as a cost-efficient alternative to costly railroads. Figure 4.3 shows growth in the total length of road built in

---

BOX 4.1   History of Road Development in Mexico

Investment in roads started with the Spanish Colony (1521–1810), when roads were focused on transporting natural resources, especially silver and gold, to the port of Veracruz to ship them to Spain. Whereas the focus in the late 19th and early 20th centuries was on improving railroads throughout the country, roads started to receive more attention in the 1920s and 1930s. Subsequently, the focus shifted again to reconstructing and enlarging the road network, which had been damaged during the Mexican Revolution (Bess 2016a, 2016b). In the 1940s and 1950s, with great hope in the promises of industrialization and a generalized drive toward economic modernization, Mexico perceived road construction as necessary to allow market growth and improve the accessibility of subnational regions (Bess 2014). This conception led to the building of new roads in Mexico by state road-building agencies, which mobilized large public spending and private domestic—and foreign—investment.[a]

In the early 1950s, the first freeway, from Mexico City to Acapulco, was opened and became a model for building future freeways. During this period, road building played a key role in modernizing the Mexican economy and in developing major commercial industries

(Bess 2014). In the 1960s, roads were built to respond to the needs of private firms and to serve the national and state governments' objective to build strategic relationships with rural communities (Bess 2017). A government-owned company was set up to build more than 1,000 km of toll roads in the center of Mexico.

In the first half of the 1990s, a very ambitious program of road construction was launched, which led to the construction of 5,800 km of privately financed highways (Foote 1997).[b] Road-building policies were pursued in the following decades in continuity with past policies, including a program for basic infrastructure in the 2000s and the construction and renovation of more than 23,000 km of roads in the second half of the decade as part of a program to address rural poverty. In 2014, the federal government launched the 2014–2018 National Infrastructure Program,[c] projecting a more than 20 percent increase in the average annual investment in this sector relative to the previous 20 years (Pérez-Cervantes and Sandoval-Hernández 2017). The most ambitious part of this new program focuses on the south of the country—no large project is planned for the north. The center of Mexico—more populated and richer—receives smaller projects.

a. The United States, for example, invested millions of dollars directly in Mexican transport industry and infrastructure.
b. The extremely high tolls that made this investment possible, however, ended up preventing trucks from using these new roads, later forcing the government to restructure the highway network and implement a toll road rescue plan to help state-owned Mexican banks finance roads on nonmarket terms (Foote 1997).
c. *Programa Nacional de Infraestructura.*

MAP 4.1 **The Evolution of the Road Network in Mexico, 1985–2016**

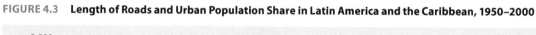

Source: Blankespoor, Bougna et al. 2017.

FIGURE 4.3 **Length of Roads and Urban Population Share in Latin America and the Caribbean, 1950–2000**

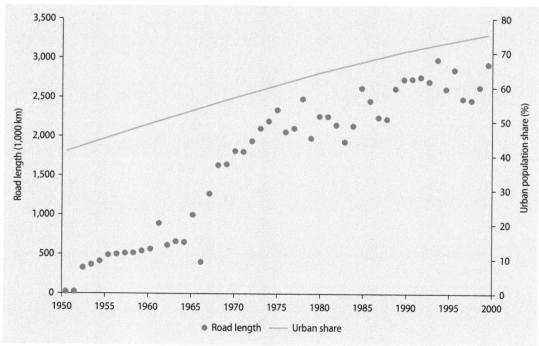

Source: Calculations based on the MOxLAD database (http://www.lac.ox.ac.uk/moxlad-database).

the LAC region as well as the rate of urbanization between 1950 and 2000.[9] Put into perspective with figure 4.1, figure 4.3 reveals two notable patterns. First, road investment began to take off the moment railroads in operation stagnated, corroborating the idea that roads substituted for declining rail services (Summerhill 2006). Second, unlike railroads, the development of road networks in the LAC region occurred concurrently with urbanization (figure 4.3). This matches recent empirical findings from research documenting the *causal* effect of road improvements on urban population growth in Africa (Jedwab and Storeygard 2017a, 2017b; Blankespoor, Mesplé-Somps et al. 2017).[10]

The upward trend in the aggregate road length between 1950 and 2000 (see figure 4.3) hides some interesting features of the current state of transport infrastructure. On road density, the infrastructure stock in the LAC region has consistently remained below that of other regions, except for SSA and MENA. In 1961, for example, average road density per 100 km² of land was about 4.2 km in the LAC region, 1.7 km in SSA, and 1.2 km in MENA (table 4.1). Between 1961 and 2000, road density grew at an average annual rate of about 6.5 percent in the LAC region, which, in relative terms, was below the annual growth rate in SSA (9.2 percent), MENA (15.4 percent), and South Asia (16.0 percent). Unlike South Asia, this rate of investment

was far from enabling the LAC region to catch up with Western Europe and the United States. In short, LAC and South Asia were not too different in road density in 1961 but became far apart in 2000. Road density in the LAC region in 2000 was only marginally greater than that in South Asia in 1961. This may reflect the recent high growth experience in South Asia, which translated into much greater infrastructure investment.

Yet, LAC countries continue to rely increasingly on roads as the main mode of passenger transport and surface freight. LAC has the highest road occupancy rate in the world with more than 800,000 vehicle-km to paved lane–km (Dulac 2013)—nearly four times the rate in China and about twice that in Africa. Similarly, ownership of motorized vehicles is also on the rise and is expected to accelerate because of the increasing size of the middle classes in Latin America (Fay et al. 2017). In comparison to rail, road is today the dominant mode of land transport, with some 80 percent of the 1,920 billion ton-km of total surface freight (table 4.2). However, the relative importance of roads in surface freight varies widely across LAC countries.[11] For example, although roads account for nearly all surface freight in Argentina, Costa Rica, and Uruguay, railroads remain an important complement mode of transport to roads in Brazil, Colombia, and Mexico, with nearly 20 percent of average surface freight (figure 4.4).

TABLE 4.1 Density of All Roads (Paved and Nonpaved) in Regions of the World, 1961–2000

| Region | Road density (kilometers per 100 km² of land) | | Annual growth rate (%) |
	1961	2000	1961–2000
Latin America	4.22	14.97	6.53
East Asia and Pacific	12.04	19.98	1.69
Western Europe	84.55	135.38	1.54
United States	62.85	69.51	0.27
Middle East and North Africa	1.17	8.18	15.42
South Asia	12.85	93.06	16.00
Sub-Saharan Africa	1.74	7.97	9.17

Source: Calculations based on Mitchell 2007.

TABLE 4.2   Modal Share of Surface Freight, by Region, 2015

Region	Road (%)	Rail (%)
Africa	80.74	19.26
Asia Pacific	56.77	43.23
Europe	55.96	44.04
Latin America	78.28	21.72
Middle East	97.23	2.77
North America	62.41	37.59

Source: International Transport Forum 2017.
Note: The modal share of surface freight indicates the split of goods transported by road or rail, excluding waterways, which were not available for the analysis.

FIGURE 4.4   Modal Split of Surface Freight in Latin America and the Caribbean, 2012

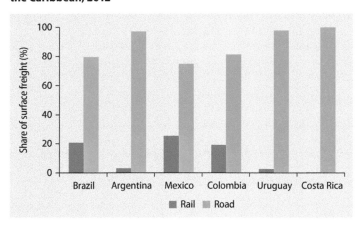

Source: Calculations based on Freight Transport and Logistics Yearbook 2015 (https://publications.iadb.org/handle/11319/6885).

FIGURE 4.5   Investment in Transport Infrastructure in Latin America and the Caribbean, 2000–13

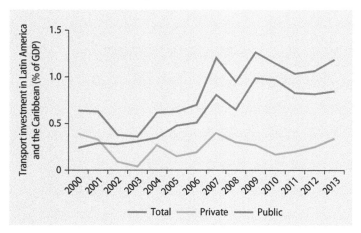

Source: Fay et al. 2017 based on the INFRATALAM database (www.infralatam.info).

Current State of Transport: Growing Investment

Recent data for 2000–2013 suggest that the LAC economies recently witnessed a vigorous pickup in total infrastructure investment after two decades of stagnation (Fay et al. 2017). In 2008–2013, annual average infrastructure spending accounted for 2.7 percent of LAC GDP, suggesting a regain in policy interest for infrastructure. Similarly, transport investment in particular exhibited an increasing trend in 2000–2013 (figure 4.5): for example, transport spending as a share of regional GDP went up threefold, from a mere 0.4 percent in 2003 to about 1.3 percent in 2009, led by public investment. This is all the more remarkable given the region's past performance, characterized by a decline in transport investment at an annual 0.69 percent in 1980–2002 (Calderón and Servén 2004b). Two factors might explain this recent trend: the increasing interest of the public sector and the growth momentum of 2003–2013, sometimes referred to as the "Latin American decade," which may have contributed to fiscal space for infrastructure development.[12]

The upward regional trend in transport spending hides wide differences among countries and subregional groups (figure 4.6). In most subregions, no trend is discernible in spending except for the Andean countries, where transport investment more than doubled in 2008–15. Specifically, such investment increased by the equivalent of 1.30 percent of GDP in Bolivia, 2.16 percent in Colombia, and 2.27 percent in Peru. Transport investment declined, however, in all countries of the Southern Cone, except for Paraguay and Uruguay, which saw increases equivalent to about 0.6 percent and 0.7 percent of their respective GDPs.

Similar to recent trends in road building (see previous section), spending in total transport infrastructure (road, rail, waterways, air) in most LAC countries was largely devoted to roads in 2008–2015 (table 4.3). Panama is an exception, given that the largest share of its infrastructure investment went to water

FIGURE 4.6   Change in Transport Investment as a Share of GDP, 2008–15

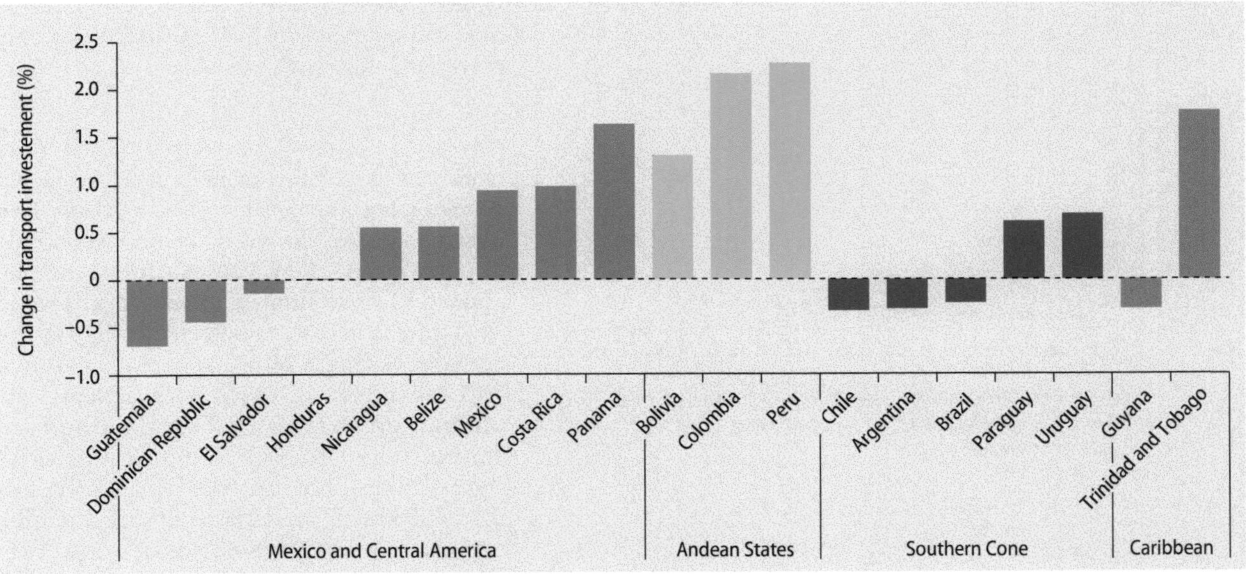

Source: Calculations based on the INFRALATAM database, www.infralatam.info.
Note: Total transport investment includes private and public spending. The baseline and end-line years are 2008 and 2015 for most countries, except for Chile (end-line year is 2014), Dominican Republic (baseline year is 2009), and Uruguay (end-line year is 2012). Growth is calculated as percentage change over the period considered.

TABLE 4.3   Transport Infrastructure Investments, by Sector, 2008–15
% of GDP

Subregion	Country	Roads	Railroads	Air	Waterways	Total
Andean States	Bolivia	3.41	0.10	0.10	0.02	3.84
	Columbia	2.40	0.01	0.06	0.09	2.56
	Peru	2.03	0.60	0.11	0.13	2.88
Southern Cone	Argentina	0.07	—	0.00	0.00	0.75
	Brazil	0.70	0.20	0.07	0.08	1.06
	Chile	1.26	0.28	0.05	0.09	1.69
	Paraguay	1.73	—	0.05	0.03	1.80
	Uruguay	0.30	0.01	0.00	0.06	0.45
Central America and the Caribbean	Belize	0.94	—	—	0.09	0.97
	Costa Rica	0.99	0.01	0.07	0.18	1.25
	El Salvador	0.87	—	0.03	0.04	0.93
	Guatemala	1.15	0.00	0.02	0.07	1.23
	Guyana	0.90	—	—	—	0.90
	Honduras	1.67	—	0.06	0.48	2.21
	Mexico	0.68	0.05	0.01	0.04	0.77
	Nicaragua	1.95	—	0.03	0.03	1.99
	Panama	1.43	—	0.07	2.19	3.68
	Dominican Republic	0.37	—	—	0.12	1.32
	Trinidad and Tobago	0.59	—	—	—	0.59

Source: Calculations based on the INFRALATAM database (www.infralatam.info).
Note: These figures are calculated as the average of total spending (private and public) as a share of GDP. — = missing data.

FIGURE 4.7 **Evolution of Paved Road Density, Selected Regions, 1961–2000**

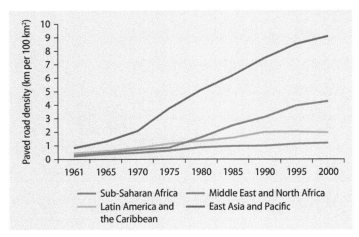

Source: Calculations based on Mitchell 2007.

transport, the bulk of which served to maintain and expand the Panama Canal. The Andean states, including Bolivia, Columbia, and Peru, emerged as the largest investors in roads with an average subregional investment of about 2.61 percent of GDP.

The breakdown of spending by sector also showcases the increasing recognition of the economic benefits of integrated networks (Leal and Pérez, 2012), combining national and transcontinental road systems with railroads and ports. In Brazil, Chile, Honduras, Panama, and Peru, higher investments in road coexist with nonroad spending in rail, air, and water transport. Prominent examples of road-integration achievements include the Trans-Amazonian Highway in Brazil and the Pan-American Highway corridor connecting Latin America to North America.

Current Challenges

Road quality has improved, but not enough. Despite its prominence in recent infrastructure policies, road development in the LAC region has not translated into better networks. In the 1960s, for example, LAC had similar paved road densities to regions like East Asia and Pacific (EAP), MENA, and SSA (figure 4.7).[13] However, the gap in paved

roads between LAC and EAP and MENA widened until 2000. The LAC region's increase in paved road density in 1960–2000 was only marginally higher than SSA's.

Cities are poorly connected. Poor road networks can have large effects on local development and productivity, as they often obstruct access to markets and economic opportunities. LAC cities, for example, appear to have limited access to improved road infrastructure, as reflected in the average cumulative length of primary roads within a 100 km radius of cities with at least one million inhabitants.[14] This indicator of connectivity to surrounding markets (figure 4.8, blue circles), is slightly less than 500 km in LAC cities, and varies in other regions from 530 km (South Asia) to 1,439 km (North America). In short, except for SSA where the length of primary roads around large cities is about 213 km, LAC cities fall short on their surrounding road infrastructure.

The ranking of LAC and SSA based on this indicator does not change if city population is considered, as shown by the kilometers of roads per 1,000 people (see the orange dots in figure 4.8). Within LAC, Peru has the least road infrastructure around large cities (200 km), Puerto Rico, Honduras, and Chile the most (768 km, 734 km, and 730 km). Surprisingly (figure 4.9), Argentina, Mexico, and Brazil, among the economic leaders of the region, each has a surrounding road indicator below the regional average of 499 km (428 km, 397 km, and 348 km).[15]

Transport costs are too high in the LAC region. Stylized facts abound on the prevalence of exorbitant transport costs in the LAC region, reflecting physical and nonphysical factors and acting as barriers to trade. In most LAC countries, transport costs more than export tariffs (Mesquita Moreira, Volpe Martincus, and Blyde 2008). This can be seen in figure 4.10, where data on intraregional exports among LAC countries (orange dots) and exports to the United States (blue dots) suggest that freight expenditures exceed tariff

FIGURE 4.8   **Average and Per Capita Road Length in a 100-Kilometer Radius around Cities with at Least 1 Million Inhabitants**

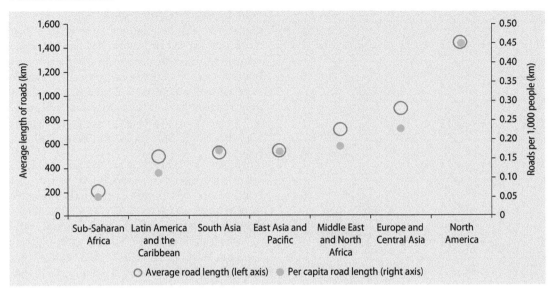

Source: Calculations based on DeLorme 2015 and Blankespoor, Khan, and Selod 2017.
Note: Road length within 100 km radius of a city's center does not measure density because effective land area may vary, for example, for coastal cities in the presence of water surface.

FIGURE 4.9   **Average Road Length in a 100-Kilometer Radius around Cities with at Least 1 Million Inhabitants**

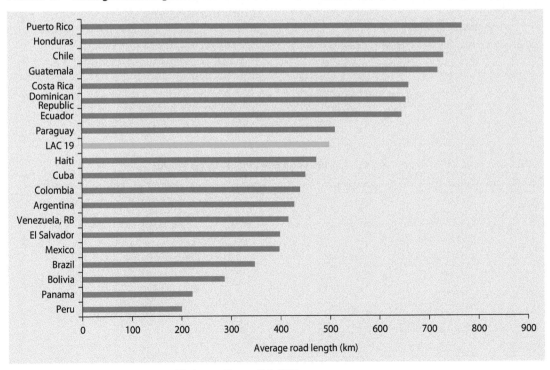

Source: Calculations based on DeLorme 2015 and Blankespoor, Khan, and Selod 2017.
Note: The y-axis shows the 19 individual countries and their collective label "LAC 19." The x-axis shows the average road length in kilometers within 100 kilometers radius of a city's center. Road length within a 100-kilometer radius of a city's center does not measure density because effective land area may vary, for example, in the presence of water surface.

FIGURE 4.10 Ad Valorem Freight and Real Tariffs for Intraregional Exports and Exports to the United States, 2005

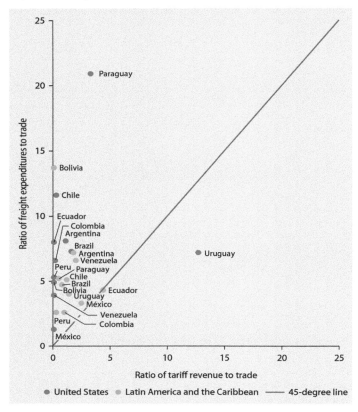

● United States   ● Latin America and the Caribbean   —— 45-degree line

Source: Mesquita Moreira, Volpe Martincus, and Blyde 2008.

costs in most LAC countries, except for Uruguay (exports to the United States) and Ecuador (intraregional exports).[16] LAC also tends to exhibit higher transport costs than developed countries because of poor infrastructure, weak competition in the trucking industry and dysfunctional customs. Freight expenditures are about 7.2 percent of regional import value in the LAC region, about twice the 3.7 percent in the United States (Mesquita Moreira, Volpe Martincus, and Blyde 2008).

The costs of urban congestion. In LAC cities, transport is associated with high congestion. Although regional rates of motorization in LAC (about 100–300 vehicles per 1,000 people) fall short of existing rates in developed nations (about 500–700 in Canada, Europe, and the United States), they are nonetheless linked to congestion, accidents, and pollution that are among the highest in the world (Barbero 2012). On congestion, the 2016 TomTom traffic index shows that Mexico City, with an extra travel time of 66 percent against the noncongested situation, is the most congested city in the world. Eight other LAC cities are among the world's top 100 congested places (table 4.4).

High congestion and related social and environmental challenges can be extremely

TABLE 4.4 LAC Cities Are among the Top 100 Congested Places in the World

World rank	City	Country	Congestion	Morning peak	Evening peak
1	Mexico City	Mexico	66	96	101
8	Rio de Janeiro	Brazil	47	63	81
17	Santiago de Chile	Chile	43	73	88
19	Buenos Aires	Argentina	42	64	68
28	Salvador	Brazil	40	63	70
43	Recife	Brazil	37	60	65
47	Fortaleza	Brazil	35	56	57
71	São Paulo	Brazil	30	42	53
99	Belo Horizonte	Brazil	27	42	59

Source: TomTom traffic index (www.tomtom.com).
Note: The TomTom index for congestion measures the percentage of extra travel time (relative to a free-flow situation) as a result of traffic congestion. The TomTom data cover 48 countries and 390 cities worldwide.

expensive for the economy of the LAC region. Bull and Thomson (2002), for example, estimate that the costs of negative externalities linked to traffic congestion in large cities are nearly 3.5 percent of the LAC region's aggregate GDP. Policy efforts to reduce such negative externalities have often favored investments in large public transport systems and hard-to-enforce regulations—and the latter, such as restrictions on vehicle use, have seen mixed outcomes in many LAC cities. Gasoline emissions, for example, were reduced by 9–11 percent during peak hours and by 6 percent during the day after vehicle use restrictions in Quito, Ecuador (Carrillo, Malik, and Yoo 2016). Although similar regulations induced a shift to public transport in Santiago de Chile (De Grange and Troncoso 2011), they failed to reduce emissions or vehicle use in Mexico (Eskeland and Feyzioglu 1997; Davis 2008). Combining these regulation-based policies with price incentives may be more efficient at reducing congestion and related externalities (Berg et al. 2017).

Roads and Agglomeration Economies: Evidence from Mexico

Bridging the transport infrastructure gap in Latin America could generate large economic gains. To illustrate them, this section presents a case study on Mexico. As already discussed in box 4.1, Mexico has invested heavily in roads over recent decades, and may therefore offer a learning opportunity for similar investments in other LAC countries.[17]

Geographic Patterns of Economic Activity

Industries are increasingly concentrated. Mexico's 2014 Economic Census indicates that most formal employment is in services (44.2 percent), commerce (29.6 percent), manufacturing (23.5 percent), agriculture (0.9 percent), and mining (0.8 percent).[18]

The geographic distribution of economic activities is highly uneven, with a large concentration in the Mexico City Metropolitan Area, which in 2010 contributed a quarter of national gross value added, although it covered less than 0.3 percent of national territory. This spatial concentration, especially in the center of the country and the periphery of Mexico City, can be seen in formal establishments (map 4.2, panel a). Manufacturing firms are even more concentrated (panel b), consistent with theories of agglomeration (Redding and Turner 2014). Most of the clustering is in central Mexico where the transport network is denser (facilitating the shipment of goods) and where major agglomeration centers are located (potentially supplying labor).[19] As expected, firms in other sectors (mainly in commerce and services) are less concentrated than firms in manufacturing (maps not shown).

A small number of studies have documented rising geographic concentration of industries in Mexico (Unger 2003). A look at the Ellison and Glaeser index at the 6-digit industry classification level (Ellison and Glaeser 1997; see box 4.2 for details) reveals patterns akin to these findings. First, industries in Mexico have become more geographically concentrated over the past decade, as reflected in the increase of the mean value of the index (across all industries), from 0.381 in 2004 to 0.430 in 2014 (a significant 10.3 percent increase). Second, the mean value of the Ellison and Glaeser index for manufacturing industries in Mexico is, on average, 12–15 percent higher than the mean value of the same index calculated for all industries, confirming that manufacturing industries are on average more concentrated than other industries. Finally, comparison with commonly agreed-on thresholds in the literature (see box 4.2) suggests that about 98–100 percent of industries (for overall industries and for manufacturing only) are concentrated (with an Ellison and Glaeser index greater than 0.05). The fraction of concentrated manufacturing industries (98 percent) in Mexico is greater than the one reported for Canada (75 percent) in Behrens and Bougna

MAP 4.2 **Spatial Distributions of Formal Establishments and Manufacturing Firms in Mexico, Overlaid on the Road Network, 2014**

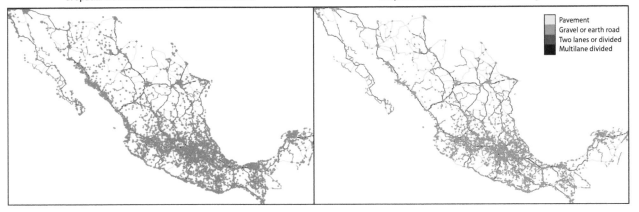

a. Spatial distribution of formal establishments

b. Spatial distribution of manufacturing firms

Pavement
Gravel or earth road
Two lanes or divided
Multilane divided

Source: DeLorme, AAA, DENUE, and INEGI. Reproduced from Blankespoor, Bougna et al. 2017.
Note: Universe of all formal firms (panel a) and of manufacturing firms only (panel b) for 2014. Firm locations (dots) are overlaid on 2016 roads. AAA = American Automobile Association; DENUE = Directorio Estadístico Nacional de Unidades Económicas; INEGI = Instituto Nacional de Estadísticas y Geografía.

BOX 4.2   Measuring Industrial Concentration: The Ellison and Glaeser Index

The Ellison and Glaeser index defines concentration as agglomeration above what would be observed if plants simply chose locations randomly. This measure provides an unbiased estimate of agglomerative forces independently of their source. It can be interpreted as the probability that a firm choosing its location follows the prior firm rather than locating randomly, and is given by the following:

$$\gamma_i = \frac{G_i - \left(1 - \sum_r x_r^2\right) H_i}{\left(1 - \sum_r x_r^2\right)\left(1 - H_i\right)}$$

where $G_i = \sum_r (S_{ri} - x_r)^2$ is the spatial Gini coefficient of industry i, S_{ri} is the share of employment of locality r in industry i, x_r is the share of total employment in each locality r, $H_i = \sum_j Z_{ji}^2$ is the Herfindahl index of the plant size distribution of industry i, and Z_{ji} represents the employment share of a particular firm j in industry i.

Following Ellison and Glaeser (1997), an industry is said to be strongly concentrated if the index is greater than 0.05, weakly concentrated if the index is 0–0.05, and not concentrated if the index is negative.

Source: Ellison and Glaeser 1997; Blankespoor, Bougna et al. 2017.

(2015) and about the same as the one reported for other developed countries (Ellison and Glaeser 1997; Duranton and Overman 2008).

Cities are increasingly specialized. The other important stylized fact, along with firm concentration, is the increasing specialization of Mexican localities. Using different spatial scales, some studies indicate an important increase in local specialization in recent years

(Pérez and Palacio 2009; Kim and Zangerling 2016). To contribute to this line of inquiry, the present study relies on the Krugman Specialization index at city level, which provides a tractable way to quantify specialization and potential changes in specialization patterns over time (box 4.3).[20]

The computed index indicates a fall in the proportion of weakly specialized localities (with an index lower than 0.35) in Mexico from 90.7 percent in 2004 to 84.7 percent

Source: Blankespoor, Bougna et al. 2017.
Note: We calculate specialization indexes for a reconstructed sample of localities by merging municipalities that belong to the same metropolitan area, leading to a universe of 316 reconstructed metropolitan areas and 1,832 standalone municipalities.

BOX 4.3 Measuring Municipality Specialization: The Krugman Specialization Index

The Krugman Specialization index is widely used. It measures deviation of industry shares by computing the share of employment that would have to be relocated to achieve an industry structure equivalent to the average structure of the reference group. It is given by the following formula:

$$KSI_i = \sum_{i=1}^{M} \left| S_m^i - \overline{S^i} \right|$$

where S_m^i is the output or employment share of industry i in locality m, and $\overline{S^i}$ is the average share of industry i in the total output or employment across all localities (in Mexico).

The index can take values between zero and two. If the relative specialization measure is zero, the economic structure of a locality is identical to the economic structure of the overall economy. The higher the index, the more the economic structure of the locality deviates from the overall economy (reference group) and the more that locality is specialized. Localities for which the specialization index is higher than 0.75 are considered highly specialized, whereas localities for which the specialization index is below 0.35 are considered weakly specialized.

in 2014. As for highly specialized localities, their percentage increased from 6 to 9.2 percent over the period. Together, these findings provide evidence of increased specialization in Mexican localities. Map 4.3 shows the spatial distribution of the Krugman Specialization index for all localities in Mexico in 2014, revealing clusters of specialized localities near one another (the red dot showing high specialization). There is some indication from zooming on the map that specialized localities are often near larger roads (two-lane or multi-lane roads), consistent with the empirical findings presented later in table 4.6.

Roads and Market Access

As roads link cities and cities to ports, access to international and domestic markets is a function of local road infrastructure. The growth of road networks (see box 4.1), and the current state of the roads network depicted on the map of firm concentration (see map 4.2) show recent road investments in Mexico.

Subsequent improvements in access to international markets can be directly measured by a reduction in the time and cost of travel. For example, Blankespoor, Bougna et al. (2017) report that average travel time to the nearest port of entry to the United States (among 44 entry ports) from any of the 2,094 Mexican localities decreased by more than an hour and half between 1986 and 2014. Similarly, travel time to the nearest port (among six major Mexican ports) decreased by more than 40 minutes over the same period.[21] These are nonnegligible decreases in the average minimum travel time to the United States border (about 8 percent) and to ports (about 6 percent).

Improvements in access to national markets can be measured using a market access indicator. By design, for a particular area, this indicator reflects a discounted sum of population or income of the surrounding areas, where the discount factor is proportional to travel time (box 4.4).[22] The rationale behind this indicator is to numerically gauge the size of surrounding markets for locally produced goods, accounting for the ease with which such goods can be transported to these adjacent domestic markets. A higher value indicates greater market access. From 1994 to 2014, the indicator

MAP 4.3   **Output Locality Specialization, Overlaid on the Road Network, 2014**

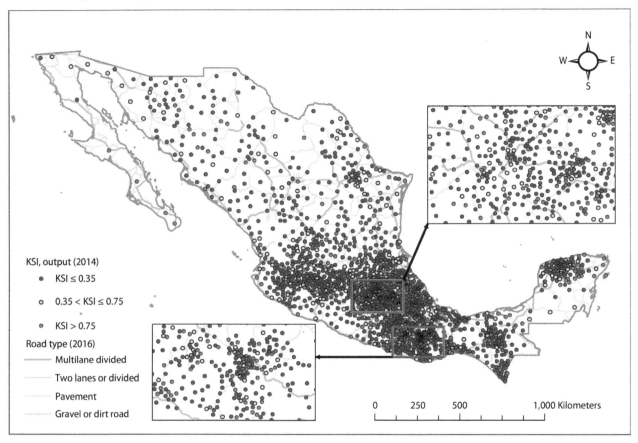

Source: DENUE (INEGI).
Note: KSI is the Krugman Specialization index described in box 4.4. DENUE = Directorio Estadístico Nacional de Unidades Económicas; INEGI =Instituto Nacional de Estadísticas y Geografía.

BOX 4.4   **Market Access**

Market access is defined in each locality as follows:

$$MA_{it} \sum_{i \neq j} P_{jt} \tau_{ijt}^{-\theta}$$

where P_{jt} is the population of locality j at time t (which proxies for the size of the local market in j), τ_{ijt} is the time required to travel between locality i and j given the state of the road network at time t, and θ is

a measure of trade elasticity. Travel times τ_{ijt} are calculated on the countrywide road network assuming that speed is a function of road type (Blankespoor, Bougna et al. 2017). For the trade elasticity parameter, lacking a specific study for Mexico, we use the same value suggested by Donaldson (forthcoming) for India ($\theta = 3.8$). The same market access indicator is used in different empirical works (Jedwab and Storeygard 2017a, 2017b).

Source: Blankespoor, Bougna et al. 2017.
Note: The measure of market access excludes the population of the locality for which it is being calculated.

MAP 4.4 Changes in Market Access in Mexico, 1986–2014

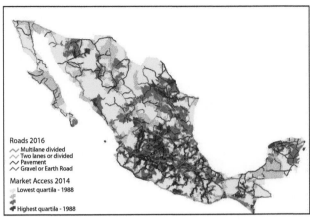

a. 1986

b. 2014

Source: DeLorme, American Automobile Association, and Economic Censuses (Instituto Nacional de Estadísticas y Geografía).
Note: On both panels, the colors describe the quartiles of the 1986 distribution of the index, with darker shades indicating higher degrees of market access.

more than doubled among the 2,094 Mexican localities analyzed in Blankespoor, Bougna et al. (2017).[23] The change between 1986 and 2014 is shown in map 4.4. Overall, as suggested by the spatial distribution of the index, most improvements in market access occurred predominantly in the center of Mexico.

The Economic Impacts of Road Improvement

This section investigates the effects of improved market access from road investment on employment, specialization, and local productivity (as measured by nighttime lights) in Mexican cities. A balanced panel data set of 2,094 localities is analyzed over different periods, depending on data constraints. The specification with employment as the explained variable covers six periods of five-year intervals from 1986 to 2014. The specification with specialization as the explained variable covers 2004, 2009, and 2014. The specification with nighttime lights comprises the years 1996, 2000, and 2010. All specifications include time-varying locality characteristics (education, population, oil-reserves, and the pre-/post–North American Free Trade Agreement [NAFTA]

period) interacted with the measure of market access, as well as time and location fixed effects.

Despite a rich set of controls and fixed effects, two factors undermine causal inference: the bias arising from nonrandom placement of roads and the recursion problem inherent to using a market access indicator when the explained variable is a function of population (Baum-Snow et al. 2017). We address these issues by resorting to instrumentation.[24]

Employment. Table 4.5 summarizes the ordinary least square (OLS) and instrumental variable (IV) results for the specification, with employment the dependent variable. The effect of market access on employment is positive and statistically significant. Specifically, the IV result suggests that a 10 percent increase in market access results in a 1.6 percent increase in employment. Other interesting findings include the interaction between market access and relevant indicators of population and human capital. For example, more urbanized areas (the metropolitan center and populated localities) and areas with less than the average level of education are likely to benefit more from increased market access. The latter may

TABLE 4.5   The Effects of Market Access on Employment

Variables	Total employment	
	OLS	IV (Road count)
Market access	0.149***	0.163***
	(0.0111)	(0.0202)
Market Access × Population Dummy	0.0717***	0.0629***
	(0.0117)	(0.0154)
Market Access × Education Dummy	−0.0468***	−0.0474***
	(0.00334)	(0.00329)
Market Access × NAFTA Dummy	−0.114***	−0.115***
	(0.00233)	(0.00213)
Market Access × Capital City	−0.0225	−0.0228
	(0.0226)	(0.0250)
Market Access × Oil Dummy	0.839**	0.832**
	(0.385)	(0.399)
Education dummy	0.155***	0.155***
	(0.0581)	(0.0522)
Population dummy	0.851***	0.805***
No. of observations	11,379	11,251
Adjusted R^2	0.423	0.424

Source: Blankespoor, Bougna et al. 2017.
Note: Standard errors are clustered at the locality level to adjust for heteroscedasticity. The road count is the number of roads intersecting a circle with a 10 km radius. Education and population controls are measured at the initial date (1986). Constant is not shown. IV = instrumental variable; OLS = ordinary least square.
***$p < 0.01$. **$p < 0.05$. *$p < 0.1$.

suggest that, with roads, cities may attract low-skilled labor. The estimates also provide evidence that the positive effect of improved domestic market access on employment is partially attenuated after NAFTA came into force. Finally, cities in oil-producing regions seem to benefit more from improved access to domestic markets than cities in other regions.

Specialization. Table 4.6 presents the results of the regression of city-level specialization on market access. It suggests a positive and statistically significant response of specialization to improved market access.[25] A 10 percent increase in market access, the findings suggest, translates into a 7 percent increase in output specialization, as reflected in the IV estimation result.[26]

Local productivity. As shown in table 4.7, the elasticity of local productivity, as measured by nighttime lights, with respect to market access is positive and statistically significant.[27] Specifically, the result from the IV regression indicates that a 10 percent increase in market access increases nighttime luminosity by 0.9 percent, controlling for the population of the locality, suggesting that market access is an important driver of city-level productivity. This finding is consistent with previous studies documenting a sizable impact of transport infrastructure on productivity in Mexico (Becerril -Torres, Álvarez-Ayuso, and del Moral-Barrera 2010; Brock and German-Soto 2013; Duran-Fernandez and Santos 2014a, 2014b). Relevant channels through which these effects materialize include spatial concentration and specialization (Dávila 2008; Monge 2012).

TABLE 4.6 The Effects of Market Access on Local Specialization

Variable	Krugman Specialization index (output)	
	OLS	IV (doughnut)
Market access	0.455***	0.704***
	(0.176)	(0.231)
Observations	4,303	3,628
Adjusted R^2	0.0234	0.0233

Source: Blankespoor, Bougna et al. 2017.
Note: The reported results are for the instrumentation with the "doughnut," which is calculated as the market access when excluding all localities within a 25 km circle (for details, see Blankespoor, Bougna et al. 2017). Education and population variables are measured at the initial date (1986). Constant not shown. IV = instrumental variable; OLS = ordinary least square. Standard errors are clustered at the locality level to adjust for heteroscedasticity.
***$p < 0.01$. **$p < 0.05$. *$p < 0.1$.

TABLE 4.7 The Effects of Market Access on Nighttime Lights

Variable	Nighttime lights	
	OLS	IV (road count)
Market access	0.044**	0.086**
	(0.022)	(0.044)
No. of observations	5,144	4,965
Adjusted R^2	0.084	0.081

Source: Blankespoor, Bougna et al. 2017.
Note: The road count is the number of roads intersecting a circle with a 10 km radius. Education and population variables are measured at the initial date (1986). Constant not shown. IV = instrumental variable; OLS = ordinary least square.
Standard errors are clustered as the locality level to adjust for heteroscedasticity.
***$p < 0.01$. **$p < 0.05$. *$p < 0.1$.

Conclusions

This chapter confirms that LAC suffers from a significant transport infrastructure gap. Bridging it may have local effects on the growth of jobs, the specialization of cities, and economic development, as shown by the Mexico case study. Complementary policies could also have an impact, such as policies that encourage competition, improve customs procedures, and improve efficiency via price-based regulations.

The extremely high congestion is likely to exert a toll on city productivity, because of the time and money lost in intracity transport, and on environmental and health costs affecting workers. Because regulations to reduce congestion and pollution have had only mixed success in the LAC region, it will be important to come up with alternative cost-efficient ways to reduce these externalities, possibly using price instruments.

Notes

1. Localization economies are the positive externalities associated with the clustering within a city of firms from the same industry (Marshall 1890). Urbanization economies are the positive externalities associated with the geographic concentration of different industries within a given city (Jacobs 1969). See Graham (2005) and Redding and Turner (2014) for a detailed discussion of transport and agglomeration economies.

2. The pricing of externalities, however, may be resisted by those facing higher transport costs.

3. See Graham (2005) for a review of the relevant papers.

4. The period 1870–1914 also coincided with the world's first wave of globalization in trade and finance.

5. From the work of Fogel (1962), the concept of "social savings" refers to a growth accounting approach to assess the historical implications of a new technology on economic growth. In practice, the rate of social savings is derived from estimating the cost savings induced by the new technology (in this case, railroads) relative to the next best alternative. The social savings approach has been extensively used to analyze the impact of innovations in transport, especially railroads. A few exceptions include Von Tunzelmann (1978), who focuses on the effects of steam power in the United Kingdom, and Bogart (2009) who focuses on the impacts of turnpike trusts set up to levy road tolls in England.

6. Export density is defined as the average export value per square kilometer of land area, and railroad density measures the average number of km of railroads per 1,000 km^2 of land area.

7. The Belle Époque (from the end of the Franco–Prussian War in 1871 to the eruption of World War I in 1914) coincided with a significant flow of foreign capital into Latin America and the economic modernization of most countries in the region.

8. These figures come from Mitchell (2007) and are based on 18 Latin American countries.

9. The urban share in figure 4.3 is from World Urbanization Prospects data and may overestimate the actual rate (see chapters 1 and 2).
10. To our knowledge, no similar study exists for Latin America. The georeferenced and historic data that would be needed to explore how roads influenced urbanization in the LAC region has not yet been compiled.
11. Data on airborne and maritime freight transport were not available for this analysis.
12. External debt, net of foreign exchange reserves, decreased from 28.6 percent of GDP in 1998–2002 to 5.7 percent in 2008 (Ocampo 2015).
13. Paved road density is the length of roads in km per 100 km^2 of land area.
14. Cities refer here to urban agglomerations. The data come from World Urbanization Prospects, georeferenced by Blankespoor, Khan, and Selod (2017).
15. This is a local indicator of infrastructure availability that does not measure overall connection to other cities or positions of the transport network. It also fails to account for road quality or congestion.
16. Freight expenditures do not include insurance and are defined as the costs of transporting goods to the international port of the country of origin and of delivering them to the port of the country of destination.
17. This section draws largely on Blankespoor, Mesplé-Somps et al. (2017), commissioned as a background paper. It deals only with the agglomeration impacts of improved transport accessibility, and does not focus on measuring other impacts.
18. Figures for informal employment are unavailable. Looking at formal employment data only, as seen in previous chapters, the notable trend over the past two decades has been the decrease in the share of formal manufacturing employment, showing that Mexico is following a trend of tertiarization similar to that experienced by developed economies in previous decades.
19. Unger and Chico (2004) note that the clustering of firms in Mexico often occurs in places where the required labor skills can be found, highlighting labor market pooling (the "matching" argument put forward in economic geography) as a mechanism of agglomeration.
20. Patterns of specialization measured with the Krugman Specialization index for *employment* are very similar and we do not show

them here (see Blankespoor, Mesplé-Somps et al. 2017 for a detailed presentation of local specialization in Mexico).
21. These figures are theoretical measures based on network extent and road type, but they do not account for congestion.
22. See Blankespoor, Mesplé-Somps et al. (2017) for the use of an alternative measure, market potential, which they define as a discounted sum of surrounding *incomes*, where the discount factor is a function of transport costs. All the results in this chapter are robust to the use of either the market access or market potential indicator.
23. Contrary to the measures of access to international markets, measures of access to domestic markets also change with concurrent changes in the population distribution. The doubling of the market access indicator thus reflects not only road improvements but also population increases.
24. To address the recursion problem, market access is instrumented with the number of roads intersecting a circle of 10 km radius around each locality. Sources of changes in accessibility are then only due to variation in roads. To address the endogeneity of road placement in the specification regressing specialization, a "doughnut" market access, excluding all localities within a 25 km radius, is instrumented. See Baum-Snow et al. (2017) and Blankespoor, Mesplé-Somps et al. (2017) for a detailed discussion about these issues and the strategies to overcome them.
25. For this result on specialization and the next on local productivity, only the estimated elasticities of the variables of interest with respect to market access are presented. See Blankespoor, Mesplé-Somps et al. (2017) for other estimated coefficients.
26. For employment specialization, Blankespoor, Mesplé-Somps et al. (2017) report a smaller elasticity of about 3 percent.
27. Nighttime lights are defined and measured as in chapter 6; see box 6.1.

References

Aschauer, D. A. 1993. "Genuine Economic Returns to Infrastructure Investment." *Policy Studies Journal* 21 (2): 380–90.
Banerjee, A., E. Duflo, and N. Qian. 2012. "On the Road: Transportation Infrastructure and Economic Growth in China." Working Paper

No. 17897, National Bureau of Economic Research, Cambridge, MA.

Baum-Snow, N. 2007. "Did Highways Cause Suburbanization?" *The Quarterly Journal of Economics* 122 (2): 775–805.

Baum-Snow, N., L. Brandt, J. V. Henderson, M. A. Turner, and Q. Zhang. 2012. "Roads, Railroads and Decentralization of Chinese Cities." *Review of Economics and Statistics* 99 (3): 435–48.

Baum-Snow, N., J. V. Henderson, M. A. Turner, Q. Zhang, and L. Brandt. 2017. "Does Investment in National Highways Help or Hurt Hinterland City Growth?" Unpublished manuscript.

Barbero, J. 2012. *Infrastructure in the Development of Latin America*. Caracas: Development Bank of Latin America.

Becerril-Torres, O., I. Álvarez-Ayuso, and L. del Moral-Barrera. 2010. "Do Infrastructures Influence the Convergence of Efficiency in México?" *Journal of Policy Modeling* 32 (1): 120–37.

Behrens, K., and T. Bougna. 2015. "An Anatomy of the Geographical Concentration of Canadian Manufacturing Industries." *Regional Science and Urban Economics* 51 (C): 47–69.

Berg, C. N., U. Deichmann, Y. Liu, and H. Selod. 2017. "Transport Policies and Development." *The Journal of Development Studies* 53 (4): 465–80.

Bess, M. 2014. "Routes of Conflict: Building Roads and Shaping the Nation of Mexico, 1941–1952." *The Journal of Transport History* 35 (1): 78–96.

———. 2016a. "'Neither Motorists nor Pedestrians Obey the Rules: Transit Law, Public Safety, and the Policing of Northern Mexico's Roads, 1920s-1950s." *The Journal of Transport History* 37 (2): 155–74.

———. 2016b. "Revolutionary Paths: Motor Roads, Economic Development, and National Sovereignty in 1920s and 1930s Mexico." *Mexican Studies/Estudios Mexicanos* 32 (1): 56–82.

———. 2017. *Routes of Compromise: Building Roads and Shaping the Nation of Mexico, 1917–1952*. Lincoln, NE: University of Nebraska Press.

Bird, J., and S. Straub. 2014. "The Brasilia Experiment: Road Access and the Spatial Pattern of Long-Term Local Development in Brazil." Policy Research Working Paper 6964, World Bank, Washington, DC.

Blankespoor, B., A. Khan, and H. Selod. 2017. *A Consolidated Dataset of Global Urban Populations: 1969–2015*. Technical note. World Bank, Washington, DC.

Blankespoor, B., S. Mesplé-Somps, H. Selod, and G. Spielvogel. 2017. "Roads and Structural Transformation in Mali." Unpublished manuscript.

Blankespoor, B., T. Bougna, R. Garduno-Rivera, and H. Selod. 2017. "Roads and the Geography of Economic Activities in Mexico." Policy Research Working Paper WPS 8226, World Bank, Washington, DC.

Bogart, D. 2009. "Turnpike Trusts and Property Income: New Evidence on the Effects of Transport Improvements and Legislation in Eighteenth-Century England." *The Economic History Review* 62 (1): 128–52.

Brock, G., and B. German-Soto. 2013. "Regional Industrial Growth in Mexico: Do Human Capital and Infrastructure Matter?" *Journal of Policy Modeling* 35 (2): 228–42.

Bull, A., and I. Thomson. 2002. "Urban Traffic Congestion: Its Economic and Social Causes and Consequences." *Cepal Review* 76: 105–116.

Bulmer-Thomas, V., J. Coatsworth, and R. Cortes-Conde, eds. 2006. *The Cambridge Economic History of Latin America, Volume II*. Cambridge, U.K.: Cambridge University Press.

Calderón, C., and L. Servén. 2004a. *The Effects of Infrastructure Development on Growth and Income Distribution*. Washington, DC: World Bank.

———. 2004b. "Trends in Infrastructure in Latin America, 1980–2001." Policy Research Working Paper 3401, World Bank, Washington, DC.

Cardenas, E. 1987. "La Industrialización Mexicana durante la Grande Depresión." Working Paper, El Colegio de México, Mexico City.

Carrillo, P. E., A. S. Malik, and Y. Yoo. 2016. "Driving Restrictions that Work? Quito's Pico y Placa Program." *Canadian Journal of Economics* 49 (4): 1536–68.

Chandra, A., and E. Thompson. 2000. "Does Public Infrastructure Affect Economic Activity? Evidence from the Rural Interstate Highway System." *Regional Science and Urban Economics* 30 (4): 457–90.

Coatsworth, J. H. 1979. "Indispensable Railroads in a Backward Economy: the Case of Mexico." *The Journal of Economic History* 39 (4): 939–60.

Datta, S. 2012. "The Impact of Improved Highways on Indian Firms." *Journal of Development Economics* 99 (1): 46–57.

Dávila, A. 2008. "Los Clústeres Industriales del noreste de Mèxico (1993–2003). Perspectivas de desarrollo en el marco de una mayor integración económica con Texas?" *Región y Sociedad* 20 (41): 57–88.

Davis, L. 2008. "The Effect of Driving Restrictions on Air Quality in Mexico City." *Journal of Political Economy* 116 (11): 38–81.

De Grange, L., and R. Troncoso. 2011. "Impacts of Vehicle Restrictions on Urban Transport Flows: The Case of Santiago, Chile." *Transport Policy* 18 (6): 862–69.

DeLorme. 2015. "Digital Atlas of the Earth Database." Yarmouth, ME.

Deng, T. 2013. "Impacts of Transport Infrastructure on Productivity and Economic Growth: Recent Advances and Research Challenges." *Transport Reviews* 33 (6): 686–99.

Donaldson, D. Forthcoming. "Railroads of the Raj: Estimating the Impact of Transportation Infrastructure." *American Economic Review.*

Dulac, J. 2013. *Infrastructure Requirements: Estimating Road and Railway Infrastructure Capacity and Costs to 2050.* Paris: International Energy Agency.

Duran-Fernandez, R., and G. Santos. 2014a. "Road Infrastructure Spillovers on the Manufacturing Sector in Mexico." *Research in Transportation Economics* 46 (C): 17–29.

———. 2014b. "Regional Convergence, Road Infrastructure, and Industrial Diversity in Mexico." *Research in Transportation Economics* 46: 103–10.

Duranton, G., and H. Overman. 2008. "Exploring the Detailed Location Patterns of U.K. Manufacturing Industries Using Micro-Geographic Data." *Journal of Regional Science* 48 (1): 213–43.

Duranton, G., and M. A. Turner. 2011. "The Fundamental Law of Road Congestion: Evidence from US Cities." *American Economic Review* 101 (6): 2616–52.

———. 2012. "Urban Growth and Transportation." *Review of Economic Studies* 79 (4): 1407–40.

Duranton, G., P. M. Morrow, and M. A. Turner. 2014. "Roads and Trade: Evidence from the US." *Review of Economic Studies* 81 (2): 681–724.

Ellison, G., and E. Glaeser. 1997. "Geographic Concentration in U.S. Manufacturing Industries: A Dartboard Approach." *Journal of Political Economy* 105 (5): 889–927.

Eskeland, G., and T. Feyzioglu. 1997. "Rationing Can Backfire: The 'Day without a Car' in Mexico City." *World Bank Economic Review* 11 (3): 383–408.

Faber, B. 2013. "Trade Integration, Market Size, and Industrialization: Evidence from China's National Trunk Highway System." Working Paper, University of California, Berkeley.

Fay, M., L., A. Andres, C. Fox, U. Narloch, S. Straub, and M. Slawson. 2017. *Rethinking Infrastructure in Latin America and the Caribbean.* Washington, DC: World Bank.

Fernald, J. G. 1999. "Roads to Prosperity? Assessing the Link between Public Capital and Productivity." *American Economic Review* 89 (3): 619–38.

Fogel, R. 1962. "A Quantitative Approach to the Study of Railroads in American Economic Growth: A Report of Some Preliminary Findings." *Journal of Economic History* 22 (2): 163–97.

Foote, W. 1997. *Mexico's Troubled Toll Roads.* ICWA Letters, February 3. Hanover, NH: Institute of Current World Affairs.

Garcia-Mila, T., T. J. McGuire, and R. H. Porter. 1996. "The Effect of Public Capital in State-Level Production Functions Reconsidered." *The Review of Economics and Statistics* 78 (1): 177–80.

Ghani, E., A. G. Goswami, and W. R. Kerr. 2016. "Highway to Success: The Impact of the Golden Quadrilateral Project for the Location and Performance of Indian Manufacturing." *The Economic Journal* 126 (591): 317–57.

Gonzalez-Navarro, M., and C. Quintana-Domeque. 2016. "Paving Streets for the Poor: Experimental Analysis of Infrastructure Effects." *Review of Economics and Statistics* 98 (2): 254–67.

Graham, D. J. 2005. "Transport Investment, Agglomeration and Urban Productivity." Unpublished manuscript.

———. 2007. "Agglomeration, Productivity and Transport Investment." *Journal of Transport Economics and Policy* 41 (3): 317–43.

Gramlich, E. M. 1994. "Infrastructure Investment: A Review Essay." *Journal of Economic Literature* 32 (3): 1176–96.

Holl, A. 2004. "Transport Infrastructure, Agglomeration Economies, and Firm

Birth: Empirical Evidence from Portugal." *Journal of Regional Science* 44 (4): 693–712.

Holtz-Eakin, D. 1994 "Public-Sector Capital and the Productivity Puzzle." *Review of Economics and Statistics* 76 (1): 12–21.

Hsu, W. T, and H. Zhang. 2012. "The Fundamental Law of Highway Congestion: Evidence from National Expressways in Japan." Working paper, Department of Economics, The National University of Singapore.

International Transport Federation. 2017. *Capacity to Grow: Transport Infrastructure Needs for Future Trade Growth.* Paris: Organisation for Economic Co-operation and Development.

Jacobs J. 1969. *The Economy of Cities.* New York: Random House.

Jedwab, R., E. Kerby, and A. Moradi. 2015. "History, Path Dependence and Development: Evidence from Colonial Railroads, Settlers and Cities in Kenya." *The Economic Journal* 127 (603): 1467–94.

Jedwab, R., and A. Moradi. 2016. "The Permanent Effects of Transportation Revolutions in Poor Countries: Evidence from Africa." *Review of Economics and Statistics* 98 (2): 268–84.

Jedwab, R., and A. Storeygard. 2017a. "Economic and Political Factors in Infrastructure Investment: Evidence from Railroads and Roads in Africa 1960-2015." Unpublished manuscript.

Jedwab, R., and A. Storeygard. 2017b. "The Average and Heterogeneous Effects of Transportation Investments: Evidence from Sub-Saharan Africa 1960–2010." Unpublished manuscript.

Kim, Y., and B. Zangerling. 2016. *Mexico Urbanization Review.* Washington, DC: World Bank.

Leal, E., and G. Pérez. 2012. "Port-Raill Integration: Challenges and Opportunities for Latin America." *FAL Bulletin* 310 (7).

Mesquita Moreira, M., C. Volpe Martincus, and J. Blyde. 2008. *Unclogging the Arteries: the Impact of Transport Costs on Latin American and Caribbean Trade.* Washington, DC: Inter-American Development Bank.

Mesquita Moreira, M., J. Blyde, C. Volpe, and D. Molina. 2013. *Too Far to Export: Domestic Transport Costs and Regional Export Disparities in Latin America and the Caribbean.* Washington, DC: Inter-American Development Bank.

Michaels, G. 2008. "The Effect of Trade on the Demand for Skill—Evidence from the Interstate Highway System." *Review of Economics and Statistics* 90 (4): 683–701.

Mitchell, B. 2007. *International Historical Statistics 1750–2005: Americas.* New York: Palgrave Macmillan.

Monge, M. 2012. "Analisis de la Cadena Productiva de Tequila: El caso de Jalisco." License Dissertation, Departamento de Economía, Universidad Autónoma Metropolitana-Azcapotzalco, Mexico City.

Ocampo, J. A. 2015. "Uncertain Times." *Finance and Development* 52 (3): 6–11.

Pages-Serra, C. 2010. *The Age of Productivity: Transforming Economies from the Bottom Up.* Washington, DC: Inter-American Development Bank.

Pérez, S., and M. Palacio. 2009. "Desarrollo Regional y Concentración Industrial: Impacto en el Empleo (1994–2004)." Observatorio de la Economía Latinoamericana No. 117.

Pérez-Cervantes, F., and A. Sandoval-Hernandez. 2017. "Short-Run Market Access and the Construction of Better Transportation Infrastructure in Mexico." *Economía* 18 (1): 225–50.

Redding, S. J. and M. A. Turner. 2014. "Transportation Costs and the Spatial Organization of Economic Activity." Working Paper No. 20235, National Bureau of Economic Research, Cambridge, MA.

Roberts, M., U. Deichmann, B. Fingleton, and T. Shi. 2012. "Evaluating China's Road to Prosperity: A New Economic Geography Approach." *Regional Science and Urban Economics* 42 (4): 580–94.

Storeygard, A. 2016. "Farther on Down the Road: Transport Costs, Trade and Urban Growth in Sub-Saharan Africa." *Review of Economic Studies* 83 (3): 1263–95.

Straub, S. 2011. "Infrastructure and Development: A Critical Appraisal of the Macro-level Literature." Journal of Development Studies 47 (5): 683–708.

Summerhill, W. R. 2006. "The Development of Infrastructure." In *The Cambridge Economic History of Latin America, Volume II,* edited by V. Bulmer Thomas, J. H. Coatsworth, and

R. Cortes Conde, 293–326. Cambridge, U.K.: Cambridge University Press.

Trebilcock, M., and M. Rosenstock. 2015. "Infrastructure Public-Private Partnerships in the Developing World: Lessons from Recent Experience." *Journal of Development Studies* 51 (4): 335–54.

Unger, K. 2003. "Los Clústeres Industriales en Mèxico: Especializaciones Regionales y la Política industrial. " Documento de trabajo número 278, División de Economía, Centro de Investigación y Docencia Económicas, Mexico City.

Unger, K., and R. Chico. 2004. "La Industria Automotriz en tres Regiones de México. Un análisis de clùsteres." *El Trimestre Económico* 71 (284): 909–41.

Venables, A. J. 2007. "Evaluating Urban Transport Improvements: Cost–Benefit Analysis in the Presence of Agglomeration and Income Taxation." *Journal of Transport Economics and Policy* 41 (2): 173–88.

Von Tunzelmann, G. N. 1978. Steam Power and British Industrialization to 1860. Oxford, U.K.: Oxford University Press.

Human Capital in Cities | 5

María Marta Ferreyra

Introduction

Cities benefit individuals, and individuals benefit cities. By bringing individuals and firms together, cities make individuals more productive. Yet, it is not just the number of individuals that makes a city productive; it is also their "quality"—their human capital. In other words, although all individuals contribute to city productivity, they do not all contribute equally.

In this chapter, we investigate the role of aggregate human capital in cities' productivity. When choosing where to live in a country, individuals compare locations on the basis of multiple attributes, including job opportunities, housing values, and amenities such as cultural attractions and neighbors' demographic characteristics. Individuals thus sort across locations, and skilled individuals are more likely to sort into cities than into rural areas.[1]

Because skilled individuals are more productive than their unskilled counterparts, their sorting into cities could, in principle, lead to higher productivity there than in rural areas. Yet cities in Latin America and the Caribbean (LAC) are more productive than

rural areas even after taking this sorting into account. Moreover, a strong determinant of city productivity is aggregate human capital—stronger, in fact, than population density and market access (see chapter 3).

Cities with larger stocks of human capital might be more productive for two main reasons. First, a greater share of skilled workers should raise the productivity of unskilled workers, to the extent that skilled and unskilled workers are complementary. For example, when a construction company hires college-educated managers, these new hires might streamline and speed up the production process, raising the productivity (and wages) of the unskilled construction workers. These complementarity effects are usually reflected in skilled workers' wages. This would be the case, in our example, if the college-educated managers were compensated for their contribution to the productivity of their less-skilled colleagues.

The second reason is the effects of human capital externalities (HCEs). In a city with a higher share of skilled workers, all workers have greater opportunity to learn from skilled workers—for example, by exchanging ideas,

The author gratefully acknowledges the excellent research assistance of Angelica Sanchez Diaz.

knowledge, and information even if they do not belong to the same firm. Because skilled workers are usually not paid for contributing to the productivity of others outside their firm, their presence yields positive externalities.

Given the importance of aggregate human capital in city productivity, this chapter first examines the distribution of human capital across cities (more specifically, areas) in the region.[2] It then presents estimates of the productivity gains due to aggregate human capital (henceforth, "returns to aggregate human capital"), and of their variation across countries. It considers two measures of aggregate human capital: the share of college-educated workers (henceforth, "college share"), and average years of schooling.

Because the estimated returns might not necessarily reflect externalities, this chapter then investigates possible channels of productivity gains from aggregate human capital. For unskilled workers, a college share increase is expected to raise productivity because of both complementarities and externalities. For skilled workers, in contrast, a college share increase raises their aggregate supply. This, by itself, would lead to a wage decline for skilled workers. As a result, if a college share increase raises wages for skilled workers, it must be due to externalities.[3] We therefore explore whether the response to a college share increase varies among workers of different educational attainments because this can provide us with evidence about the existence of HCEs.

When these externalities exist, the policy maker may want to subsidize policies that raise an area's aggregate human capital, either by forming it locally, or by attracting it from other areas. Yet, to attract or retain skilled workers, the area must offer the attributes sought by these individuals. For this reason, we investigate individuals' valuation of locational attributes. Crucially, these include the college share because college-educated individuals may contribute to others not only by raising their productivity but also by enriching social interactions, becoming civically involved, and contributing to lower crime.

We examine the case of Brazil, a country with large regional disparities in average income and college share. Because we find that college-educated workers gravitate toward areas with high college shares, the question arises as to how areas with low college shares can attract college-educated workers. One possibility is to implement policies that raise the demand for such workers. We run a simulation of such a policy for one area.

The chapter's main findings are as follows:

- Relative to small areas, large areas have higher shares of skilled individuals, and their income distributions are more unequal. Migrants to large areas are more skilled than migrants to small areas. In order to acquire skilled human capital, small areas rely more than large areas on "importing" it. Most individuals in large areas work in services, but skilled and unskilled individuals work in different type of services. Urban shares of population across countries differ mostly depending on the urban share of their unskilled population.

- On average in the LAC region, an additional year of average education raises nominal wages (henceforth, "wages") by 9.2 percent, and an additional percentage point in the college share raises wages by 2 percent. These returns are commensurate with private returns, although they are larger for average years of schooling than for college share. Returns to aggregate human capital are heterogeneous across countries. They are U-shaped with respect to the country's average aggregate human capital.[4]

- In the LAC region, wages for college-educated workers rise with an increase in college share. This supports the existence of HCEs in the LAC region. Returns to college share are U-shaped relative to a person's educational attainment and are highest for the least educated. Returns to average years of schooling are also U-shaped relative to a person's number of years of schooling, yet they are highest for workers with the highest number of years of schooling.

- In Brazil, workers of all educational attainments value college-educated neighbors and intercity connectivity. They value density only to the extent that it raises the share of college-educated neighbors.
- In Brazil, simulation results for a policy that raises demand for college-educated workers show that such a policy would benefit not only these workers but also others, who would gain in welfare and productivity through the greater presence of college-educated workers.

Some Stylized Facts

The unit of observation in this section (as in chapter 3 and in the section below titled "Returns to Aggregate Human Capital") is an administrative unit, except in a few cases in which administrative units have been merged.[5] For most countries, the administrative unit is a municipality; we present information for the most recent year with data (see annex 5A for further details). For simplicity, we use the term "area" for the unit of observation. We measure area size by population; we thus consider an area larger than another when it has a greater population. We consider an area to be small, medium, or large when its population is below the country's median, between the country's median and 75th percentile, and above the country's 75th percentile, respectively.[6] In figures that compare urban and rural areas, Argentina is not included because that country's household surveys do not cover rural areas.

We define the adult population as individuals age 25–64 years. In this section, "skilled" individuals are those who have some higher education, regardless of whether they have completed it; thus "unskilled" individuals are those who have at most completed high school and have not started higher education. We classify individuals by their educational attainment into those with elementary, secondary, and higher education when they have completed elementary, secondary, or higher education at most, respectively, and have not started the following level. "Average" refers to a simple (unweighted) average, unless

indicated otherwise. Income and wages are measured in nominal terms.

Stylized Fact 1. Human Capital Is Unequally Distributed across and within Countries

In LAC areas, the average share of skilled adult population is equal to 13 percent. Behind this average lies substantial variation across and within countries: the median share of skilled adult population in Argentina is 32 percent, against 3.7 percent in Honduras (figure 5.1, panel a). The variation across areas is lowest in the countries with the lowest and the highest average share of skilled adult population, yet is high in countries with intermediate levels of average share of skilled adult population. Similar patterns hold for average years of schooling (figure 5.1, panel b), as we would expect from the high area-level correlation (equal to 0.87) between the share of skilled adult population and average years of schooling. Human capital is more unequally distributed within LAC countries than in comparator countries such as Poland or Turkey.

Even among the largest areas in the region, the share of the skilled adult population varies widely (figure 5.2). Ciudad de Buenos Aires tops the distribution, with a 60 percent share of skilled population. Its surrounding area, Gran Buenos Aires, reaches only 23 percent. A country's largest areas are not necessarily the most educated. For example, the largest areas in Brazil—Rio de Janeiro and São Paulo—have around the same share of skilled adult population (about 30 percent) as Campinas, a medium-sized area that hosts multiple higher education institutions. Moretti (2004b) similarly notes that, in the United States, small and medium-sized areas that host large higher education institutions have disproportionately large shares of skilled individuals.

Stylized Fact 2. Skilled Individuals Are More Likely Than Others Are to Live in Urban Areas

Skilled individuals have a greater tendency than unskilled individuals to live in urban

FIGURE 5.1   Distribution of Human Capital at the Area Level, circa 2014

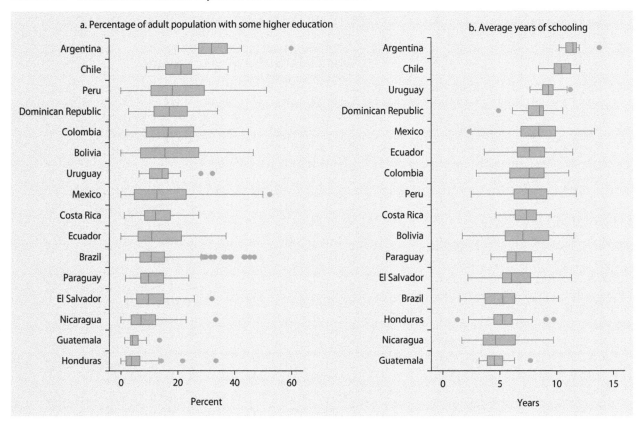

Source: Calculations based on SEDLAC (for countries other than Brazil) and IPUMS (for Brazil).
Note: Panel a shows a box plot per country for the distribution of the percentage of population with some higher education at the area level. Panel b shows a box plot per country for the distribution of the average years of schooling at the area level. Indicators are calculated for the population age 25–64 years. See annex 5A for the years used for each country. Countries are sorted by median values for each indicator. Outliers are indicated by dots. When there are no outliers, the left and right caps show the minimum and maximum value, respectively, and the box indicates the 25th and 75th percentiles (with the median indicated inside the box). In the cases of outliers, the left and right caps are the minimum and maximum values excluding the outliers. To identify outliers, we calculate the interquartile range; values outside the range defined by (25th percentile − 1.5 * interquartile range, 75th percentile + 1.5 * interquartile range) are considered outliers.

areas (figure 5.3). Of the skilled adult population, 92 percent lives in urban areas, against only 67 percent of the unskilled adult population.

For each country, the red diamond shows the overall propensity of the adult population to live in urban areas, and the vertical difference between the orange and blue bars below shows the gap in the propensity to live in urban areas between the skilled and unskilled. Although the fraction of skilled population living in urban areas varies little across countries, the fraction of unskilled population varies more, driving the differences across countries in the overall

propensity to live in urban areas. Absent other changes, countries with low shares of urban population will become more urban to the extent that their unskilled population moves to urban areas.

Stylized Fact 3. The Higher the Area Population, the Greater the Share of Skilled Individuals

As shown in figure 5.4, a greater share of the population is skilled in large areas than in small or medium-sized areas (Argentina is the exception). On average, a 1 percent increase in population is associated with

FIGURE 5.2 Population and Human Capital in the Largest Areas, circa 2014

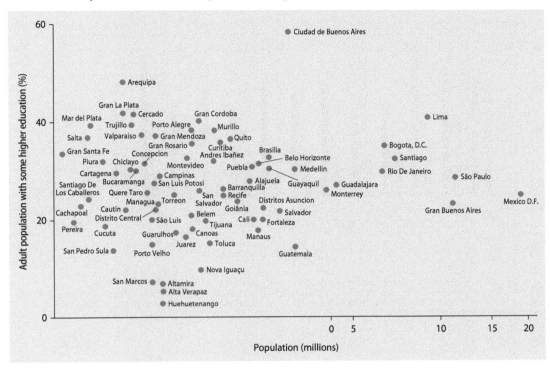

Source: Calculations based on SEDLAC (for all countries other than for Brazil) and IPUMS (for Brazil).
Note: For each of the largest areas, the figure shows population (in millions) and percentage of adult population with some higher education. The figure shows selected areas in the region where population is greater than a given threshold (equal to 1 million for Brazil, Guatemala, and Mexico, and 500,000 for the remaining countries). The horizontal axis is in (natural) logarithmic scale. IPUMS = Integrated Public Use Microdata Series; SEDLAC = Socio-Economic Database for Latin America and the Caribbean.

FIGURE 5.3 Percentage of the Adult Population Living in Urban Areas, circa 2014

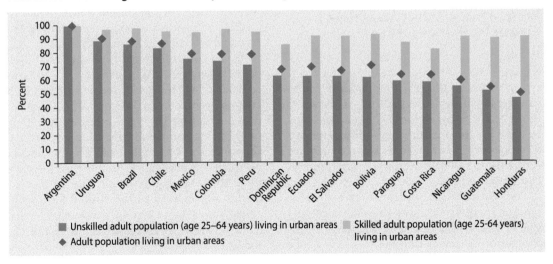

Source: Calculations based on SEDLAC (for countries other than for Brazil) and IPUMS (for Brazil).
Note: Skilled population has at least some higher education. Urban areas are defined by national statistics offices. IPUMS = Integrated Public Use Microdata Series; SEDLAC = Socio-Economic Database for Latin America and the Caribbean.

FIGURE 5.4   **Percentage of Skilled Population, by Area Size, circa 2014**

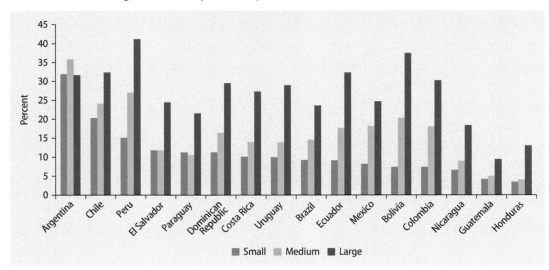

Source: Calculations based on SEDLAC (for countries other than Brazil) and IPUMS (for Brazil).
Note: The figure shows the average percentage of the adult population (age 25–64 years) with some higher education, by area size. Area size classification follows country-specific population thresholds, as explained in annex 5A. IPUMS = Integrated Public Use Microdata Series; SEDLAC = Socio-Economic Database for Latin America and the Caribbean.

a 0.29 percent increase in the share of skilled adult population.[7] The corresponding increase is lower (equal to 0.12 percent) in the United States (Behrens and Robert-Nicoud 2015).

Stylized Fact 4. Larger Areas Have Greater Income Inequality

We measure income inequality for each area through the Gini coefficient (whose value ranges between 0 and 1; higher values indicate greater income inequality). As shown in figure 5.5, in most countries larger areas tend to have greater income inequality. The pattern does not hold, or holds less strongly, for Argentina, Bolivia, Ecuador, Guatemala, Paraguay, and Peru.

As it turns out, large cities are more unequal largely because they have greater shares of skilled population. We arrive at this conclusion by estimating the elasticity of the Gini coefficient with respect to area population, with and without controlling for the share of skilled population.

On average, the elasticity of the Gini coefficient with respect to area population is equal to 0.03.[8] In other words, on average a 1 percent increase in population is associated with a 0.03 percent increase in inequality (as measured by the Gini coefficient). The elasticity is lower for the United States (equal to 0.012), indicating a stronger tendency toward income inequality in large LAC cities.

When controlling for the share of skilled population, the LAC elasticity of the Gini coefficient with respect to area population falls on average from 0.03 to 0.017, and from 0.012 to 0.009 for the United States. This implies that the share of skilled population accounts for 43 percent of the association between city population and income inequality in the LAC region yet for only 25 percent of this association in the United States. So education is more strongly associated with income inequality in large LAC cities than in the United States.

The fact that city population, skills, and inequality are more strongly associated in the LAC region than in the United States reflects

FIGURE 5.5 Average Gini Coefficient, by Area Size, circa 2014

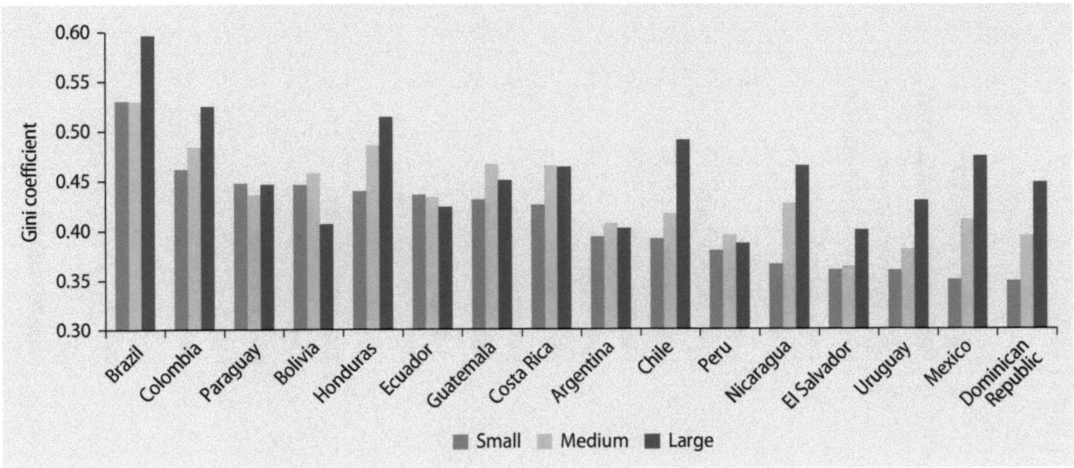

Source: Calculations based on SEDLAC (for countries other than Brazil) and IPUMS (for Brazil).
Note: The figure shows the average Gini coefficient by area size (weighted average; weight is area size). Area size classification follows country-specific population thresholds, as explained in annex 5A. IPUMS = Integrated Public Use Microdata Series; SEDLAC = Socio-Economic Database for Latin America and the Caribbean.

the LAC region's relative skill scarcity. In LAC countries, the share of skilled population is lower than in the United States. For example, the share of individuals with some higher education in the average LAC country (18.4 percent) is roughly one-third of that in the United States (59 percent). Second, returns to higher education are higher in the LAC region than in the United States. For example, returns to complete higher education are equal to 104 percent for the average LAC country, more than twice as high as in the United States.[9]

Stylized Fact 5. Migrants to Large Areas Are More Skilled Than Migrants Are to Small Areas

The migration that fuels areas' growth in the LAC region is of domestic rather than foreign origin. Only 2.8 percent of these areas' adult population is foreign born. Argentina and Costa Rica are the countries whose areas attract most international migration (see annex 5D). In contrast, in comparator countries in East Asia and Pacific (EAP) and Europe and Central Asia

(ECA), 11 percent of the population living in urban areas is foreign born.[10] Hence, here we focus on domestic migrants.

On average, 7.16 percent of household heads age 25–35 years have migrated within their countries in the last five years.[11] In most countries, migrants to large areas are more likely to be skilled than migrants to medium or small areas (except in Ecuador, El Salvador, and Paraguay) (figure 5.6). In other words, large areas benefit from the inflow of skilled migrants at a higher rate than medium or small areas. This, in turn, reinforces large areas' advantage in human capital.[12]

Stylized Fact 6. To Acquire Skilled Human Capital, Small Areas Rely More Than Large Areas Are on Migration

In most countries, the share of skilled population that arrived via migration is larger in smaller areas (figure 5.7)—smaller areas are more likely to "import" their skilled population. This might be because larger areas are more likely to host higher education institutions and so develop their own skilled population, which then stays in the area.[13]

FIGURE 5.6   **Percentage of Skilled Migrants, by Area Size, circa 2014**

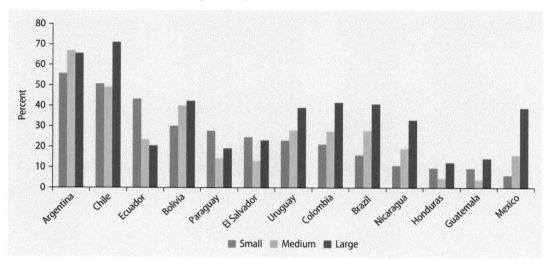

Source: Calculations using IPUMS (for Brazil, Colombia, El Salvador, and Mexico) and SEDLAC (for all other countries).
Note: The figure shows, among household heads age 25–35 years who have migrated within the past five years, the percentage who are skilled (who have at least some higher education) by size of their destination area. Area size classification follows country-specific population thresholds; as explained in annex 5A. IPUMS = Integrated Public Use Microdata Series; SEDLAC = Socio-Economic Database for Latin America and the Caribbean.

FIGURE 5.7   **Percentage of Skilled Individuals Who Are Migrants, by Area Size, circa 2014**

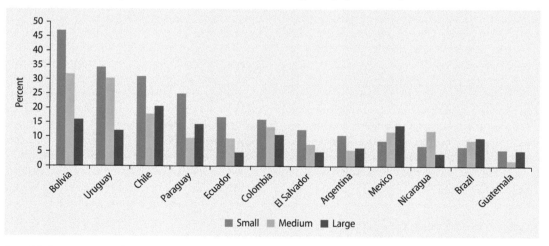

Source: Calculations using IPUMS (for Brazil, Colombia, El Salvador, and Mexico) and SEDLAC (for all other countries).
Note: The figure shows, for each area size, the percentage of skilled individuals who are migrants. A migrant is someone who has moved within the past five years from a different department (Admin-1 unit) except in the case of Bolivia, where migrations are from any other place in the country. The sample consists of household age 25–35 years. Area size classification follows country-specific population thresholds, as explained in annex 5A. IPUMS = Integrated Public Use Microdata Series; SEDLAC = Socio-Economic Database for Latin America and the Caribbean.

Stylized Fact 7. The Larger the Area, the Greater the Employment Share in Services

As figure 5.8 shows, in larger areas, a greater share of the adult population is employed in services (except in Argentina). This is due to two reasons. First, larger areas host larger shares of skilled individuals (stylized fact 3), who are more likely than their unskilled counterparts to work in services regardless of area size (annex 5B).[14] Second, in larger areas, individuals of *all* skill levels are more likely to work in services (annex 5C).

FIGURE 5.8   **Percentage of Employment in Services, by Area Size, circa 2014**

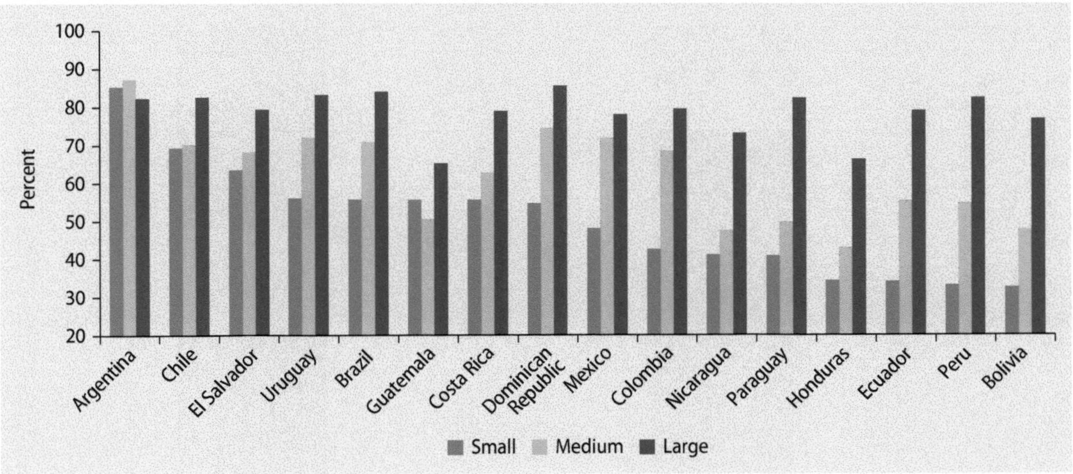

Source: Calculations based on SEDLAC (for countries other than Brazil) and IPUMS (for Brazil).
Note: The figure shows the employment share (in percent) of the service sector, by area size. Area size classification follows country-specific population thresholds; as explained in annex 5A. The sample consists of workers age 25–64 years. IPUMS = Integrated Public Use Microdata Series; SEDLAC = Socio-Economic Database for Latin America and the Caribbean.

Nonetheless, the specific service sector where individuals work in large areas depends on their skill level (figure 5.9). Skilled individuals are most likely to work in public administration, education, health, social work, financial intermediation, and real estate; unskilled individuals in whole-sale, retail, hotels, restaurants, transport and communications. In services in large areas, skilled individuals are also more likely than unskilled individuals to work in the public sector, mainly in public administration and education.

Structural transformation in the LAC region seems to have shifted an increasing share of workers into low-productivity service sectors since 1960 (see chapter 1). Although both skilled and unskilled individuals may be vulnerable to this trend, unskilled individuals seem to be more vulnerable given the service sectors where they tend to work. Data from the Groningen Growth and Development Center (GGDC), also used in chapter 1, show that, among activities that usually

take place in cities, labor productivity is lowest in wholesale, retail, hotels, and restaurants—namely, in the service sectors where unskilled individuals are most likely to work.[15]

Summary

In the LAC region, skilled individuals tend to sort into large areas, and migrants to large areas are more skilled than migrants to small areas. Large areas are also more likely than small areas to develop their own human capital than to "import" it from other areas.

Larger areas have more unequal income distributions, largely because they have greater shares of skilled individuals. Put differently, the greater inequality of larger areas is a consequence of their ability to attract high-earning, "successful" individuals. Importantly, the sorting of skilled individuals into large areas does not necessarily mean that these individuals have a taste for size (or population density) in itself; rather, it may

FIGURE 5.9   **Percentage of Service Workers, by Sector in Large Areas and by Skill Level, circa 2014**

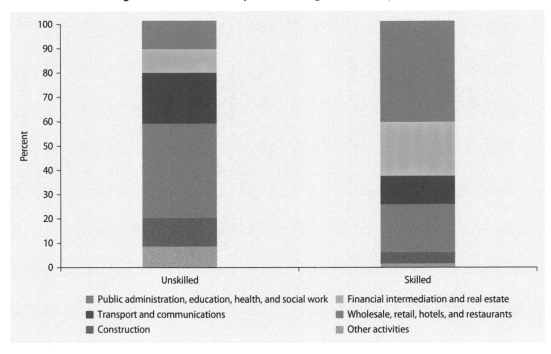

Source: Calculations based on SEDLAC (for countries other than Brazil) and IPUMS (for Brazil).
Note: For each skill level, the figure shows the distribution of employees across subsectors in the service sector in Latin America and the Caribbean. Unskilled workers are those who have completed high school at most, and skilled workers have at least some higher education. The sample consists of workers age 25–64 years who work in the service sector and live in large areas in Latin America and the Caribbean. Large areas are determined following country-specific population thresholds; see annex 5A for further information. IPUMS = Integrated Public Use Microdata Series; SEDLAC = Socio-Economic Database for Latin America and the Caribbean.

reflect a preference for locational attributes that they more typically find in large areas, including job opportunities, cultural amenities, and a high college share. It may also reflects their greater ability to pay for housing because housing prices are usually higher in large areas. We revisit these issues later in the chapter.

Although the positive association between area size, education, and inequality has been documented for the United States as well, we find that it is stronger for LAC. This may be because a smaller share of the population in the LAC region is skilled, and returns to higher education are substantially higher. Yet, it is also possible that locational attributes may be less evenly distributed across a country's areas in the LAC region than in the United States. For example, it is possible that only a few areas offer good job opportunities to college graduates.

Across LAC countries, differences in the share of urban population are mostly driven by the unskilled. It is possible that, as a country's share of skilled population grows (because, perhaps, of the expansion of education in the country), the share of urban population grows simply because skilled population sort into large areas. But this share may also rise as the unskilled move to urban areas. Because the services in which the unskilled typically work in large areas (wholesale, retail, hotels, and restaurants) are of low productivity, urbanization may thus continue the trend of shifting workers into low-productivity service sectors (see chapter 1).

Returns to Aggregate Human Capital

Through education, workers become more productive and earn concomitantly higher salaries. Using the same sample of LAC workers as in Quintero and Roberts (2017) and as in chapter 3, we find that a worker's additional year of schooling increases her or his salary, on average, by 8.92 percent.[16] This is on a par with estimates from other researchers. For example, when estimating returns to education for nations all over the world, Montenegro and Patrinos (2014) find an average return of 10 percent for high-income economies, and of 9.2 percent for LAC.

Education benefits society as well. For example, more-educated individuals may contribute to the generation and dissemination of ideas, knowledge, and products. They may be more informed and engaged citizens, and may advocate for greater quality (and perhaps variety) of public goods. They may be less likely to engage in criminal activities.

In this section, we focus on a specific kind of social benefit from education, namely the returns that a person's human capital has on the productivity (and hence wages) of others *in her or his area*. Although a person's human capital could also benefit others in larger geographic units (such as the state and the country), we focus on benefits *in the area* because this is the geographic unit in which most of a person's interactions are likely to take place.

To estimate these social benefits, researchers have often compared wages for workers who live in areas with different levels of aggregate human capital, controlling for other area-level characteristics and for workers' characteristics. We use the term "return to aggregate human capital" to refer to these wage differences. Returns to aggregate human capital, however, may reflect not only HCEs but also complementarities between skilled and unskilled human capital. When these complementarities are present, higher aggregate human capital raises productivity (and hence wages) for the unskilled and, perhaps, for the skilled as well. Moreover, the return to aggregate human capital may be entirely due to these complementarities, without any role for HCEs.

A critical distinction between complementarities and HCEs is that the former are likely internalized in skilled workers' wages, but the latter are not. For example, if a skilled worker raises the productivity of unskilled workers inside his or her firm by sharing her or his knowledge and skills, that worker is likely to be paid for it. In contrast, if the skilled worker raises the productivity of a worker *in another firm*, most likely that skilled worker is not paid for it.

The distinction between complementarities and HCEs is important for policy. Because HCEs are a market failure, their correction requires policy intervention—for example, through government subsidies to the formation of human capital. Complementarities, in turn, do not require policy intervention.

A form of complementarity arises when a greater share of college-educated individuals raises demand for the services provided by less skilled individuals, that is, when college-educated individuals take more cab rides, or hire more house cleaners and nannies, than less-educated individuals. Because salaries for the unskilled adjust to reflect this greater demand, this phenomenon does not constitute a market failure.

In an area, HCEs can arise through interactions among individuals. For example, they can arise when workers from different companies interact in formal settings such as conferences, public presentations, and joint projects among companies. They can also arise when workers from different companies interact in informal settings such as school meetings, civic associations, or even the neighborhood. All these interactions provide learning opportunities for workers, who thus exchange ideas and share relevant knowledge and skills. Verbal exchanges may not even be required for learning because a worker can learn from another merely by observing that person.

HCEs can also arise from the actions and behaviors of skilled individuals that benefit all individuals in the area. For example, because skilled individuals are less likely to engage in crime than unskilled individuals, an area with more aggregate human capital is likely safer. To the extent that safety contributes to productivity, this might be reflected in wages.[17] Similarly, college-educated individuals are more likely to be civically engaged and to demand better public services from local authorities. To the extent that these improve productivity, they might be reflected in wages as well.

Estimated Returns to Aggregate Human Capital

When measuring returns to aggregate human capital, researchers have used two measures: average years of schooling of those living in an area, and the share of individuals with some higher education (whether they completed it or not). In our investigation of the determinants of area-level productivity in chapter 3, we used (log) average years of schooling, and share of individuals in the working-age population (WAP) with completed higher education.[18]

In table 5.1, columns 1 and 2 show the coefficients on two alternative measures of aggregate human capital, namely average years of schooling and share of individuals in the WAP with completed higher education (or college share). Both regressions control

for individual-level characteristics and for other area characteristics, including population density and market access.

Two caveats are in order. The first is that it is possible that area density, aggregate human capital, and market access are endogenous, that is, they are correlated with some unobserved area or individual characteristic (see chapter 3). Lacking instruments for the whole region, we proceed as if endogeneity were not a concern (with the same caveats made in that earlier chapter), and use the term "returns to aggregate human capital" to denote the coefficient on aggregate human capital. The second caveat is that, as indicated above, the returns to aggregate human capital may not only (if at all) reflect HCEs. We return to this point in the next section.

As column 1 shows, an additional year of average schooling in our sample is associated with a salary increase of 9.2 percent, which is slightly larger than the estimated average private return to education in the LAC region (recall that this is equal to 8.92 percent in our sample). This finding is consistent with other studies, both for the developed and developing world, which have estimated returns to aggregate human capital in the range of 50–100 percent of private returns (Duranton 2014). The estimated return for the LAC region is large: if all individuals acquired an extra year of schooling, each of them would reap a salary increase of about 18 percent, in roughly equal parts from own and aggregate human capital.

In our sample, a 1 percentage point increase in the college share is associated with a 2 percent average salary increase (column 2). As with the average number of years of schooling, the estimated return to college share is in line with the private returns to higher education: on average in the LAC region, a higher education graduate earns 104 percent more than a high school graduate, controlling for observed characteristics (Ferreyra et al. 2017). Thus, a 1 percentage point increase in college share will raise *average* wages by about 1 percent, which is commensurate with our estimated return to the college share.

Our estimated return to college share in the LAC region is somewhat larger than that

TABLE 5.1 Returns to Aggregate Human Capital, 2000–14

	(1)	(2)
Average no. of years of schooling	0.092***	
	(0.012)	
% WAP with completed higher education		0.020***
		(0.003)
Adjusted R^2	0.832	0.803
No. of observations	5,050	5,050

Source: Calculations using SEDLAC for all countries except for Brazil, and IPUMS for Brazil. Sample is the same as that used by Quintero and Roberts 2017. Column 2 reports the same results as those of column 5 in table 3.2.
Note: This table regresses estimated area-level productivity on aggregate human capital. The coefficients represent returns to aggregate human capital; when multiplied by 100, returns are expressed in percent. In these regressions, a unit of observation is an area; all Latin American and Caribbean areas are pooled in the regressions. Both regressions control for population density, market access, air temperature, terrain ruggedness, and precipitation; both include country fixed effects. Area-level productivities are estimated by regressing, for each country, log wages on individual-level characteristics (age, age squared, years of schooling, gender, and marital status) and year fixed effects. Average years of schooling is calculated for individuals in the WAP. IPUMS = Integrated Public Use Microdata Series; SEDLAC = Socio-Economic Database for Latin America and the Caribbean; WAP = working-age population (individuals age 14–65 years).
*** $p < 0.01$, ** $p < 0.05$, * $p < 0.1$. Standard errors are clustered by country.

in Moretti (2004a) for the United States (which is in a range of 0.6–1.2 percent), yet of similar magnitude. The estimate might be larger for LAC because, in the average LAC area, only 5 percent of the WAP has completed higher education, against 23 percent in U.S. cities (Moretti 2004b).[19]

To provide context for the estimated return to college share, an area would, on average, need to raise its college share by 4.6 percentage points to attain the same social benefit derived from an extra year of average schooling. Relative to the average college share (equal to 5 percent), this is a very sizable increase. It is approximately equal to the increase in college share in the LAC region between 2002 and 2012, during the region's remarkably large and fast higher education expansion (Ferreyra et al. 2017).

Hence, returns to aggregate human capital appear large when aggregate human capital is measured by average years of schooling, but not as large when measured by college share. This might be because the average educational attainment is low in the region: the average

area has an average number of years of schooling of 7.35, which in most countries is equivalent to just having finished elementary education. With such low educational attainment, an additional year of average education might have high returns in wages but might not affect the college share.[20] It is reassuring, however, that country-level estimates of returns to human capital using average years of schooling and college share are highly and positively correlated (correlation = 0.75).[21]

Returns to aggregate human capital are heterogeneous across countries (see chapter 3). In figure 5.10, we investigate whether this heterogeneity is related to countries' aggregate human capital, measured as the average (across areas) of aggregate human capital. For both measures of aggregate human capital, there seems to be a U-shaped association between a country's average aggregate human capital and its return to aggregate human capital. In other words, as aggregate human capital rises, returns to aggregate human capital first fall, and then rise. One possible explanation for this pattern is that aggregate

FIGURE 5.10   Returns to Aggregate Human Capital, 2000–14

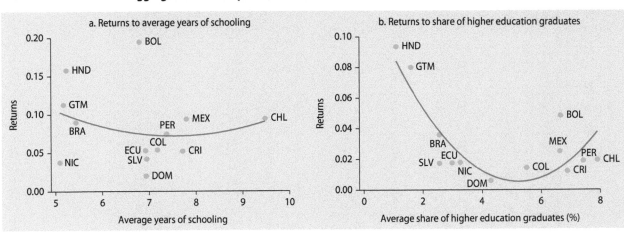

Source: Calculations using SEDLAC for all countries except for Brazil, and IPUMS for Brazil. Panel a sample and panel b returns are from Quintero and Roberts 2017.
Note: The vertical axis shows, for each country, the estimated returns to aggregate human capital. The horizontal axis shows, for each country, the average of the corresponding variable; the average is calculated over the country's areas. Average years of schooling, and share of higher education graduates, correspond to individuals age 14–65 years. Returns can be expressed in percent if multiplied by 100. To obtain these returns, for each country we regress area-level productivity on the corresponding measure of aggregate human capital; these regressions control for area density, market access, air temperature, terrain ruggedness, and precipitation. Area-level productivities are estimated by regressing, for each country, log wages on individual-level characteristics (age, age squared, years of schooling, gender, and marital status) and year fixed effects. We do not run these regressions for Argentina, Panama, or Uruguay because they have few areas. Coefficients from the quadratic specification in panel b are significantly different from zero. Coefficients from the quadratic specification in panel a are not significantly different from zero (if a linear specification is fitted to the data in panel a, the corresponding coefficient is not significantly different from zero either). IPUMS = Integrated Public Use Microdata Series; SEDLAC = Socio-Economic Database for Latin America and the Caribbean. For a list of country abbreviations, see annex 2A.

human capital has decreasing returns when it is low, but increasing returns once it surpasses a certain threshold—perhaps indicating the need for a critical share of skilled workers (or for workers with a minimum number of years of schooling) who can benefit from the presence of other skilled workers.

Complementarities Versus Human Capital Externalities

Although the evidence above indicates positive returns to aggregate human capital, we recall that this association might not be due—at least not solely—to HCEs. Consider, for example, the return to college share. This return could be positive not only because of HCEs, but also because of workers' complementarities with college-educated workers.

To distinguish between the two factors, it is useful to investigate whether the return to college share varies by own education (Moretti 2004a). On the assumption that workers of different skills are complementary, an increase in the share of skilled

workers benefits unskilled workers because of complementarities and HCEs. Because the two effects work in the same direction, a return to the share of skilled workers for the unskilled does not provide evidence of HCEs because it could be entirely due to complementarities.

In contrast, an increase in the share of skilled workers depresses the wages of other skilled workers because it raises their relative supply, yet also raises their wages via HCEs. For skilled workers, the net effect is positive only if HCEs are sufficiently large.[22] Thus, a positive return to college share for skilled workers provides evidence of the presence of HCEs.

When he investigates whether the return to college share varies by educational attainment in the United States, Moretti (2004a) finds that this return is positive for college-educated individuals, thus confirming the presence of HCEs. Furthermore, he finds that the return declines with a worker's educational attainment.

For LAC, we also find that returns to college share are positive for college-educated

FIGURE 5.11   Returns to Aggregate Human Capital, by Individual's Own Education, 2000–14

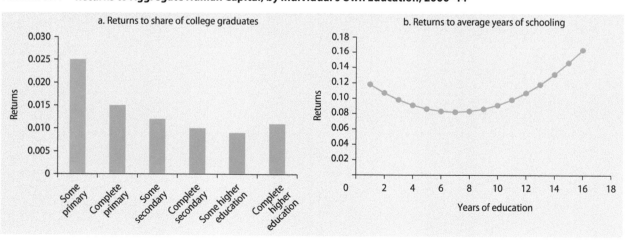

Source: Calculations based on Socio-Economic Database for Latin America and the Caribbean for all countries except for Brazil, and IPUMS for Brazil. Sample is the same as used by Quintero and Roberts 2017.
Note: Panel a shows, for each educational attainment, the return to the share (in percent) of college graduates. In both panels, returns can be expressed in percent if multiplied by 100. To construct panel a, we pool data from all countries and regress log wages on individual characteristics (age, age squared, indicators of educational attainment, gender, and marital status) interacted with country dummies, area-level characteristics (density, share of college graduates, market access, air temperature, terrain ruggedness, and precipitation), country-year fixed effects, and the interaction between indicators of individual educational attainment and the area share of college graduates. Individuals with completed primary (secondary) have not started secondary (higher) education. Panel b shows, for each value of own years of schooling, the return to average years of schooling. To construct panel b, we pool data from all countries and regress log wages on individual characteristics (age, age squared, years of schooling, years of schooling squared, gender, and marital status) interacted with country dummies, area-level characteristics (density, average years of schooling, market access, air temperature, terrain ruggedness, and precipitation), country-year fixed effects, the interaction between own years of schooling and average years of schooling, and the interaction between own years of schooling squared and average years of schooling. All relevant coefficients for these panels are significantly different from zero.

workers, thus providing evidence of the presence of HCEs (figure 5.11, panel a). Unlike Moretti (2004a), we find that the returns to college share are U-shaped relative to own educational attainment: they are highest for the least educated and decline with educational attainment, as in Moretti (2004a), but rise again for college-educated workers. The fact that, in the LAC region, returns are higher for college-educated workers than for workers with complete secondary education, or some higher education, suggests that human capital externalities might be higher for college-educated workers than for workers with those other attainments. But, more important, returns to college share are highest for the least educated—either because a higher college share implies greater demand for their services (for example, as restaurant workers or cab drivers), because it allows them to work in the same firms as skilled college educated workers, or because it allows them to learn from college educated workers outside the firm.

This U-shaped pattern also holds for the alternative measure of aggregate human capital, namely average years of schooling (figure 5.11, panel b). In particular, an individual can reap increasing returns from average years of schooling once she or he completes at least seven years of schooling (roughly equivalent to finishing elementary school). With 9.36 years of schooling, the average individual has already surpassed this threshold.

Although the returns to both measures of aggregate human capital are U-shaped in own human capital, who enjoys the highest returns varies depending on the measure: people with the lowest educational attainment benefit the most from college share (figure 5.11, panel a), yet people with the highest number of years of schooling benefit the most from average years of schooling (figure 5.11, panel b). These differences may be related to the region's level of educational attainment and with the fact that workers might not be perfect substitutes within a given skill level.

To see this, recall that the average years of schooling equals 7.35 years (roughly equal to elementary school) in the average area in the region, which makes the average worker in this area unskilled. Thus, an additional year of average education does not alter the average college share in the LAC region, but it changes the average skill of the unskilled. For example, a person with five years of schooling may not benefit if average years of schooling rises from seven to eight years because this would make other unskilled workers more educated (and hence employable). This would explain the descending portion of figure 5.11, panel b. However, the same situation may benefit a person with 16 years of schooling because it may allow her to specialize in complex activities and leave easier ones to the average worker, who is now more educated. Thus, the returns to average years of schooling may capture more complementarity effects than the returns to college share because of the low number of average years of schooling in the region. In contrast, the returns to college share may capture more HCEs because it is plausible that college-educated workers would generate more positive externalities than workers who have only finished elementary school.[23]

The U-shape of the return to aggregate human capital for own education (see figure 5.11, panels a and b) is reminiscent of the U-shape of the returns for a country's average aggregate human capital (see figure 5.10). In other words, aggregate human capital has high returns for an individual (or average area) with low education; these returns fall as the individual (or a country's average area) acquires more education, and finally rise once the individual (or average area) has acquired sufficient education.

To summarize, the evidence suggests that an area's aggregate human capital raises average productivity and that at least part of this return can be attributed to HCEs. The least skilled individuals benefit the most from an increase in college share, and individuals with the highest years of schooling benefit the most from an increase in average years of schooling. By enhancing workers' productivity, areas with high aggregate human capital are thus attractive to all individuals, holding other locational attributes constant.

Attracting Skilled Individuals to Cities

Given the evidence that skilled human capital raises aggregate productivity, it seems as though local leaders would be interested in attracting such individuals to local communities. These efforts, however, can be successful only to the extent that the communities offer the locational attributes sought by skilled individuals. This issue may be of particular importance to medium-sized and small areas, which rely more than large areas on migration to raise college share (stylized fact 6).

In this section, we study the determinants of location choice among individuals of different skill levels in Brazil. We also study the productivity spillovers of college graduates onto other workers and consider the effects of a hypothetical program that attracts college graduates to an area.[24] We draw largely on Fan and Timmins (2017), a background paper for this book. Box 5.1 describes their model.

Fan and Timmins (2017) use data from a 5 percent sample of the 2010 Population Census in Brazil. They focus on the locational choices of household heads age 25–35 years, who choose among almost 1,400 municipalities in 27 states.[25] Lacking better data, they consider a person as having moved if she or he resides in a municipality outside her or his birth state.

BOX 5.1   An Equilibrium Model of Household Sorting for Brazil

Fan and Timmins (2017) study how individuals choose their municipality (or locality) of residence in Brazil. They develop an equilibrium model of household locational choice and local labor markets. They estimate the parameters of individuals' utility functions and of local labor markets' productivity, and use the parameter estimates to perform counterfactuals.

In the model, when choosing among locations, individuals consider natural attributes such as elevation and climate, and others such as job opportunities (proxied by their expected income in the specific location), housing values, population density, density of college graduates, connectivity with other locations, and other attributes not observed by the researcher.[a] Importantly, preferences over these attributes are allowed to vary by educational attainment—for example, the density of college graduates may be more valuable to college graduates than to less-educated individuals. The model accounts for the fact that moving is costly, which in turn makes people more likely to remain in a location, even when it is not their preferred one.

Some local attributes, such as elevation and precipitation, do not depend on people's collective decisions, yet others do. Such is the case for a municipality's population density, the density of college graduates, and housing prices. In other words, some local attributes are the outcome of individuals' sorting and are thus *endogenous*. This poses a challenge in the estimation of preferences for local attributes. By using state-of-the-art methods, the authors overcome this challenge and recover preferences over these attributes.

One local attribute considered by people is their expected income in that location. The authors model it as a function of individual characteristics and a local productivity term that varies by educational attainment (for example, the composition of economic activity of a given municipality may be particularly fitting for college graduates). Expected income is also an outcome of individuals' sorting. For example, local productivity for high school graduates depends on the local density of high school graduates (because an increase in this density would render them less scarce and hence less valuable) and on the local density of college graduates (because an increase in this density could make them more productive, as we saw in the previous section).

The model accounts for the fact that changes in locational attributes (including labor market conditions) may lead people to change their locational choices, which in turn changes the local attributes resulting from individuals' sorting and leads to further re-sorting. The model, then, can be used to evaluate the equilibrium impact of specific policies on population density, skill composition of the population, housing prices, incomes, and utilities.

a. A municipality's density of college graduates is defined as the municipality's number of college graduates divided by the municipality's area. Thus population density is equal to the density of college graduates plus the density of less-educated individuals.

Brazil is a country with large regional disparities. Incomes for the average individual in the midwest or southeast (the richest regions) are almost twice as high as in the northeast (the poorest region). In the sample, 16.9 percent of individuals have moved. Moving is most likely among college-educated individuals and among individuals born in the northeast region. The southeast attracts the highest share of migrants.

Preferences for Locational Attributes

An important finding from the model's estimation is that moving costs are steep. These costs may not only be pecuniary but also reflect other considerations such as the difficulty of separating from family members and friends. Fan and Timmins (2017) also uncover a pattern of individuals' preferences in locational attributes.

In principle, individuals might like dense places, perhaps because greater density facilitates social interaction. The authors find that whether density is liked or not depends on the composition of the additional population, and on whether it leads to a greater or lower share of college-educated individuals. People like population growth, or changes in population composition, so long as they do not lower the college share.

Importantly, individuals of all skill levels enjoy living in locations with a higher share (and density) of college graduates. Preference for college graduates captures not only an intrinsic preference for more educated neighbors but also a preference for local attributes associated with the presence of such neighbors in the community. As Fan and Timmins (2017) document, in Brazil the density of college graduates is positively and significantly correlated with the provision of trash collection, sewage, and water, perhaps because governments are more likely to provide these services to areas with a relatively large share of middle- and high-income individuals who exert political pressure to receive these services and can pay for them, or because these individuals can afford housing in areas with high service provision. Similarly, the authors document that the share of college graduates

is positively and significantly correlated with the number of museums, theaters, and restaurants. Even if less-educated individuals cannot afford all these amenities, they may still enjoy their presence. Finally, preferences for college-educated individuals might also reflect the preference for other, unmeasured amenities that are correlated with the presence of such individuals, as is the case of lower crime.

Individuals who completed at least high school prefer locations with additional university buildings. This might reflect the value they attach to institutions that their children might attend because about 80 percent of higher education students in the LAC region live with their parents while attending higher education (Ferreyra et al. 2017). It might also reflect university spillovers in the community, for example, through extension activities with the community at large, or through research and innovations that benefit the community.

Most individuals value additional road and rail density, reflecting the value they place on the connectivity of the location with others. All individuals value the presence of a shoreline. Although they like higher temperatures and more abundant winter rain, they dislike summer rain.

Thus, people weigh multiple locational attributes when choosing where to live. Critical attributes, however, are the presence of college-educated neighbors and intercity connectivity. This suggests that areas seeking to attract such individuals can resort to policies that raise the local demand for college-educated workers, improve intercity connectivity, or expand higher education. Moreover, that college share is highly and positively correlated with the presence of other urban amenities, such as public services and cultural attractions, indicates that expanding the provision of these amenities may also raise the college share.

To the extent that household preferences in Brazil are similar to those in other LAC countries, the estimates suggest that the sorting of skilled individuals into large areas observed in the LAC region (see the stylized facts earlier in the chapter) does not reflect their taste for area size;

rather, it mainly reflects their taste for the locational attributes more usually found in large areas, including a high college share.

Labor Demand

Fan and Timmins (2017) also estimate labor demand for individuals in local labor markets. How much employers are willing to pay to those of a given educational attainment depends on local labor market conditions. Table 5.2 shows that, as expected, employers are willing to pay less to workers with less than completed higher education when the local labor market displays a greater density of those skills (see the first three coefficients in row 1). Employers are willing to pay slightly more to college graduates when the density of college graduates is higher, although this effect is not significantly different from zero.

The table further shows that employers are willing to pay more to workers of *any* skill level when the local labor market displays a greater density of higher education graduates. The positive spillovers of college graduates on less-skilled workers might be due to both complementarities and HCEs (as seen). As in Moretti (2004a), these spillovers are larger than those on college-educated workers.

The Overall Effects of Raising the Share of Higher Education Graduates

Because the presence of higher education graduates raises the attractiveness and productivity of a community, local leaders might be interested in attracting such individuals,

for which reason Fan and Timmins (2017) explore the effects of a hypothetical program that expands the demand for higher education graduates in Feira de Santana, a mid-sized municipality in Brazil's relatively poor northeast. The program raises wages offered to higher education graduates by 50 percent. Hiring college instructors for a local college, or hiring physicians and researchers for a local hospital, would exemplify this type of program.

Table 5.3 shows average program effects for individuals by educational attainment in the municipality. The program increases the number of higher education graduates in Feira de Santana by 17.2 percent. Further, it raises the density and share of college graduates. The inflow of higher education graduates attracts less-educated individuals as well, who arrive in the municipality to enjoy the presence of a greater share of higher education graduates and to benefit from the greater labor demand induced by their presence. Most immigrants are from neighboring towns. The table shows average effects for individuals in Feira de Santana, which, after the program, also includes immigrants from other municipalities.

As intended, average income rises by about 50 percent for college graduates yet also rises for less-educated individuals. For higher education graduates, the increase in income is the total outcome of the positive effect of the program itself, which raises labor demand for college graduates, and the positive (albeit small) effect of the greater presence of college graduates. For less-educated individuals, two competing forces

TABLE 5.2   **Local Labor Demand, Brazil, 2010**

Percent salary increase that employers are willing to pay in locations with:	Individual's educational attainment			
	Less than primary	Completed primary	Completed high school	Completed higher education
An additional 1 percent density of workers with the same educational level	−0.717	−0.795	−0.291	0.013[a]
An additional 1 percent density of college graduates	0.613	0.831	0.376	n.a.

Source: Calculations based on Fan and Timmins 2017. Data are from IPUMS.
Note: a. Preference coefficients for the corresponding attribute that are not significantly different from zero.
Results are for household heads age 25–35 years.

TABLE 5.3   The Effects of Raising Labor Demand for Higher Education Graduates in Feira de Santana, Brazil, 2010

Effects in Feira de Santana	Individual's educational attainment			
	Less than primary	Completed primary	Completed high school	Completed higher education
Percent increase in population	13.43	11.43	9.69	17.20
Percent increase in income	0.67	4.83	3.36	50.20
Percent increase in income due to change in density of own type of worker	−9.19	−9.39	−2.81	0.20
Percent increase in income due to change in density of higher education graduates	9.86	14.22	6.17	n.a.
Change in quality of life (expressed as a percent of income)	19.14	17.71	54.31	29.06
Due to change in population density[a]	−15.95	−12.85	−36.96	−22.26
Due to change in share of higher education graduates[a]	59.58	49.95	147.18	85.40
Total welfare change (expressed as a percent of income)[b]	19.81	22.54	57.67	79.26

Source: Calculations based on Fan and Timmins 2017. Data are from IPUMS.
Note: Estimates are for household heads age 25–35 years. Quality of life is the component of utility from a particular location that is common to all individuals of a given educational attainment. It is a function of location characteristics, net of housing prices.
a. This represent the contribution of change in population density and change in share of higher education to the total change in quality of life.
b. This represents the sum of percent increase in income and change in quality of life.

are at play: the supply increase of individuals of their skill level (which lowers their wages), and the positive spillovers from higher education graduates (which raises their wages). The latter effect prevails.

Moreover, thanks to the program, all individuals experience greater satisfaction with their location (alternatively, they gain "quality of life"). Although Feira de Santana becomes denser and housing prices rise, it also becomes more attractive given the greater presence of higher education graduates, and the latter effect prevails.

The total welfare effect of the program is the net effect of income growth and of change in quality of life. Because income grows and quality of life rises for all individuals, the program raises welfare for all individuals. Furthermore, Fan and Timmins (2017) show that if individuals did not value the presence of college-educated neighbors, quality of life would actually fall for all individuals. This would in turn result in lower population growth because some of this growth is due to the increased college share.

Thus, raising the demand for higher education graduates in Feira de Santana benefits not only those workers but also others. Benefits accrue to the original residents of

Feira de Santana as well as to those who move in (mainly from neighboring municipalities), regardless of their educational attainment. In contrast, individuals who stay in the neighboring municipalities experience (net) negative effects. On the one hand, these "stayers" benefit from lower density and lower housing prices; but, on the other hand, they lose quality of life and labor demand spillovers from the college share decline. Although the net effect of these forces is negative, on average each of these municipalities loses relatively little because individuals from numerous neighboring municipalities move to Feira de Santana.

Through this simulation, the authors illustrate how an area can benefit from policies that raise demand for highly educated individuals. An important message is that increasing college share has the potential of raising both quality of life and incomes. It can raise quality of life because individuals of all skill levels enjoy having skilled neighbors, either because they enjoy interacting with them or because their presence is associated with a greater volume of urban amenities. It can raise incomes because skilled individuals raise the productivity of all others.

Several caveats are in order. First, to conduct a full cost-benefit analysis of such a simulation, one would need additional information, such as the fiscal cost of the program. Second, in principle the total effect of this type of program (taking into account both the positive effects on Feira de Santana and the negative effects on the neighboring municipalities) can be either positive or negative. This depends on whether the gains of college graduates to Feira de Santana outweigh the losses to other municipalities, which in turn depends on the initial distribution of population and amenities (including college share) across municipalities. Third, one must exercise caution if designing policies favoring a specific location because these policies have a mixed track record.[26] Fourth, if all locations implemented this type of policy without increasing the country's aggregate human capital, the country as a whole might not gain. In particular, raising the share of higher education graduates in *each* location would ultimately require a nationwide increase in college share.

Conclusions

As in other regions of the world, in the LAC region, larger geographic areas attract more-skilled individuals. These individuals may not be interested in area size (or density) in itself but rather in the amenities, jobs, and college share typically found in large areas (as is the case in Brazil). Yet, by virtue of attracting more skilled individuals, larger areas are places with greater inequality. Migration patterns are part of this picture because migrants to large areas are more likely to be skilled than migrants to small areas. Large areas are also more likely than small areas to develop their own human capital than to "import it" from other areas.

Although the positive association between area size, education, and inequality has been documented for the United States as well (Behrens and Robert-Nicoud, 2015), we find that it is stronger for LAC. This may be because a smaller share of the population in the LAC region is skilled, and returns to

higher education are substantially higher. Yet it is also possible that locational attributes may be less evenly distributed across a country's areas in the LAC region than in the United States. For example, it is possible that only a few areas offer good job opportunities to college graduates.

Across LAC countries, differences in the share of urban population are mostly driven by the unskilled. When living in large areas, the unskilled tend to work in low-productivity services, such as wholesale, retail, hotels, and restaurants. To the extent that urban population shares continue to grow, fueled by the migration of unskilled workers to urban areas, the concern is that they will shift into low-productivity sectors. This will continue the trend (chapter 1) of shifting workers into low-productivity sectors.

Our estimates show that individuals of all skill levels prefer to live in areas with greater shares of skilled people. The latter contribute not only to quality of life in an area but also to workers' productivity. On average, returns to aggregate human capital in the LAC region are large, of about the same size as private returns. HCEs account for at least part of the returns to aggregate human capital. The least-skilled individuals benefit the most from an increase in college share, and individuals with the highest years of schooling benefit the most from an increase in average years of schooling.

Because at least part of the estimated returns to aggregate human capital are due to HCEs, it is efficient to enact policies that correct the market failure—for example, by subsidizing the formation or acquisition of skilled human capital in an area. This seems particularly true for small areas, which tend to have lower shares of skilled population and largely import their skilled human capital. Further research, however, is required to quantify the exact size of HCEs and of the optimal subsidy.

If returns to aggregate human capital were solely due to complementarities between skilled and unskilled human capital, policy intervention would not be required to correct a market failure. Nonetheless, policy makers might still want to enact policies to raise aggregate human capital because of the positive impact of skilled workers on the productivity and welfare of all workers.

Attracting skilled individuals to areas with low college shares may seem difficult, given that these individuals have a preference for areas with high college shares. Yet, the evidence in this chapter indicates that such areas (as well as others) can attract skilled human capital in the short run by improving connectivity with other areas, increasing the supply of amenities desired by skilled individuals, and raising demand for skilled human capital. In the medium and long run, however, their best strategy might be to develop human capital locally. As seen in this chapter, even keeping students in school for an extra year can yield large returns.

Annex 5A: Areas Used in the Stylized Facts

Country	Year	Administrative unit	Merged administrative units	Median (thousands)	75th percentile (thousands)
SEDLAC					
Argentina	2014	Urban agglomerate	n.a.	315	2,263
Bolivia	2011	Province	Cercado and Quillacollo; Andres Ibañez and Warnes; Ingavi and Murillo.	40	290
Chile	2013	Province	Some districts in Maramarga and Valparaiso; Santiago Metropolitan area and some districts of Cahapoal.	154	1,159
Colombia	2010	Municipalities	Pereira, La Virginia and Dosquebradas; Cucuta, Los Patios, El Zulia, and Villa del Rosario; Giron, Piedecuesta, Bucaramanga and Floridablanca; Soledad Barraquilla and Malambo; Palmira, Yumbo, and Cali; Valle del Aburra metropolitan area; Bogotá, Sibate, and Mosquera.	26	637
Costa Rica	2010	Canton	San José city covering selected districts from the following provinces: Alajuela, Cartago, Heredia, and San José.	27	316
Dominican Republic	2014	Municipalities	La Calena, Santiago de los Caballeros and Pedro García; National Districto and selected municipalities of San Cristobal and Santo Domingo.	12	225
Ecuador	2012	Canton	Guayaquil and Duran.	23	256
El Salvador	2014	Municipalities	San Salvador Metropolitan area and Cuscatlan.	10	110
Guatemala	2014	Department	n.a.	455	1,084
Honduras	2012	Municipalities	San Pedro Sula and La Lima.	11	93
Mexico	2014	Municipalities	Eighteen groupings in total. Examples: Tuxtla Gutierrez, Berriozabal, and Chiapa de Corzo; Morelia and Tarimbaro; Ramos Arizpe and Saltillo; Distrito Federal and selected municipalities of Mexico and Hidalgo.	34	835
Nicaragua	2005	Municipalities	n.a.	23	125
Paraguay	2008	Municipalities	Districts of Asuncion and additional municipalities from Central Area (such as Limpio, Villa Elisa, Luque)	13	202
Peru	2013	Province	Metro area of Lima and Callao.	50	705

(continued)

ANNEX 5A **Areas Used in the Stylized Facts** (continued)

Country	Year	Administrative unit	Merged administrative units	Population threshold 1 (thousands)	Population threshold 2 (thousands)
Uruguay	2011	Aggregated city ("localidad agregada")	n.a.	12	159
IPUMS					
Brazil	2010	Municipalities >20,000 inhabitants	n.a.	44	448
Colombia	2005	Municipalities >20,000 inhabitants	n.a.	34	458
El Salvador	2007	Municipalities >20,000 inhabitants	n.a.	36	95
Mexico	2010	Municipalities	n.a.	13	145

Note: n.a. = not applicable, indicating countries in which there was no merge of administrative units. IPUMS = Integrated Public Use Microdata Series; SEDLAC = Socio-Economic Database for Latin America and the Caribbean.

Annex 5B: Percentage of Employment in Services, by Educational Attainment

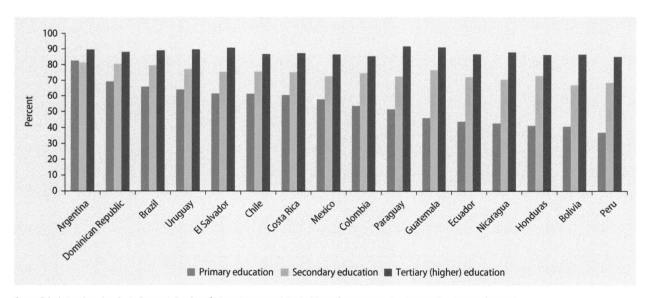

Source: Calculations based on Socio-Economic Database for Latin America and the Caribbean (for countries other than Brazil) and IPUMS (for Brazil).
Note: Figure refers to workers in the adult population (age 25–64 years). The figure shows the percentage of individuals of each educational attainment who are employed in services. For the definition of educational attainments, see the "Some Stylized Facts" section earlier in this chapter.

Annex 5C: Probability of Working in the Service Sector for Skilled and Unskilled Workers, by Area Size

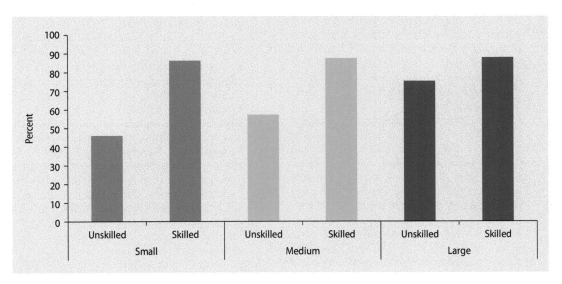

Source: Calculations based on SEDLAC (for countries other than Brazil) and IPUMS (for Brazil).
Note: For areas of a given size, the figure shows the percentage of workers employed in services for skilled and unskilled workers. The figure refers to workers in the adult population (age 25–64 years). Skilled workers have at least some higher education. IPUMS = Integrated Public Use Microdata Series; SEDLAC = Socio-Economic Database for Latin America and the Caribbean.

Annex 5D: Percentage of Urban Population Born Abroad

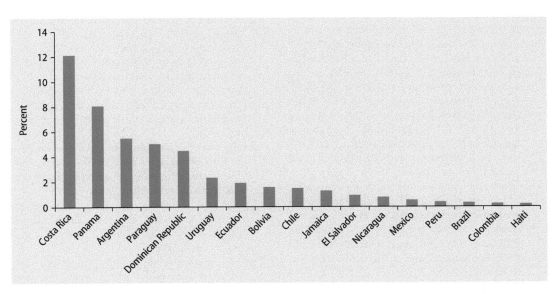

Source: Calculations using IPUMS.
Note: The figure shows, for each country, the fraction of individuals who were born abroad among those who are classified as urban by national statistics offices. Because households are not classified as urban or rural in Argentina or Uruguay, figures for Argentina and Uruguay are for total population. IPUMS = Integrated Public Use Microdata Series.

Notes

1. In this chapter, "skilled" individuals are those with postsecondary education. More specifically, the term comprises individuals with completed or unfinished higher education as discussed in the section on stylized facts and individuals with completed higher education as discussed in the subsequent two sections.
2. The definition of a "city" is in the "Some Stylized Facts" section.
3. Of course, this positive effect could also arise if skilled workers were complements among themselves. Following the literature (Moretti 2004a; Guo, Roys, and Seshadri 2016; Ciccone and Peri 2006), we assume that workers of different skill levels are complements and that workers of the same skill level are substitutes.
4. For each country, we calculate the average (over cities) of cities' average years of schooling, and cities' share of college-educated workers.
5. Specifically, we use level-2 administrative units. We follow the same criteria as in chapter 6 on the merging of administrative units (see table in annex 5A for details).
6. We adopt these cut-offs because the distribution of area size is highly skewed to the right. In other words, most areas are small, and a few areas are large. With these thresholds, the group of "small" areas comprises a large number of areas, and the group of "large" areas comprises a small number of areas. The groups are not equally sized, but they are relatively homogeneous on area size. To facilitate comparisons with the United States (Moretti 2004a; Behrens and Robert-Nicoud 2015), we define groups by population instead of by population density. Annex 5A lists the population thresholds used to build the area groups.
7. This value is the coefficient of the regression of log area share of skilled individuals on log area population, pooling data for all areas and countries. When country fixed effects are included, the coefficient is equal to 0.28. Both coefficients are significantly different from zero.
8. This is the average of country-specific elasticities, estimated separately by country. When pooling data for all countries, the estimated elasticity is 0.029; if country fixed effects are included in this regression, the estimate is 0.042.

9. Percent of skilled population is calculated relative to the population age 25-65 years in each country. Sources for LAC: SEDLAC for all countries other than Brazil; IPUMS for Brazil. Source for the United States: U.S. Census Bureau, Current Population Survey 2010. Returns to higher education in the LAC region are from Ferreyra et al. (2017). Returns to higher education in the United States are based on Card (2001) and Heckman et al. (2006).
10. Comparator countries include Indonesia, Kyrgyz Republic, Malaysia, Slovenia, Thailand, and Ukraine. Source: IPUMS. In selecting comparators, we apply a different criterion from that in chapter 2. Following other World Bank studies (such as Ferreyra et al. 2017), our comparators for LAC are developing countries from EAP and ECA with information on international migration at the area level in IPUMS.
11. In the data, recent migration can be measured by whether an individual currently resides in a different place from five years ago, in which case she or he has moved some time during the past five years. Following related work (Bayer, Kehoe, and Timmins 2009; Lall, Timmins, and Yu 2009), we focus on the 25–35-year-old group to capture own migration decisions (as opposed to one's parents), during the years in which individuals are most mobile (because they are less likely to migrate once they start a family).
12. Migrants might actually become skilled at their destination. Although we have no data to assess this possibility, Ferreyra et al. (2017) document that 80 percent of higher education students live with their parents during college, in which case they most likely do not move for college.
13. For example, in Colombia all large areas have at least one higher education institution, only 30 percent of medium-sized areas have one, and virtually no small areas have one.
14. The share of individuals employed in services averages 55 percent, 74 percent, and 87 percent among those with primary, secondary, and higher education.
15. We measure labor productivity as the ratio between value added and employment, using the GGDC 10 sector database for 2011 for the LAC countries with available data (Argentina, Brazil, Costa Rica, and Peru). We consider agriculture and mining as nonurban sectors.
16. These estimates arise from the first stage of the estimation of the determinants of city

productivity (see chapter 3). Returns to education are estimated as the coefficient on years of schooling in the regression of log wages on years of schooling, age, age squared, gender, marital status, and an area fixed effect. Because a separate regression is run for each country, we obtain returns to schooling for each country. These range from about 6 percent in the Dominican Republic, Nicaragua, and Peru, to about 11 percent in Brazil and Uruguay; across countries, their average is 8.92 percent.

17. Box 3.3 documents that this is indeed the case in Colombia, based on Balat and Casas (2017).
18. As in Ferreyra et al. (2017), higher education comprises both short-cycle and bachelor's programs, akin to associate and bachelor's programs, respectively, in the United States.
19. The U.S. average is for individuals age 25 and older. The LAC average is for individuals age 14–65; it is the average of the area college shares for the areas (and years) included in the regressions that estimate returns to aggregate human capital.
20. However, returns to aggregate human capital also appear relatively low in the United States when aggregate human capital is measured by the share of higher education graduates. Although the average city share of higher education graduates is larger in the United States (23 percent), it is still quite low. It is possible that returns to the share of higher education graduates are relatively low for the observed range of this share, but might be higher for higher ranges.
21. To obtain country-level returns, for each country we regress area-level productivity on the corresponding measure of aggregate human capital; these regressions control for area density, market access, air temperature, terrain ruggedness, and precipitation. To estimate area-level productivities, for each country we regress log wages on individual characteristics (age, age squared, years of schooling, gender, and marital status) and year fixed effects. We do not run these regressions for Argentina, Panama, or Uruguay because they have few areas.
22. This net effect might be positive as well because of complementarities among skilled workers. We follow Moretti (2004a, 2004b), Ciccone and Peri (2006), and Combes and Gobillon (2015) in assuming that skilled workers are substitutes among themselves and that an

increase in their share would drive down their wages, holding other things constant, by virtue of increasing their relative supply.
23. It is possible, however, that the high returns to an additional year of schooling reflect externalities arising from crime reduction. To the extent that people are more productive in safer places (see chapter 3), this might give rise to HCEs and be reflected in the returns to average years of schooling.
24. The estimation of these spillovers bears similarities to that of the estimation of returns to aggregate human capital, though it is not exactly the same.
25. These municipalities, with 97 percent of Brazil's population, are those with data.
26. See, for example, Neumark and Simpson (2015). In the same spirit, the World Bank's 2009 World Development Report argues in favor of spatially blind policies and mainly against spatially targeted policies except when countries are fragmented for linguistic, political, religious, or ethnic reasons (World Bank 2009).

References

Balat, J., and C. Casas. 2017. "Firm Productivity and Cities: The Case of Colombia." Background paper for this book. World Bank, Washington, DC.

Bayer, P., N. Keohane, and C. Timmins. 2009. "Migration and Hedonic Valuation: The Case of Air Quality." *Journal of Environmental Economics and Management* 58 (1): 1–14.

Behrens, K., and F. Robert-Nicoud. 2015. "Agglomeration Theory with Heterogenous Agents." In *Handbook of Regional and Urban Economics, Volume 5,* edited by Gilles Duranton, J. Vernon Henderson, and William C. Strange, 171–87. Amsterdam: Elsevier.

Card, D. 2001. "Estimating the Return to Schooling: Progress in Some Persistent Econometric Problems." *Econometrica* 69 (5): 1127–60.

Ciccone, A., and G. Peri. 2006. "Identifying Human-Capital Externalities: Theory with Applications." *Review of Economic Studies* 73 (2): 381–412.

Combes, P., and L. Gobillon. 2015. "The Empirics of Agglomeration Economies." In *Handbook of Regional and Urban Economics, Volume 5,* edited by Gilles Duranton, J. Vernon Henderson, and William C. Strange, 247–348. Amsterdam: Elsevier.

Duranton, G. 2014. "Growing through Cities in Developing Countries." *World Bank Research Observer* 30 (1): 39–73.

Fan, L., and C. Timmins. 2017. "A Sorting Model Approach to Valuing Urban Amenities in Brazil." Background paper for this book. World Bank, Washington, DC.

Ferreyra, M. M., C. Avitabile, J. Botero, F. Haimovich, and S. Urzua. 2017. *At a Crossroads: Higher Education in Latin America and the Caribbean.* Washington, DC: World Bank.

Guo, J., N. Roys, and A. Seshadri. 2016. "Estimating Aggregate Human Capital Externalities." Working Paper, University of Wisconsin–Madison.

Heckman, J., L. Lochner, and P. Todd. 2006. "Earnings Functions, Rates of Return, and Treatment Effects: The Mincer Equation and Beyond." In *Handbook of the Economics of Education*, Volume 1, edited by E. A. Hanushek. New York: Elsevier.

Lall, S. V., C. Timmins, and S. Yu. 2009. "Connecting Lagging and Leading Regions: The Role of Labor Mobility." *Brookings-Wharton Papers on Urban Affairs* 2009 (1): 151–74.

Montenegro, C. E., and H. A. Patrinos. 2014. "Comparable Estimates of Returns to Schooling around the World." Policy Research Working Paper 7020, World Bank, Washington, DC.

Moretti, E. 2004a. "Estimating the Social Return to Higher Education: Evidence from Longitudinal and Repeated Cross-Sectional Data." *Journal of Econometrics* 121 (1–2): 175–212

———. 2004b. "Human Capital Externalities in Cities." In *Handbook of Regional and Urban Economics, Volume 4*, edited by J. V. Henderson and J. F. Thisse, 2243–91. Amsterdam: Elsevier.

Neumark, D., and H. Simpson. 2015. "Place-Based Policies." In *Handbook of Regional and Urban Economics, Volume 5*, edited by Gilles Duranton, J. Vernon Henderson, and William C. Strange, 1197–1287. Amsterdam: Elsevier.

Quintero, L., and M. Roberts. 2017. "Explaining Spatial Variations in Productivity: Evidence from 16 LAC Countries." Background paper for this book, World Bank, Washington, DC.

World Bank. 2009. *World Development Report: Reshaping Economic Geography.* Washington, DC: World Bank.

Urban Form, Institutional Fragmentation, and Metropolitan Coordination

6

Nancy Lozano-Gracia and Paula Restrepo Cadavid

Introduction

This chapter attempts to explain the effect of urban form and institutional structure on productivity. Urban form has multiple spatial dimensions, such as the geometric *shape* of a city's urban extent; the *internal structure* of the city as determined, for example, by its transport network; and the *land use patterns* as reflected through the spatial distribution of population and buildings within a city. This approach goes beyond the economic literature's frequent focus on a single dimension of urban form: density. This chapter also explores an institutional aspect of urban form, namely the fragmentation of governance in large metropolitan areas and concomitant attempts at metropolitan coordination.

As with chapters 2 through 5, we focus on city-level productivity measures and introduce identification methods that aim to assess the links between urban form and a city's institutional structure, on the one hand, and city-level productivity on the other.

The same channels—sharing, matching, and learning—identified by Duranton and Puga (2004) to explain the emergence of

agglomeration economies are also at the core of the links between the spatial aspects of urban form and city productivity. Cities can use a given area of land and space in very different ways. Such differences are closely linked to the way transport systems are designed, the transport modes used (private or public), commuting times, matching between workers and firms, how firms interact with each other, and the type and intensity of human interaction.

In the economics literature, urban form has been linked to economic performance (Parr 1979; Ciccone and Hall 1996), sustainability (Breheny 1992; De Roo and Miller 2000), quality of life (Squires 2002), commuting costs (Wheeler 2001), and knowledge spillovers through human interactions (Lynch 1981; Jaffe, Trajtenberg, and Henderson 1993; Glaeser 1998). Overall, denser cities are thought to improve labor productivity through better matching of firms and workers and enhanced interactions that facilitate the spread of tacit knowledge, both of which are thought to occur more easily the closer people and firms are to each other (see Ciccone and Hall 1996; Rosenthal and Strange 2004;

This chapter is based on background papers by Duque et al. (2017a), Duque et al. (2017b), and Duque et al. (2017c). The authors thank Grace Cineas, Jane Park, and Wilson A. Velasquez for excellent research assistance provided for the work on this chapter.

Cervero 2001). Furthermore, recent work has shown that density of employment and population can lift innovation and overall metropolitan productivity. All else equal, the number of inventions (measured as patents) per capita is about 20 percent higher in a metropolitan area that is twice as dense—with density measured as employment density—as another metropolitan area in the United States (Carlino, Chatterjee, and Hunt 2007). Metropolitan sprawl is also associated with lower average labor productivity (Fallah, Partridge, and Olfert 2011).

However, although the links for the relationship between density and productivity are well established in the developed world, little research has been done for developing countries, including, prior to this book, for countries in Latin America and the Caribbean (LAC) (see chapter 3). Although such links have been established between density and productivity, much less is known about the links between other spatial dimensions of urban form, and productivity. Recent steps in this direction are presented in the works of Harari (2016) and Tewari, Alder, and Roberts (2016). The former focuses on the geometry of urban extents of over 450 Indian cities and finds that more compact cities, with an urban geometry conducive to shorter potential within-city trips, are characterized by larger populations, lower wages, and higher housing rents. These findings suggest that a city's residents value compactness as a consumption amenity. By contrast, firms do not appear to be directly affected by city shape in their location choices, and no evidence is found of a significant effect on the productivity of firms for that subset of Indian cities. In their analysis of urban development patterns of Indian cities, Tewari, Alder, and Roberts (2016) find a robust and positive relationship between a city's initial compactness and its subsequent economic growth, estimated using nighttime lights data.

The chapter's main findings are as follows:

- Although the average LAC city is rounded, has smooth borders (perimeters), has a dense street network, and tends to be compactly built, the region's cities show a great diversity of urban form.

- Beyond density, other spatial dimensions of urban form matter for productivity. Smooth, rounded, compact, and internally well-connected cities tend to have higher productivity levels than rugged or elongated cities, or cities with poorly connected streets.
- Large metropolitan areas in the LAC region comprise, on average, just over nine administrative units. Half of them have a metropolitan governance body. The fragmentation levels observed in the region are detrimental for productivity. However, unlike what Ahrend et al. (2014b) find for Organisation for Economic Co-operation and Development (OECD) countries, we find no evidence that the presence of a governance body at the metropolitan level mitigates the negative effects of fragmentation. This may point to ineffective governance arrangements or institutions that do not effectively support interjurisdictional coordination.

Urban Form and Productivity
Measuring Urban Form

In this section, we focus on spatial aspects of urban form; in the next section, we focus on its institutional aspects. Hence, "urban form" in this section refers to spatial urban form.

Economists have commonly focused on only one dimension of urban form: population density. In the economics literature, the common conclusion is that less dense cities face higher commuting rates (Wheeler 2001) and have lower knowledge spillovers (Lynch 1981; Jaffe, Trajtenberg, and Henderson 1993; Glaeser 1998), negatively affecting a city's productivity levels. Some authors argue that improved highways, public transit services (Glaeser and Khan 2004; Chatman and Noland 2014), and advances in communication technologies (Partridge et al. 2009) have helped reduce the productivity costs of sprawling.[1]

Density alone, however, does not describe all the multiple dimensions of urban form. Because it is measured as an average, it does not capture how density varies over space within cities as a result of the interwoven decisions of individuals, firms, and government on where to live, locate, or build infrastructure—often affecting, for example, street layout and land use patterns.

The urban planning and geography literature has long discussed different ways of characterizing urban form. For Batty and Longley (1994), for example, it has many dimensions because it includes all elements that form the spatial layout of cities, such as streets, buildings, or open spaces.

Cities may be characterized in three key, interrelated, dimensions of urban form:

1. The border's *shape* and *perimeter* (Angel, Parent, and Civco 2010a)
2. The *internal structure of the urban area*
3. The *land use* patterns observed within city boundaries and reflecting the use of space and the distribution of population within the city (see Whyte 1968; Batty and Longley 1994; Batty 2008; Prosperi, Moudon, and Claessens 2009)

These dimensions link to the efficiency of city transport, the cost of providing urban infrastructure and services, and environmental sustainability.

Border shape and perimeter
Whether the border of a city is shaped as a circle or as a tentacle-like shape has implications for trip lengths, as does the smoothness of its perimeter.

A perfect circle—the most compact geometric shape—has geometric properties such as a minimum surface area and a maximum accessibility from and to any interior point (see Thompson 1952; Angel, Parent, and Civco 2010b). A circular form can reduce trip lengths and increase accessibility compared with an elongated form.[2] Better accessibility improves matching between workers and jobs, consumers and goods, and firms and output markets, affecting productivity. Cities with compact and circular shapes also have lower costs per capita in providing basic infrastructure, which benefits from economies of density (Litman 2015).

A roundness index can be calculated to measure the degree to which the shape of an urban area deviates from its equal-area circle. It is calculated as the share of the total area of the urban extent that is inside the equal-area circle about its center of gravity.[3] The roundness index equals 1 for a perfect circle. As the index moves toward 0, the urban area becomes more irregular and less compact (see annex 6B).[4] For example, for all forms shown in the first row of table 6.1, the shape shown in column a will have a roundness value closer to 1, whereas that in column c will have a value closer to zero.

The smoothness of the perimeter provides another way to measure a city's compactness (Harari 2016), resting on the fact that, among all shapes of a given area, the circle has the minimal length of contact with its periphery. In a walled city, for example, looking at the smoothness of the perimeter would be a natural measure of its compactness, all else being equal (Angel, Parent, and Civco 2010b).

A smoothness index can be calculated as the ratio of the perimeter of the equal-area circle and the perimeter of the shape (Angel, Parent, and Civco 2010a). A smoothness index equal to 1 indicates a totally smooth perimeter found in a perfect circle. A smoothness index close to 0 indicates a highly irregular perimeter, which is very common in cities that have grown unplanned or are in rugged topography.[5] The shapes in the smoothness index row of table 6.1 provide examples of varying levels of smoothness. The shape in column a will have a value closer to 1 compared with those in columns b and c.

Internal structure of the city
The internal structure of the city affects the way people and products move within a city. A key element in this structure relates to two aspects of its connective infrastructure: the structure given by the layout of the road network in the city and the degree to which all segments in the network are interconnected. Figures shown under the "Internal structure" row in table 6.1 provide an example of street networks with different layouts and levels or connectedness of the network segments.

TABLE 6.1   **Examples of Urban Areas with High, Medium, and Low Values of the Indexes That Describe Urban Form**

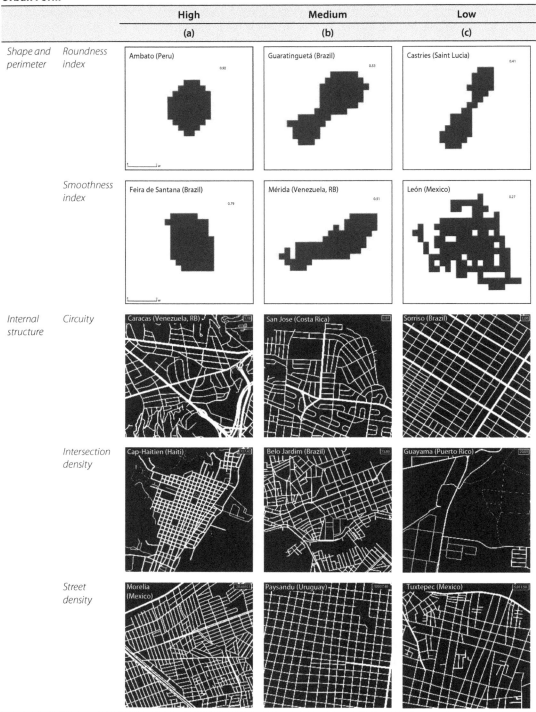

TABLE 6.1   Examples of Urban Areas with High, Medium, and Low Values of the Indexes That Describe Urban Form *(continued)*

		High	Medium	Low
		(a)	(b)	(c)
Land use	*Sprawl*	Ciudad Bolívar (Venezuela, RB)	Barcelona (Venezuela, RB)	Kingston (Jamaica)
	Fullness index	Kingston (Jamaica)	Maturin (Venezuela, RB)	Antofagasta (Chile)

Source: Duque et al. 2017a.
Note: Roundness and smoothness images represent the urban area. Circuity, street density, and intersection density show the layout of road networks in an urban area. Fullness pixels represent density of built-up area and sprawl pixels represent population density. See annex 6C for correlation matrix between urban form indicators.

Cities where the road network has grown unplanned—such as table 6.1, third row ("Circuity"), column a—are usually associated with longer commuting times and lower accessibility indicators than cities where the road network follows a grid pattern—such as table 6.1, third row, column c (see Boeing 2017). Regular urban structures and high-density street networks are associated with more efficient, shorter, and cheaper trips, which reduce congestion costs and allow for nonmotorized modes of transport (see Mills and Hamilton 1989; Bogart 1998; Bertaud 2004; Giacomin and Levinson 2015; Huang and Levinson 2015; Cervero and Kockelman 1997). Reducing the costs of interaction through better-connected networks and providing denser intersections can potentially improve matching and learning in cities.

To assess the degree of connectivity for all segments, we can use measures of intersection density and street density as indicators of a city's internal structure. Both metrics can provide information on the ease of movement within a city because circular roads and networks with many dead-end streets make it harder to reach all points in a city (see Boeing 2017). High values of these two measures are associated with high walking rates and an increased use of nonmotorized modes (Cervero and Kockelman 1997).

For this work, we calculate two indexes to reflect the internal structure of cities:

1. *Circuity of the road network.* This measure indicates how circular the street network's layout is. It is calculated as the average ratio between the lengths of each segment and the

straight-line distance between the two nodes it links (Boeing 2017). The circuity value is equal to 1 when all the streets in the network are straight and greater than 1 when the street network has curved roads.

2. *Intersection density and street density.* These indexes assess the degree of connectivity of the road network. Intersection density is calculated as the number of nodes divided by the area the network covers, considering only the set of nodes with more than one street emanating from them and thus excluding streets with a dead end (Boeing 2017). Street density is calculated as the sum of all segments of the street network (in km) in the undirected representation of the street network, divided by the area of the city in square kilometers (Boeing 2017).[6]

Land use patterns

How cities distribute and organize land can affect the way firms and households in a city interact. Cities can grow by sprawling, with population locating in patches of land that leapfrog through empty spaces, such as Ciudad Bolivar in República Bolivariana de Venezuela—table 6.1, sixth row, column a. Sprawling cities are inefficient in providing infrastructure and public services because the per-unit cost of development increases with sprawl (Knaap and Nelson 1992; Knaap, Ding, and Hopkins 2001; Fallah, Partridge, and Olfert 2011). Having less sprawl is conducive to lower commuting times, easier interactions, and higher productivity (Wheeler 2001). Land use interventions that contribute to the colocation of residences and jobs have the potential to increase employment accessibility (see Avner and Lall 2016; Quirós and Mehndiratta 2015). However, some separation of land uses may be desirable because allowing for the colocation of firms potentially leads to agglomeration economies. Given the difficulties in accessing information on effective land uses and the distribution of jobs for a broad set of cities,[7] we focus on two indicators of land use that look at the distribution

of the population (sprawl) and of the built-up areas (fullness of the form) within a city's boundaries (table 6.1):

1. *Sprawl.* The population distribution within city boundaries gives an indication of how land is used in a city (Fallah, Partridge, and Olfert 2011). A sprawl index that measures the degree of evenness in that distribution can provide a good measure of land use within cities. It takes a value close to 1 when the population is highly concentrated in a portion of the urban area. The sprawl index is calculated as the normalized difference between the share of areas with population density below the regional, or LAC, average density and the share of areas with population density above that (Fallah, Partridge, and Olfert 2011).[8] The population counts for each area within the city were retrieved from high-resolution population grid layers for 1990, 2000, and 2015 within the derived urban extents.[9]

2. *Fullness of the form.* This indicator measures the presence of built-up areas within the urban extent as a fraction of the total area. A fuller city where built-up area is denser, as shown in column a of the last row of table 6.1, may be conducive to more interactions; however, a high fullness can also suggest a city with little open space, which may undermine productivity.[10] A fullness index equals 1 for a city where all land is fully built up; an index close to 0 is indicative of a city with many unbuilt areas within its boundaries.

Measuring Productivity

One of the key challenges in studying urban form, and the relationship between such form and productivity, is the lack of comparable data across countries and over time. As seen in part I of this book, national definitions of urban areas vary, often dramatically, across countries; within a country, cities' administrative boundaries seldom conform to the actual extent of a city. And, although cross-sectional analysis measured productivity at city level in chapters 2 and 3, productivity is harder to measure over time; and that measurement over time is needed to tease out the links between cities' form and their productivity. Recent advances in Geographic Information Science (GIScience) and Computational Geometry provide some valuable methods for our purposes.

In a first attempt to provide a comprehensive characterization of urban form in the LAC region over time, we use nighttime lights (NTL) imagery, for 1996, 2000, and 2010, to identify all urban areas in the region, outline their borders, and extract indicators of their form.[11] This effort allows us to provide a standardized characterization of the urban form of 919 LAC cities.

As a starting point, all cities with more than 50,000 people in 2010 were identified and their shapes drawn using the areas outlined from NTL imagery for the three years (box 6.1). Further, similar to Tewari, Alder, and Roberts (2016) and chapter 2 of this book, we used an aggregate measure of luminosity extracted from NTL data to calculate an estimate for city output (Y) per square kilometers, which we take as a proxy measure of productivity.[12] Specifically, the sum of luminosity within the defined city boundaries extracted (see box 6.1) is calculated and then divided by the area in square kilometers.[13]

A Variety of Urban Forms in the LAC Region

Using the above indexes we now characterize urban form of LAC cities along the three key dimensions: shape, internal structure, and land use. The shape indicators for 2010 generally indicate that LAC cities are more rounded

---

BOX 6.1   Outlining Urban Extents Using Nighttime Lights

Two nighttime lights (NTL) products are available from the Defense Meteorological Satellite Program nighttime lights Operational Linescan System (DMSP-OLS) for the years included in this analysis: the so-called "ordinary" product (the NTL) and the radiance-calibrated product. For this work, we use radiance-calibrated yearly composites for 1996, 2000, and 2010 from the National Centers for Environmental Information of the National Oceanic and Atmospheric Administration to delineate urban extents. We chose the radiance-calibrated product over the ordinary product because the radiance-calibrated data correct for saturation issues found in the NTL product, avoiding underestimation of total light for the largest, and hence brightest, cities (Zhang, Schaaf, and Seto 2013). Previous work also suggests that the radiance-calibrated product is a better proxy than the ordinary product for socio-economic variables (Hsu et al. 2015; Ma et al. 2014). The composites used for this work have a spatial resolution of 30 arc-seconds (about 1 km at the equator).

Before the radiance-calibrated data can be used for analysis at the city level, including the delinea-

tion of city boundaries and later the aggregation of luminosity levels within such boundaries, several corrections are needed. First, the literature recognizes the problem of *overglow* in DMSP-OLS, which is the effect of light spilling beyond boundaries—for example, light from coastal cities appearing up to 50 km out to sea (Croft 1978; Wu et al. 2014).[a] To accurately allocate light intensity to a city and more accurately outline the form of cities, a correction for overglow is necessary. For this, we conducted a deblurring process by restacking the light on its source pixels (Abrahams, Lozano Gracia and Oram 2016). Yearly composites are not comparable because of the lack of the sensors' onboard calibration, so an additional intercalibration is necessary for a multitemporal analysis of urban form and city productivity in the LAC region (Cao et al. 2016; Hsu et al. 2015; Pandey, Joshi, and Seto 2013; Zhang and Seto 2011). Following Duque et al. (2017a), we used a threshold approach to delineate urban extents each year for LAC cities with more than 50,000 inhabitants in 2010. Map B6.1.1 shows three examples of the urban extents obtained using the NTL for 2010.

(continued)

BOX 6.1   Outlining Urban Extents Using Nighttime Lights *(continued)*

MAP B6.1.1   **Examples of Urban Extents over the DMSP-OLS Radiance-Calibrated 2010 Composite**

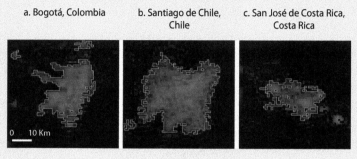

a. Bogotá, Colombia   b. Santiago de Chile,   c. San José de Costa Rica,
                                          Chile   Costa Rica

0   10 Km

Source: Elaboration based on Duque et al. 2017b.
Note: All maps are at the same spatial scale. The yellow line shows the urban boundary. Lighter-shaded (whiter) areas are those that have greater nighttime lights intensity.

Note: The radiance-calibrated product is used for the analysis, but in the text we generally refer to radiance-calibrated as nighttime lights.
a. These are problems not present in the data from VIIRS sensors, but those data are constrained by their short period.

than elongated, have urban perimeters that are more smoothed than complex, and have little open space inside city boundaries.

The degree of roundness in LAC cities tends to be high or close to 1, with median and mean values above 0.5 in the three years (table 6.2).[14] A slight decrease is observed between 1996 and 2010, indicating a weak trend toward less round and more elongated urban extents.[15]

Smoothness of the city's perimeter is also observed to decrease slightly over time, from 0.67 to 0.64, indicating a trend toward less smoothed urban perimeters, which could reflect urban growth along corridors linking other cities.

Internal structure indicators suggest that most LAC cities follow regular patterns that resemble a grid, with high values of intersection density and street density and with circuity levels very close to 1. The LAC region's average circuity value in 2010 was 1.04 (a slight increase from 1996), which suggests that street networks for most LAC cities are about only 4 percent longer than if they were all composed of straight lines. This regularity is in line with the findings by Huang, Lu, and

Sellers (2007), who also find that cities in Asia and LAC have very dense city structures relative to cities like Dallas in the United States and Sydney in Australia. In terms of circuity, the typical LAC city, according to our findings, looks like Bogotá or Mexico City. A small increasing trend is observed in circuity values from 1996 to 2010, which might be due to recent growth of settlements in more rugged terrain.[16]

The sprawl indicator suggests that LAC cities do not face high degrees of sprawl but have grown with compact patterns and high density overall, with the mean for 2010 being 0.575. Huang, Lu, and Sellers (2007), find that LAC cities are among the world's least sprawling cities. This does not seem to have changed much over time, with only a slight decrease from the 1996 value of 0.598. Completing the picture of urban form, fullness values are high overall with an average of 0.602 in 2010, showing a small increase during the period. These results are consistent with previous findings (Angel, Parent, and Civco 2010a; Huang, Lu, and Sellers (2007); Inostroza, Baur, and Csaplovics 2013).[17]

TABLE 6.2 Descriptive Statistics of Urban Form in LAC Cities

Variable	Year	p25	Median	p75	Mean	SD	Min	Max
Shape and perimeter								
Roundness	1996	0.725	0.828	0.879	0.787	0.121	0.266	0.947
	2010	0.712	0.782	0.877	0.782	0.121	0.35	0.952
Smoothness	1996	0.620	0.721	0.767	0.674	0.14	0.09	0.888
	2010	0.567	0.7	0.755	0.644	0.146	0.16	0.856
Internal structure								
Intersection density	1996	46.96	64.9	84.13	65.87	28.88	0.33	184.97
	2010	36.02	51.26	66.59	51.93	23.51	0.2	148.01
Street density	1996	7,988.80	10,452.40	12,985.50	10,474.40	3,791.50	135.9	20,669.20
	2010	6,428.30	8,643.80	10,773.70	8,582.40	3,249.50	87.1	19,040.00
Circuity	1996	1.019	1.028	1.046	1.037	0.034	1.002	1.419
	2010	1.021	1.032	1.05	1.04	0.029	1.004	1.241
Land use								
Sprawl	1996	0.479	0.595	0.721	0.598	0.177	0.108	1
	2010	0.475	0.583	0.677	0.575	0.148	0.074	1
Fullness	1996	0.494	0.63	0.763	0.618	0.192	0.014	0.996
	2010	0.482	0.623	0.739	0.602	0.181	0.028	0.993

Source: Calculations based on Duque et al. 2017a.

Note: Roundness ranges from 0 to 1. A high roundness value approximates a circle; a low roundness value approximates an irregular shape. *Smoothness* ranges from 0 to 1. A high smoothness value indicates a smooth perimeter; a low smoothness value indicates a highly irregular perimeter. *Intersection density* can take on values of 0 or greater. A high intersection density value indicates a higher concentration of intersecting streets given the city area; lower intersection density indicates a lower concentration of intersecting streets given the city area. *Street density* can take on values of 0 or greater. A high intersection density value indicates a higher number of streets; a low intersection density value indicates a lower number of streets. *Circuity* can take on values of 1 or greater. A circuity value greater than 1 indicates a street network that is not straight (curvy); a circuity value of 1 or close to 1 indicates a street network that is straight. *Sprawl* ranges from 0 to 1. A high sprawl value indicates a population that is evenly distributed; a low sprawl value indicates a population that is concentrated. *Fullness* ranges from 0 to 1. A high fullness value indicates a city that is compact and built up with minimal empty spaces; a low fullness value indicates a city that is sprawling with empty spaces. See annex 6C for correlation matrix between urban form variables. LAC = Latin America and the Caribbean; SD = standard deviation.

Figure 6.1 shows three indicators, one for each dimension of urban form analyzed. The three panels illustrate the large variability in the form of LAC cities. Some cities like Santa Cruz (Bolivia) or Puebla (Mexico) have high smoothness values, whereas cities like Medellín and São Paolo have low smoothness values (panel a).

The indicators for internal structure also show variability. Cities like La Paz, Santiago de Chile, and Lima have relatively high street density values whereas cities in Central America such as San Salvador (El Salvador) and Panama City (Panama) show relatively low values (panel b). The average LAC city seems to have high fullness, with the average fullness index just above 0.6 (panel c). Cities like São Paulo and Puebla appear to have densely built urban forms whereas cities like Brasilia and Cali tend to have a higher proportion of open spaces within their urban areas.

Despite large regional variability in urban form, little change was seen between 1996 and 2010 in roundness, smoothness, circuity, fullness, and sprawl, which changed less than 5 percent between 1996 and 2010 (figure 6.2). Such small changes stress the *persistence* of urban form, highlighted in the literature and chapters 1 and 2.

The indicators that changed most over the period of analysis are intersection density and street density, both decreasing by nearly 20 percent, suggesting that LAC cities have become less connected on average,

FIGURE 6.1 Urban Form in Latin America and the Caribbean Shows Great Variability

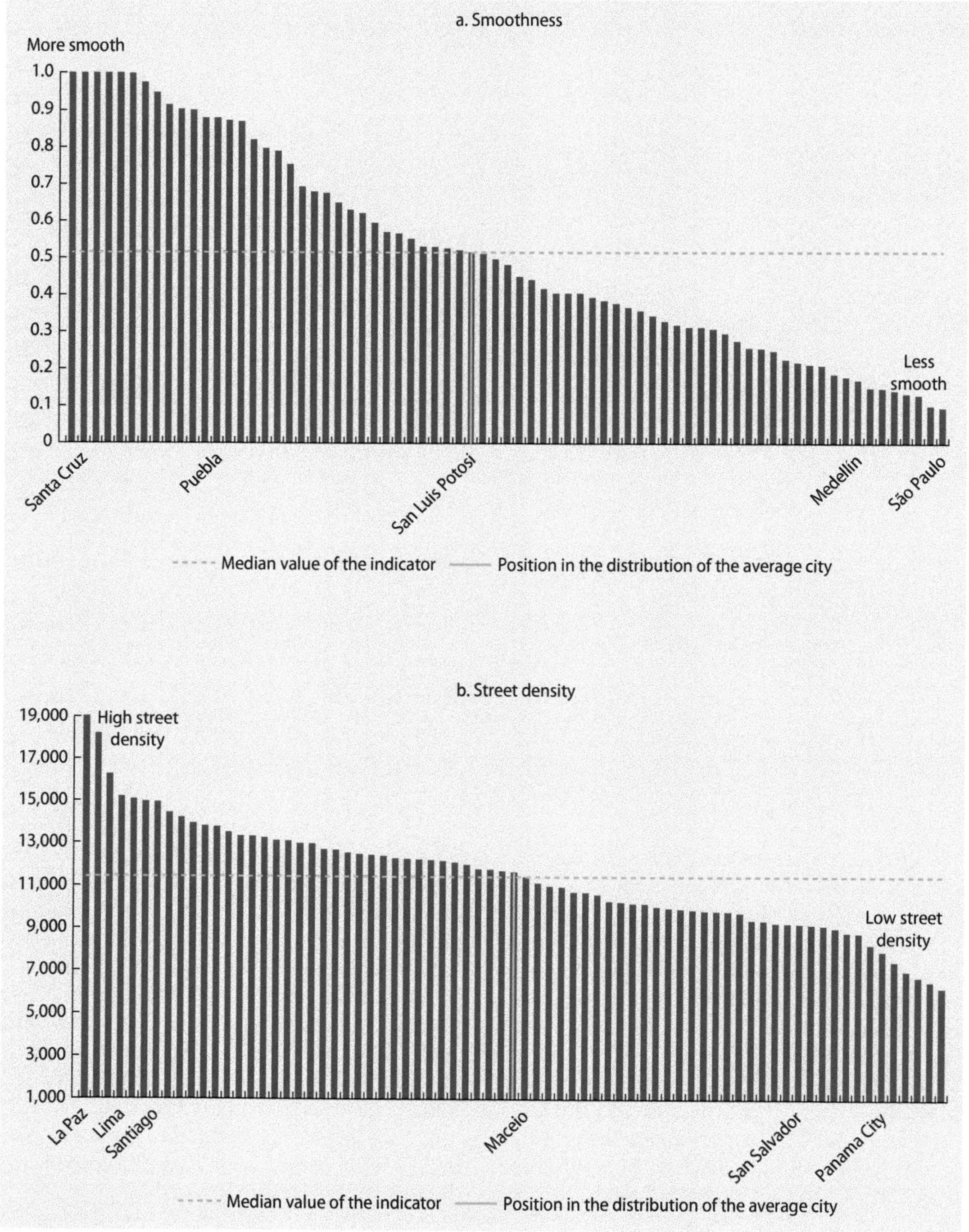
a. Smoothness
More smooth
1.0
0.9
0.8
0.7
0.6
0.5
0.4
0.3
0.2
0.1
0
Less smooth
Santa Cruz
Puebla
San Luis Potosi
Medellin
São Paulo
Median value of the indicator
Position in the distribution of the average city
b. Street density
19,000
17,000
15,000
13,000
11,000
9,000
7,000
5,000
3,000
1,000
High street density
Low street density
La Paz
Lima
Santiago
Maceio
San Salvador
Panama City
Median value of the indicator
Position in the distribution of the average city

(continued)

FIGURE 6.1 **Urban Form in Latin America and the Caribbean Shows Great Variability** *(continued)*

c. Fullness

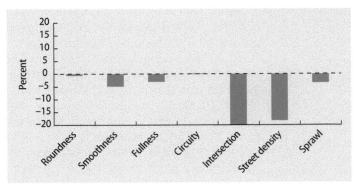

Source: Elaboration based on Duque et al. 2017a.

potentially hindering the exchange of goods and ideas. This result supports the claim in chapter 4 that transport investments in LAC cities have not enhanced city connectivity within the region.

In short, although the average city is round and tends to have smooth perimeters, a dense and gridded street network, and a densely built footprint, averages are deceiving and hide a wide diversity of urban forms in the LAC region.

Does Urban Form Matter for Productivity in the LAC Region?

Beyond describing urban form and trends in the region, we wish to establish whether there is evidence of links between the various urban form metrics and a city's productivity. Does form ultimately matter for productivity in LAC cities? To respond to this question, we estimate an empirical model that regresses city productivity on a

FIGURE 6.2 **Change in Urban Form Indicators, 1996–2000**

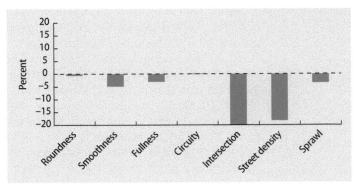

Source: Elaboration based on Duque et al. 2017a.

vector of urban form variables including shape, internal structure, and land use metrics and on a vector of control variables including geographic characteristics such as distance to the nearest international border, temperature, precipitation, and coastal location.

To construct a proxy of productivity at the city level we used the density of NTL emitted by the urban extent, controlling for population density.[18] We first regressed density of NTL on population density so as to isolate the variation in NTL density explained by population density alone. We then used the residuals from this regression as a measure of city-level productivity, where a larger residual indicates that a city of given population density is more productive. We used our sample of 919 cities across 32 LAC countries (see box 6.1).

One of the main empirical challenges in answering this question is to tackle the endogeneity of urban form when estimating its effect on productivity. City form can, in fact, be taken as the result of the interaction between decisions taken by firms, households, and government (within the constraints posed by topography); and hence both urban form and productivity stem from the interplay between agglomeration economies and congestion forces. In the simplest example, cities that grow dense can facilitate agglomeration economies by increasing proximity of firms, fostering productivity. But highly productive cities are also more likely to have governments able to invest in city centers, invest in better-planned street networks, and better manage land use patterns to reduce sprawl.

To tackle these endogeneity concerns, we adopted two alternative identification strategies. Strategy 1, as in Fallah, Partridge, and Olfert (2011), uses lagged explanatory variables from an earlier year to mitigate the direct simultaneity between the dependent and independent variables. In our case, we regressed city productivity in 2010 on urban form metrics from either 1990 or 1996, depending on data availability. Strategy 2 uses an instrumental variables (IV) approach, exploiting both temporal and cross-sectional variation in city shape. For this, we used the time variation of NTL data to build a panel of time-city observations. We followed Harari (2016) and constructed a synthetic instrument that uses the potential shape of a city as a starting point, and calculated the city form indicators on the basis of such

potential form.[19] Strategy 1 uses all seven urban form metrics, but strategy 2 is limited to using roundness and smoothness metrics only because these are the only two form variables for which instruments can be constructed (see Duque et al. 2017a).

The results confirm that shape matters for productivity in LAC cities.

Table 6.3 presents four specifications of the empirical model using strategy 1. Alternative specifications are used to disentangle the relative importance of the different urban form metrics, and to avoid problems of multicollinearity as some of the urban metrics variables are highly correlated.[20] Six of the seven form metrics are in the specifications in table 6.3. For purposes of simplicity, we do not present the variable for street density (it is highly correlated with intersection density). Similar results were found using strategy 2.

Our results confirm the importance of considering dimensions of urban form that go beyond population density when looking at city productivity. Three of the seven urban metric indicators are significant at the 90 percent level or higher in all model specifications in which they are included.

Regarding the shape of cities, we find that the coefficients for roundness and smoothness are positive and significant across all specifications.[21] Other things being equal, a more circular urban shape and a smooth perimeter are associated with higher productivity. This suggests that the way a city grows, within its boundaries and at its periphery, can have an impact on productivity. This implies that city leaders can influence the productivity of their cities with policies that shape the physical form they take. Infrastructure investments, land use, and zoning regulations not only are therefore tools for planning the form a city takes but can also—through their role in building the shape, texture, and land use of a city—influence productivity.

Changing our focus from the periphery to the internal structure, we find that having a dense street network (higher values of street density or intersection density) is associated

TABLE 6.3   Regression Results for Urban Form and City Productivity with Outliers

	(a)	(b)	(c)	(d)
Roundness (1996)			0.459***	
			(0.0656)	
Smoothness (1996)	0.496***			0.485***
	(0.1702)			(0.1584)
Fullness (1990)		0.683**	0.536*	0.433
		(0.3012)	(0.2981)	(0.3297)
Fullness^2 (1990)		−0.717***	−0.529**	−0.390
		(0.2400)	(0.2424)	(0.2607)
Circuity (1996)	0.125	−0.065	0.088	0.107
	(0.7760)	(0.7864)	(0.7815)	(0.7472)
Street density (1996)	0.406***	0.386***	0.364***	0.389***
	(0.0684)	(0.0677)	(0.0728)	(0.0749)
Sprawl (1990)	0.085			
	(0.0677)			
Constant	−0.732	−0.558	−0.634	−1.026
	(0.5758)	(0.8088)	(0.7401)	(0.7055)
N	919	919	919	919
R	0.282	0.269	0.279	0.283

Source: Duque et al. 2017a.
Note: The dependent variable is the residuals of the regression of nighttime lights density on population density. Street density 1996 has been rescaled (divided by 1×10^4). Robust standard errors clustered at the country level appear in parentheses. All models include controls for geographic characteristics as measured by natural amenities that are distances (in thousand kilometers) to international border, temperature, precipitation, and coast indicator, and include country fixed effects.
***$p < 0.01$. **$p < 0.05$. *$p < 0.1$.

with higher productivity.[22] Our results suggest that a 10 percent increase in intersection density would be associated with productivity levels that are about 39 percent higher. Although this may seem like a large effect, increasing intersection density by 10 percent would require significant efforts and investments. Rio de Janeiro, for example, increased its street density by only 4 percentage points between 1996 and 2010. On regularity of urban structure, our results show no evidence in favor, at least from a productivity perspective, of a regular gridded street network: the coefficient of circuity was found to be not significant across all specifications, after controlling for other measures of urban form.

For land use patterns, we introduce a quadratic term for the fullness variable to test whether there is a nonlinear relation between fullness and productivity. Despite having estimated coefficients for both terms of the expected sign and significance, we find the combined effect of fullness on productivity not significantly different from zero for most values of fullness. Finally, contrary to the results presented by Fallah, Partridge, and Olfert (2011), the sprawl variable is not significant across all specifications, which suggests that, after controlling for the shape and internal texture characteristics of the city, there is no evidence that the distribution of population density within cities, as measured through the sprawl index, affects their productivity. The results here suggest that building denser street networks in more elongated cities could lift these cities' productivity toward that of rounded, smoother, and more compact cities.

To summarize, urban form matters for city productivity in the LAC region, and specific characteristics (such as roundness and smoothness) appear to create more conducive urban spaces for firms and households to interact. We also confirmed the validity of moving beyond population density and broadening the measurements of urban form to include proxies of intracity connectivity and land use (such as built-up area fragmentation). The results suggest that policy makers have several instruments at hand to increase their cities' productivity by influencing the form their cities take. Although rounded, smoother, and more compact cities of a given population density tend to be more productive, the evidence suggests that a more elongated city could become more productive by improving connectivity, for example by building a denser street network.

Institutional Fragmentation, Metropolitan Coordination, and Productivity

This section moves beyond spatial urban form and focuses on institutional fragmentation.[23] In chapter 2 we saw that LAC stands out relative to other regions for its high number of multicity agglomerations (MCAs). LAC countries also stand out against those in North America and Western Europe for exhibiting a negative and significant relationship between the share of their population living in MCAs and their gross domestic product per capita. These results are consistent with the hypothesis that institutional fragmentation can have negative effects on national productivity.

In this section, we seek to assess whether the fragmentation of urban areas across different administrative units has an effect on productivity, and whether the existence of metropolitan governance bodies attenuates the negative effects of fragmentation. In contrast to chapter 2, we focus on productivity at the level of individual cities rather than at the national level, following the methods used in chapter 3 to control for the sorting of workers across different cities. We also expand the indicators of institutional

fragmentation and introduce metropolitan coordination proxies.

Most of the literature follows three lines of thought when looking at the links between the governance structures of cities and their economic performance: polycentrist, centrist, and regionalist.

The *polycentrist* view argues that institutional fragmentation in cities is equivalent to creating additional layers of decentralization that can, in fact, enhance economic growth (Fischer 1980) through two mechanisms: better information, which leads to more efficient provision of public goods (Ostrom 2010), and increased competition between individual local governments (Stansel 2005). This is consistent with the arguments put forward by Charles Tiebout in 1956, suggesting that competition between local governments leads to efficiency gains.

The *centrist* view argues that the presence of multiple local governments within metropolitan areas may generate coordination failures that reduce efficiency in providing transport infrastructure and land use planning, with negative repercussions for economic performance (Ahrend, Gamper, and Schumann 2014b). Fragmentation may also reduce a metropolitan area's ease of doing business because of the additional bureaucracy that it imposes on firms (Kim, Schumann, and Ahrend 2014) and the associated higher transaction costs and barriers to the diffusion of growth-promoting policies (Cheshire and Gordon 1996; Feiock 2009). The centrist view thus argues that the costs of fragmentation are higher than the efficiency benefits it may bring.

The *regionalist* view is a middle way between the two: it recognizes the benefits of local governments while highlighting the importance of metropolitan coordination, defined as the efforts of governmental institutions to manage and solve problems in common between municipalities (Ríos 2015). According to Grassmueck and Shields (2010), more important than the presence of multiple local governments is the way in which they interact and perceive each other. For a sample of OECD countries, Ahrend, Gamper, and Schumann (2014b) found that the presence of a governance body that coordinates municipalities halved the productivity penalty associated with fragmentation, measured by the number of municipalities in a given metropolitan area. Foster (1993) and Nelson and Foster (1999) also found empirical support for the regionalist view: they found a positive association between income growth and the presence of overarching decision-making mechanisms such as multijurisdictional, multipurpose regional governments. Also, the presence of single-purpose districts associated with large-scale infrastructure provision (such as water and wastewater systems) has been found to foster income growth.

Empirical studies looking at the role of institutional fragmentation and governance on economic performance have focused mostly on developed countries.[24] Further, their results do not *consistently* support one of the three views. In this section, we extend the interpretations to LAC, and test whether empirical data are supportive of one of these lines of thought.

Measuring Fragmentation and Coordination in LAC Cities

We focus on three variables to measure institutional fragmentation: the number of administrative units within a city; the number of administrative units per 100,000 inhabitants; and the share of the population living in the central city. Each covers different aspects of fragmentation as proposed by Hendrick and Shi (2015): fragmentation of a given urban extent; scale of institutional fragmentation; and dominance of the central city in the metropolitan region (table 6.4). All three variables are constructed using spatial data (box 6.2).

In a similar way, we focus on a subset of variables with the aim of covering the multiple dimensions of metropolitan coordination. Coordination can result from the presence of institutions (metropolitan governance bodies), coordinated planning processes (for example, for land use planning and mobility), or special-purpose entities that overlap with administrative units (usually for providing certain public services). We use three proxies (see table 6.4) to capture each of these dimensions: the presence of a metropolitan governance body; the percentage of municipalities covered by an integrated transport system; and the total number of single-purpose districts for public service provision in the metropolitan area (see box 6.2).

TABLE 6.4   Institutional Fragmentation and Metropolitan Coordination

Dimension	Description
Institutional fragmentation	
I. Size of region	Number of administrative units 2010
II. Political fragmentation	Number of administrative units per 100,000 inhabitants 2010
III. Central city domination	Central-city population share 2010, where the central city is defined as the city whose administrative area overlaps the most with the identified urban extent
Metropolitan governance	
I. Governance	Presence of a governance body
II. Land use plan and mobility	Percentage of municipalities covered by integrated transport systems (metro, bus) between municipalities and central city
III. Coordination for SPDs	Presence of an SPD for water
	Presence of an SPD for energy
	Presence of an SPD for waste collection
	SPD water + SPD energy + SPD waste = SPD sum

Note: SPD = single-purpose district.

BOX 6.2 Constructing Institutional Fragmentation and Metropolitan Coordination Variables

We used data from Defense Meteorological Satellite Program-Operational Linescan System (DMSP-OLS) NTL imagery (see box 6.1) to identify urban extents in the LAC region. We considered that a metropolitan area existed when more than one municipality or equivalent administrative unit intersected a single urban extent with more than 500,000 people in 2010. We used the administrative unit boundaries from the World Bank's LAC Geospatial Database, constructed for this book for this purpose (Branson et al. 2016). Metropolitan area boundaries were obtained by aggregation of all administrative units that intersected the same urban extent. We verified each obtained metropolitan area with ancillary information from official sources to include those municipalities that are part of the official metropolitan area denomination but were not intersected by the urban extent. Map B6.2.1 presents some examples of identified metropolitan areas: Mexico City, Rio de Janeiro, and Buenos Aires.

Using a combination of desk review and spatial data, we constructed a database to characterize the metropolitan areas in the region in terms of institutional fragmentation and metropolitan coordination. We used the administrative boundaries of local governments that conform with the metropolitan areas and distributed population data to calculate institutional fragmentation measures using geoprocessing tools in ArcGIS. Administrative boundaries were obtained from OpenStreetMap[a] and the World Bank's LAC Geospatial Database. Population counts at the administrative unit and urban extent levels were estimated using the Global Human Settlement Layer distributed population grids produced by the Joint Research Centre of the European Union (Freire and Pesaresi 2015; Pesaresi et al. 2015). All metropolitan coordination variables were obtained through a desk review using official information, further detailed in Duque et al. (2017b).

MAP B6.2.1 **Examples of Metropolitan Areas**

a. Mexico City   b. Rio de Janeiro   c. Buenos Aires

Source: Elaboration based on Duque et al. 2017b.
Note: Urban extents extracted from 2010 nighttime images (in red), over the Global Human Settlement Layer built-up layer for 2014 (Freire and Pesaresi 2015), with administrative boundaries (light purple).

a. For more information, see http://www.openstreetmap.org/copyright.

LAC Cities: How Fragmented? How Coordinated?

We limited our analysis of institutional fragmentation and coordination to metropolitan areas with more than 500,000 inhabitants in 2010 and more than one administrative unit overlapping with its urban extent. This corresponds to 110 of the 919 cities included in the urban form analysis (see the second section in this chapter, "Urban Form and Productivity"). This restriction in our city sample was to focus on "larger cities," usually thought to face the most challenging coordination issues. It also allows us to compare, albeit not perfectly, results with those from a study of institutional fragmentation and coordination in OECD countries

conducted by Ahrend, Gamper, and Schumann (2014).[25] In table 6.5 we compare the 110 metropolitan areas in the LAC region with the 225 metropolitan areas included in Ahrend, Gamper, and Schumann

TABLE 6.5 Institutional Fragmentation and Metropolitan Coordination, LAC Region versus OECD

	LAC[a]		OECD	
	Mean	SD	Mean	SD
Number of MAs > 500,000	110		225	
Average population of MA	2,257,472	3,309,093	2,072,762	3,552,573
Average population density of central city[a] (inhabitants per square kilometer)	3,339.251	2,025.94	1,877.66	1,901.62
Average population density of MAs (inhabitantss per square kilometer)	806.4	868.97	703.26	754.114
Average number of admin units per MA	9.39	11.42	86.19	135.76
Average number of admin units per 100,000 inhabitants	0.55	0.60	5.64	7.27
Share of MA population living in the central city[a]	38.83		72.98	
Share of MA with joint governance body	48.86		67.84	

Source: Elaboration based on Duque et al. 2017b and Ahrend, Gamper, and Schumann 2014a.
Note: LAC = Latin America and the Caribbean; MA = metropolitan area; OECD = Organisation for Economic Co-operation and Development; SD = standard deviation.
a. Differences may be a result of inconsistencies in how central cities are identified between Duque et al. (2017b) and Ahrend, Gamper, and Schumann (2014a).

TABLE 6.6 Top 15 Fragmented Metropolitan Areas, LAC Region versus OECD

Country	Central city	No. of admin. units[a]	MA population (2010)	Country	Central city	No. of administrative units[a]	Population (2010)
Mexico	Mexico City	76	21,242,585	France	Paris	1,375	11,693,218
Brazil	São Paulo	39	20,483,833	Korea, Rep. of	Seoul	964	22,529,435
Mexico	Puebla	38	2,805,693	United States	Chicago	540	9,461,105
Brazil	Curitiba	37	3,640,533	Czech Republic	Prague	435	1,829,843
Brazil	Ribeirao Preto	34	5,085,801	France	Toulouse	434	1,217,316
Brazil	Belo Horizonte	34	1,573,563	United States	New York	356	16,539,430
Costa Rica	San Jose	31	2,319,583	France	Rouen	346	698,385
Brazil	Porto Alegre	31	13,588,699	United States	Minneapolis	329	3,348,859
Argentina	Buenos Aires	31	4,103,952	France	Lyon	327	1,894,945
Brazil	Sorocaba	27	1,950,203	Austria	Vienna	313	2,683,251
Brazil	Londrina	25	1,041,624	Germany	Hamburg	308	2,984,966
Brazil	Brasilia	23	3,879,415	Australia	Melbourne	281	4,105,857
Brazil	Rio de Janeiro	21	12,104,842	Australia	Sydney	279	4,555,516
Brazil	Joinville	20	2,922,544	Germany	Berlin	276	4,374,708
Mexico	Oaxaca de Juarez	20	1,130,568	Spain	Madrid	272	6,507,502

Source: Elaboration using Duque et al. 2017b and Ahrend, Gamper, and Schumann 2014a.
Note: LAC = Latin America and the Caribbean; OECD = Organisation for Economic Co-operation and Development.
a. "No. of administrative units" refers to number of local governments operating in a metropolitan area.

(2014a) for 28 OECD countries (excluding Chile and Mexico).

The average metropolitan area in the LAC region and OECD has a very similar population of about 2 million. Population density is, on average, higher in the LAC region than in OECD metropolitan areas, particularly within central cities. However, metropolitan areas in the LAC region are much less fragmented than those in the OECD (table 6.6): 0.55 administrative units per 100,000 inhabitants versus 5.64. Administrative fragmentation is even more marked, with the average metropolitan area in the OECD having some 86 administrative units, against 9.39 in the LAC region.

About half of the metropolitan areas in the LAC region have a metropolitan governance body, against 68 percent in the OECD. The presence of governance bodies and other coordination mechanisms in LAC metropolitan areas is indicative by itself of an intent by policy makers in the region to foster coordination in large and fragmented urban areas. Below we examine whether these efforts are having any measurable impact.

Do Fragmentation and Metropolitan Coordination Matter for Productivity in the LAC Region?

To estimate the relationship between institutional fragmentation and metropolitan area productivity, we build on the two-stage empirical approach followed by Quintero and Roberts (2017) for LAC cities in chapter 3 and follow a similar analysis to the one conducted by Ahrend, Gamper, and Schumann (2014b) for OECD countries.

The first step consists of extracting the productivity differentials that result from population sorting: more skilled workers tend to prefer living in larger cities (see chapters 3 and 4). This is necessary because otherwise one may confound agglomeration benefits with productivity increases linked to having a more skilled workforce. From this first step we obtain the productivity differentials—which cannot be explained by workers' own observable characteristics—and regress them on institutional fragmentation variables, metropolitan coordination variables, and other control variables (table 6.4). We limit our analysis to the metropolitan areas in the previous subsection for which productivity differentials (estimated by Quintero and Roberts 2017) are available.[26] This constrains our sample to 73 LAC cities, across 14 LAC countries. Results are in table 6.7.

Columns 1 through 3 in table 6.7 replicate three of the specifications estimated in chapter 3. In all three cases, for our more limited sample of cities, we see that population density has essentially no estimated effect on productivity. This is the case even without controlling for a city's geographical characteristics and its stock of human capital (as measured by its average years of schooling).[27] Consistent with chapters 3 and 5, we also find evidence of strong human capital externalities (column 3). Columns 4 and 5 then add the fragmentation and metropolitan variables that are the core of analysis in this chapter. In both columns, this results in the estimated coefficient on the log of population density becoming both positive and strongly statistically significant. On first inspection, this would seem to imply the existence of strong agglomeration economies, even having controlled for human capital, in contradiction to results presented earlier in this book. However, this would be the incorrect takeaway because the regressions also control for area and include a variable (the number of administrative units per 100,000 inhabitants), the definition of which includes population. Given this, unlike the regressions in columns 1–3, the coefficient on population density cannot be interpreted as an estimate of the elasticity of productivity with respect to population density.

To see this, consider the implied effect of an increase in a city's population density that

TABLE 6.7 Regression of a City Productivity Premium (ln) on Institutional Fragmentation and Metropolitan Coordination Variables

Variables	(1)	(2)	(3)	(4)	(5)
Log(Population Density)	−0.002	0.005	−0.014	0.203***	0.205***
	(0.0271)	(0.0327)	(0.0259)	(0.0579)	(0.0607)
Log(Average Years of Schooling 2010)			2.011***	1.454***	1.449***
			(0.3408)	(0.3239)	(0.3414)
Log(Area km²)				0.264***	0.262***
				(0.0625)	(0.0644)
Log(Number of Admin Units 2010)				−0.172***	−0.173***
				(0.0614)	(0.0626)
Number of admin units per 100,000 inhabitants 2010				0.212***	0.210***
				(0.0700)	(0.0712)
Share of population living in central city 2010				−0.345***	−0.336**
				(0.1272)	(0.1360)
Governance body					0.021
					(0.0482)
Integrated transport system					−0.000
					(0.0006)
Sum (single-purpose districts)					0.029
					(0.0279)
log(Terrain Ruggedness)		−0.011	−0.016	−0.021	−0.022
		(0.0284)	(0.0223)	(0.0191)	(0.0204)
log(Mean Air Temperature)		−0.002	0.090	0.203***	0.189**
		(0.0960)	(0.0770)	(0.0706)	(0.0772)
log(Total Precipitation)		−0.007	−0.070	−0.112**	−0.093
		(0.0782)	(0.0623)	(0.0538)	(0.0611)
Constant	1.158***	1.166***	−3.580***	−5.450***	−5.551***
	(0.1704)	(0.2938)	(0.8357)	(0.9404)	(0.9727)
Country dummies	Y	Y	Y	Y	Y
No. of observations	71	71	71	71	71
Adjusted R²	0.641	0.619	0.768	0.832	0.826

Source: Duque et al. 2017b.
Note: City productivity premiums for metropolitan areas are estimated using Quintero and Roberts' (2017) narrow sample (restricted to prime-age men working in the private sector). Sum (single-purpose districts) refers to the presence of a single-purpose district for water, energy, and waste added together so that the max value for the variable is 3. Standard errors are in parentheses.
***p < 0.01. **p < 0.05. *p < 0.1.

results from a 1 percent decline in its area, holding everything else constant. The results in columns 4 and 5 imply that the effect of this increase in population density would be given by $\hat{\alpha}-\hat{\beta}$, where $\hat{\alpha}$ is the estimated coefficient on log (population density) and β is the estimated coefficient on log (area km²). For column 4, this value would be equal to −0.061, whereas, for column 5, it would be equal to −0.057. Hence, in both cases, an increase in population density resulting from a reduction in area is estimated to have a negative effect on productivity. This is consistent with the results presented in chapter 2, where urban areas in the LAC region are shown to be relatively dense, not so much because they have higher populations but because their populations tend to be squeezed into smaller areas.[28]

Fragmentation—as measured by the number of administrative units and the number of administrative units per 100,000 inhabitants—is found to matter for productivity. As observed in table 6.7 (columns 4 and 5) both variables are statistically significant, albeit having different signs (the first negative, the second positive). Our results, combined with the results from chapter 2, are consistent with the hypothesis that fragmentation may be dampening the benefits of agglomeration economies in LAC cities. These results

suggest the presence of nonlinearities in the relationship between the fragmentation of a metropolitan area and its productivity and that, starting from a certain level of fragmentation, the benefits of more responsive local government or greater competition can compensate for costs due to coordination failures.

Figure 6.3 visualizes the relationship between fragmentation and productivity, and sheds more light on its nonlinear characteristics. This representation of the results shown in table 6.7, column 4, summarizes the net effect of increasing the number of administrative units, holding population size constant, for cities having 500,000, 1 million, or 10 million inhabitants.

The main message from the figure is that in LAC cities the negative effects of fragmentation dominate, and, given current structures, only extreme fragmentation would

FIGURE 6.3   What Levels of Fragmentation Are Needed to Reap the Benefits?

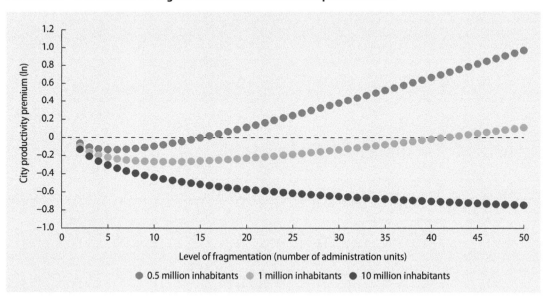

Source: Calculations based on Duque et al. 2017b.
Note: The figure displays the net effects of different fragmentation levels for metropolitan areas of different population sizes (0.5 million, 1 million, and 10 million) using the coefficients for number of administrative units and number of administrative units per 100,000 inhabitants in 2010 (from column 3, table 6.7).

lead to any benefits and only then for cities that are not too populous. A metropolitan area of 500,000 inhabitants would need at least 16 administrative units to start reaping any benefits, and a metropolitan area of 1 million inhabitants at least 42 administrative units. Because the average metropolitan area in the LAC region has 9.39 administrative units, our results suggest that, in practice, most LAC metropolitan areas are probably being affected negatively by their fragmentation (rather than benefitting from it). For a city of 10 million inhabitants, the net effect of fragmentation on productivity is negative at all levels of fragmentation. These results are similar to those in Ahrend, Gamper, and Schumann (2014b) and are consistent with the centralist view that argues for the presence of coordination failures and their negative repercussions on economic performance. Finally, we find that an increase in the central city domination—measured as the share of the population in the metropolitan area living in the central city—may negatively affect economic performance.

We find no evidence that metropolitan coordination variables have an effect on economic performance (see table 6.7, column 5).[29] In fact, contrary to what was found by Ahrend, Gamper, and Schumann (2014b), none of these variables appears significant. There is therefore no evidence in favor of the regionalist view because our results show that the presence of a governance body or integrated public services does not necessarily foster increased productivity for LAC cities. However, these last results need to be viewed with caution because they are conditioned on the variables used to measure the degree of metropolitan coordination. For example, it is quite possible that a metropolitan coordination body is in place, at least on paper, but that it is not effective in practice in solving coordination failures. To fully understand the role of such bodies in reducing the perils of fragmentation in the LAC region, one

likely needs to expand the desk review approach (used to gather the metropolitan variables in this chapter) to include variables that reflect reality on the ground, for example, through a detailed city survey.

Conclusions

This chapter suggests that the average LAC city is rounded and has smooth perimeters and a dense street network. Controlling for a city's average population density, these characteristics seem to be positively linked to a city's economic performance, likely supporting the emergence of agglomeration economies through different mechanisms. An important outcome is that a city can grow in different shapes and still achieve high productivity by guaranteeing a high rate of inner-city connectedness (equally, a compact but poorly connected city can show low productivity.) The results also underscore the fact that urban form tends to persist over time, requiring policy makers to think far ahead and ensure good accessibility within cities. This has important implications for policy makers because mayors often ask what they can do to improve the productivity of their cities. City planning and land management policies are not often regarded as instruments to foster productivity and growth in cities. The results in this chapter suggest otherwise: these are important tools that local governments have at hand to increase productivity in LAC cities.

Institutional fragmentation matters for productivity, and most metropolitan areas in the region are hurt by it; but there is no evidence of metropolitan coordination mitigating these impacts. This raises doubts over the effectiveness of current bodies for metropolitan coordination, in part stemming from overlapping responsibilities across local governments and government agencies, and from these bodies' limited authority.

Annex 6A: Seventy-Three Cities in Institutional Fragmentation and Coordination Analysis

Country	Central city
Brazil	Florianopolis
Mexico	Tuxtla Gutierrez
Colombia	Pereira (Centro Occidente)
Mexico	Morelia
Peru	Arequipa
Brazil	Joinville
Argentina	Salta
Brazil	Ribeirao Preto
Mexico	Cancun
Brazil	Londrina
Guatemala	Quetzaltenango
Mexico	Veracruz
Brazil	Sorocaba
Mexico	Saltillo
Mexico	Tampico
Colombia	Cucuta
Brazil	Cuiaba
Mexico	Chihuahua
Brazil	Sao Jose Dos Campos
Peru	Trujillo
Brazil	Aracaju
Mexico	Aguascalientes
Argentina	Tucuman
Mexico	Queretaro
Mexico	Merida
Argentina	Mendoza
Mexico	Cuernavaca
Brazil	Teresina
Bolivia	Cochabamba
Mexico	Torreon
Brazil	Joao Pessoa
Brazil	Maceio
Mexico	San Luis Potosi
Colombia	Bucaramanga
Panama	Panama City
Brazil	Natal
Brazil	Sao Luis

Country	Central city
Argentina	Rosario
Brazil	Vitoria
Bolivia	Santa Cruz
Brazil	Santos
Argentina	Cordoba (Capital)
Uruguay	Asuncion
Bolivia	La Paz
San Salvador	San Salvador
Brazil	Manaus
Colombia	Barranquilla
Brazil	Goiania
Brazil	Belem
Brazil	Brasilia
Mexico	Toluca
Costa Rica	San Jose
Brazil	Campinas
Colombia	Cali
Ecuador	Guayaquil
Mexico	Puebla
Brazil	Curitiba
Guatemala	Guatemala
Brazil	Salvador Bahia
Brazil	Fortaleza
Colombia	Medellín
Dominican Republic	Santo Domingo
Brazil	Porto Alegre
Brazil	Recife
Mexico	Monterrey
Brazil	Belo Horizonte
Mexico	Guadalajara
Chile	Santiago
Colombia	Bogotá
Peru	Lima
Brazil	Rio de Janeiro
Mexico	Mexico City
Brazil	São Paulo

Annex 6B: Urban Form Indicators

Roundness index

Draw the equal-areas circle about the proximate center C_p and calculate the area of overlap O_s of the equal-area circle and the shape. The following is the formula for calculating the Exchange Index I_x:

$$I_X = {O_s}\Big/{A}$$

(Angel, Parent, and Civco 2010b).

Smoothness index

Find the perimeter P of the shape. The following is the formula for calculating the Exchange Index I_p:

$$I_p = P_A \,/\, P = (2\sqrt{\pi A}) \,/\, R$$

(Angel, Parent, and Civco 2010b).

Fullness index

Calculate the radius r_A of a small neighborhood in the shape, so that $\pi r^2{}_A = A/100$, with

$$r_A = \sqrt{(A / 100\pi)}.$$

Find the average fullness of the shape, F_S, as the average of the fullness F_i of a small circle of radius r_A about the center of every pixel i in the shape

$$F_S = \left(\sum_{i=1}^{m} F_i\right) / n$$

(Angel, Parent, and Civco 2010b).

Circuity

Circuity divides the sum of all edge lengths by the sum of the great-circle distances between the nodes incident (element of a graph) to each edge. This is the average ratio between an edge length and the straight-line distance between the two nodes it links (Boeing 2017). The unweighted circuity of an area m is calculated as follows:

$$C_{u,m} = \frac{m^{D_N}}{m^{D_E}}$$

where

$C_{u,m}$ is the average unweighted circuity in area m,

m^{D_N} is the sum of the network distances between all origin-destination pairs in the sample, and

m^{D_E} is the sum of the Euclidean distances between all origin-destination pairs in the sample (Giacomin and Levinson 2015).

Intersection density

Intersection density is the node density of the set of nodes with more than one street emanating from them (thus excluding dead ends) (Boeing 2017).

Street density

Street density is the sum of all edges in the undirected (an undirected graph's edges point mutually in both directions) representation of the graph (an abstract representation of a set of elements and the connections between them) (Boeing 2017).

Sprawl index

Metropolitan sprawl is measured as follows:

$$Sprawl = ((L\% - H\%)+1)) \times 0.5$$

where $L\%$ is the share of the metropolitan population living in block groups with population density below the overall metropolitan median block group. $H\%$ is the share of metropolitan population living in block groups with density above that of the overall metropolitan median block group (Fallah, Partridge, and Olfert 2011).

Annex 6C: Correlation Matrix between Urban Form Variables

	(1)	(2)	(3)	(4)	(5)	(6)	(7)
Roundness (1996)	1						
Smoothness (1996)	0.7453*	1					
Fullness (1990)	−0.1573*	−0.3100*	1				
Intersection density (1996)	0.1427*	−0.0309	0.3429*	1			
Street density (1996)	0.1527*	−0.0465	0.4361*	0.9470*	1		
Circuity (1996)	−0.1993*	−0.1172*	−0.0586	−0.3901*	−0.4351*	1	
Sprawl (1990)	0.0422	0.2216*	−0.7122*	−0.5454*	−0.5939*	0.2032*	1

Note: * Denotes significance at 5 percent.

Notes

1. Sprawling is usually referred to as low-density expansion of cities, or density decline (Brueckner and Fansler 1983; Civco et al. 2000; Fulton et al. 2001).
2. *Accessibility* is defined as the number of points that can be reached in a predefined period, for example one hour.
3. The roundness index has been referred to in the geography literature as the exchange index. We refer to it here as roundness for ease of interpretation (see Angel, Parent, and Civco 2010b).
4. The Shape Metrics Toolbox was used to calculate the shape metrics of the urban extent polygons. This software is intellectual property of the Center for Land Use Education and Research at the University of Connecticut (http://clear.uconn.edu/tools/Shape_Metrics/index.htm).
5. The correlation between roundness and smoothness is 0.93, hence the measures are not used concurrently in the regressions.
6. The undirected representation of a street network considers that all nodes of the network point in all directions.
7. Ideally, one would like to build indicators that consider the variation in actual land uses, but such information is rarely available in LAC cities; and, although there is work using satellite imagery to obtain an approximation of land use through land cover classes, such efforts are time and computer intensive and require high resolution (day-time) satellite imagery (see Antos et al. 2016).
8. Because population is available at a spatial resolution of 250 meters, the distribution of reference is the distribution of 250-meter squares that fall within the boundaries of all cities in our sample. Population density levels are calculated for each square (or pixel) and hence not at the aggregate city level.
9. We used the GHS-Pop layers as outlined in Pesaresi et al. (2015). An important constraint of this indicator is that it does not take into account the actual height of buildings, but assumes that population is equally distributed in all built-up areas in an administrative unit.
10. Recent work by the World Health Organization suggests a positive relationship between urban green space and health, which may in turn affect productivity (WHO 2016).
11. NTL products have high correlation with human activities (Hsu et al. 2015), and have been used previously for regional and global analysis of urbanization (Cheng et al. 2016; Pandey, Joshi, and Seto 2013; Sutton, Cova, and Elvidge 2006; Zhang and Seto 2011; Zhou, Hubacek, and Roberts 2015; Zhou et al. 2015), population modeling (Anderson et al. 2010; Lo 2001), and economic performance (Cao et al. 2016; Forbes 2013; Henderson, Storeygard, and Weil 2012; Shi et al. 2014; Small, Elvidge, and Baugh 2013; Chen and Nordhaus 2011). NTL data are also used in chapters 1, 2, and 4 of this book.
12. For a discussion on the use of luminosity density as a proxy for economic statistics, see Chen and Nordhaus (2011).
13. Although the more recent VIIRS NTL data used in chapter 2 overcome some of the challenges of the DMSP-OLS data, they lack the time dimension needed for analyzing urban form over time (they are available only since 2013).

14. Because of space limitations, table 6.2 shows statistics for only 1996 and 2010.

15. Huang, Lu, and Sellers (2007) find that LAC cities are more elongated than those in Asia and Europe, which tend to be more circular; LAC cities are less elongated than those in the United States. Shanghai in China and Manchester in the United Kingdom represent the average circular city in their regions whereas Boston has a more elongated shape and represents the average city in the United States. Huang, Lu, and Sellers (2007) use satellite images of 77 metro areas in Asia, Australia, Europe, Latin America, and the United States to calculate seven spatial metrics that capture five dimensions of urban form. Note that Huang, Lu, and Sellers (2007) group Japan with Europe, not with Asia

16. Expansion in LAC cities in 2000–10 was in terrains with an average slope above 16 percent (Duque et al. 2017c).

17. Huang, Lu, and Sellers (2007) use a measure called porosity that measures the ratio of open space to total urban area, which can be understood as a complement to measures like fullness and sprawl used in this book. They find that LAC has less open space than Asia, Europe, and the United States, and slightly more than Australia.

18. Measured as the natural logarithm of deblurred NTL (lumens) per km². This is consistent with measures used in previous chapters; by dividing both sides of the equation by city area, this is only a rescaling exercise to facilitate comparison across cities and interpretation.

19. Following Harari (2016), the identification relies on the fact that exogenous changes in the city form over time can result from encountering topographic obstacles along its expansion path.

20. The following urban form metrics were found to be highly positively correlated: *roundness* and *smoothness*, and *intersection density* and *street density*. There is also a high and negative correlation between *fullness* and *sprawl*.

21. Similar results are found using strategy 2 for the coefficient on roundness, which is positive and highly significant at the 5 percent level. The coefficient of smoothness was found to be negative but not significant.

22. Nonlinear relationships were tested but found to be nonsignificant. Results from intersection density are not presented in the table but are similar to those of street density. This is expected because these two variables are highly positively correlated.

23. Although institutional fragmentation and metropolitan governance are, on their own, key issues to be studied and understood in depth, we focus here only on their effect on city productivity, given the overall focus of the book. We leave the in-depth study of these two topics for further research.

24. See, for example, Ahrend, Gamper, and Schumann 2014b; Carr and Feiock 1999; Parks and Oakerson 1989; Brezzi and Veneri 2014. These studies focus on metropolitan governance in the United States, OECD countries, and the European Union.

25. Analysis by Ahrend, Gamper, and Schumann (2014) includes metropolitan areas with a population of 500,000 or more, similar to the population threshold in this book. However, differences in how metropolitan areas are delineated may affect comparability of indicators. The metropolitan areas defined by Ahrend, Gamper, and Schumann (2014) are functional economic areas characterized by a densely inhabited "city" and a commuting zone whose labor market is highly integrated with the core. This analysis relies on identifying metropolitan areas through use of NTL. The city cores in Ahrend, Gamper, and Schumann (2014) are defined by the LandScan population database. Polycentric cores and the hinterlands of the functional areas are identified on the basis of commuting data (travel from home to work) in 2000 (census year) with the requirement that more than 15 percent of the resident population of any of the cores commutes to work in the other core.

26. In their study, the authors use micro data on nominal hourly wages in the main occupation. As independent variables, they use a vector of observable characteristics per worker (age, age squared, gender, marital status, and years of education completed) and municipality fixed effects.

27. In contrast, chapter 3 reports the absence of a significant relationship between productivity and population density only after controlling for geographical characteristics, human capital, and market access.

28. Similar nonlinearities determine the effect of a change in population on productivity, which

by definition, would be a function of the number of administrative units per 100k individuals and the percentage of the population in the central city. Although marginal effects for all population levels are not presented here because of space constraints, the resulting nonlinear function suggests a positive marginal effect that increases with population up to an inflection point that occurs at population levels of about 10 million people when the marginal effect starts decreasing, but remains positive.

29. Results for institutional fragmentation and metropolitan coordination variables remain the same after including a series of control variables (table 6.7, column 5).

References

Abrahams, A., N. Lozano Gracia, and C. Oram. 2016. "Deblurring DSMP Nighttime Lights." Working paper, World Bank, Washington, DC.

Ahrend, R., C. Gamper, and A. Schumann. 2014a. "The OECD Metropolitan Governance Survey." Regional Development Working Papers, Organisation for Economic Co-operation and Development, Paris.

———. 2014b. "What Makes Cities More Productive? Evidence on the Role of Urban Governance from Five OECD Countries." OECD Regional Development Working Papers, 2014/05, OECD Publishing.

Anderson, S. J., B. T. Tuttle, R. L. Powell, and P. C. Sutton. 2010. "Characterizing Relationships between Population Density and Nighttime Imagery for Denver, Colorado: Issues of Scale and Representation." *International Journal of Remote Sensing* 31 (21): 5733–46.

Angel, S., J. Parent, and D. Civco. 2010a. "The Fragmentation of Urban Footprints: Global Evidence of Urban Sprawl 1990–2000." Lincoln Institute of Land Policy Working Paper, Cambridge, MA.

———. 2010b. "Ten Compactness Properties of Circles: Measuring Shape in Geography." *Canadian Geographer* 54 (4): 441–61.

Antos, S. E., S. V. Lall, and N. Lozano Gracia. 2016. "The Morphology of African Cities." Policy Research Working Paper 7911, World Bank, Washington, DC.

Avner, Paolo, and Somik V. Lall. 2016. "Matchmaking in Nairobi: The Role of

Land Use." Policy Research Working Paper No. 7904, World Bank, Washington, DC.

Batty, M. 2008. "The Size, Scale, and Shape of Cities." *Science* 319: 769.

Batty, M., and P. Longley. 1994. *Fractal Cities: A Geometry of Form and Function.* London: Academic Press.

Bertaud, A. 2004. *The Spatial Organization of Cities: Deliberate Outcome or Unforeseen Consequence?* Berkeley, CA: Institute of Urban and Regional Development.

Boeing, G. 2017. "OSMnx: New Methods for Acquiring, Constructing, Analyzing, and Visualizing Complex Street Networks." Working Paper, University of California, Berkeley.

Bogart, W. T. 1998. *The Economics of Cities and Suburbs.* Upper Saddle River, NJ: Pearson Education Company.

Branson, J., A. Campbell-Sutton, G. M. Hornby, D. D. Hornby, and C. Hill. 2016. "A Geospatial Database for Latin America and the Caribbean," draft version 1. University of Southampton, Southampton, U.K.

Breheny, M. J., ed. 1992. *Sustainable Development and Urban Form.* London: Pion Limited.

Brezzi, M., and P. Veneri. 2014. "Assessing Polycentric Urban Systems in the OECD: Country, Regional and Metropolitan Perspectives." Regional Development Working Paper No. 2014/01, OECD, Paris.

Brueckner, J., and D. A. Fansler. 1983. "The Economics of Urban Sprawl: Theory and Evidence on the Spatial Sizes of Cities." *Review of Economics and Statistics* 65 (3): 479–82.

Cao, Z., Z. Wu, Y. Kuang, N. Huang, and M. Wang. 2016. "Coupling an Intercalibration of Radiance-Calibrated Nighttime Light Images and Land Use/Cover Data for Modeling and Analyzing the Distribution of GDP in Guangdong, China." *Sustainability* 8 (2): 1–18.

Carlino, G. A., S. Chatterjee, and R. M. Hunt. 2007. "Urban Density and the Rate of Invention." *Journal of Urban Economics* 61 (3): 389–419.

Carr, J. B., and R. C. Feiock. 1999. "Metropolitan Government and Economic Development." *Urban Affairs Review* 34 (3): 476–88.

Cervero, R. 2001. "Efficient Urbanisation: Economic Performance and the Shape of the Metropolis." *Urban Studies* 38 (10): 1651–71.

Cervero, R., and K. Kockelman. 1997. "Travel Demand and the 3Ds: Density, Design and Diversity." *Transportation Research. Part D Transportation Environment* 2 (3): 199–219.

Chatman, D., and R. Noland. 2014. "Transit Service, Physical Agglomeration and Productivity in US Metropolitan Areas." *Urban Studies* 51 (5): 917–37.

Chen, X., and W. D. Nordhaus. 2011. "Using Luminosity Data as a Proxy for Economic Statistics." *Proceedings of the National Academy of Sciences of the United States of America* 108 (21): 8589–94.

Cheng, Y., L. Zhao, W. Wan, L. Li, T. Yu, and X. Gu. 2016. "Extracting Urban Areas in China Using DMSP/OLS Nighttime Light Data Integrated with Biophysical Composition Information." *Journal of Geographical Sciences* 26 (3): 325–38.

Cheshire, P. C., and I. R. Gordon. 1996. "Territorial Competition and the Predictability of Collective (In)action." *International Journal of Urban and Regional Research* 20 (3): 383–99.

Ciccone A., and R. E. Hall. 1996. "Productivity and the Density of Economic Activity." *American Economic Review* 86 (1): 54–70.

Civco, D. L., J. D. Hurd, C. L. Arnold, and S. Prisloe. 2000. "Characterization of Suburban Sprawl and Forest Fragmentation through Remote Sensing Application." Proceedings of the ASPRS Annual Convention, Washington, DC.

Croft, T. A. 1978. "Night-Time Images of the Earth from Space." *Scientific American* 239 (1): 68–79.

de Roo, G., and D. Miller. 2000. *Compact Cities and Sustainable Urban Development: A Critical Assessment of Politics and Plans from an International Perspective.* Aldershot, U.K.: Ashgate.

Duque, J. C., N. Lozano Gracia, J. Patino, and P. Restrepo. 2017a. "Urban Form and Productivity: In What Shape Are Latin American Cities?" Background paper for this book, World Bank, Washington, DC.

———. 2017b. "Institutional Fragmentation and Metropolitan Coordination in Latin American Cities: What Consequences for Productivity and Growth?" Background paper for this book, World Bank, Washington, DC.

Duque, J. C., N. Lozano-Gracia, J Patino, P. Restrepo, and W. A. Velasquez. 2017c. "Spatio-temporal Dynamics of Urban Growth in Latin American Cities: An Analysis Using NTL Imagery." Background paper for this book, World Bank, Washington, DC.

Duranton, G., and D. Puga. 2004. "Microfoundations of Urban Agglomeration Economies." In *Handbook of Urban and Regional Economics, Volume 4*, edited by J. V. Henderson and J.-F. Thisse, 2063–2117. New York: North Holland.

Fallah, B., M. Partridge, and M. Olfert. 2011. "Urban Sprawl and Productivity: Evidence from US Metropolitan Areas." *Papers in Regional Science* 90 (3): 451–73.

Feiock, R. C. 2009. "Metropolitan Governance and Institutional Collective Action." *Urban Affairs Review* 44 (3): 356–77.

Fischer, M. M. 1980. "Regional Taxonomy: A Comparison of Some Hierarchic and Non-Hierarchic Strategies." *Regional Science and Urban Economics* 10 (4): 503–37.

Forbes, D. J. 2013. "Multi-Scale Analysis of the Relationship between Economic Statistics and DMSP-OLS Night Light Images." *GIScience & Remote Sensing* 4 (4): 165–71.

Foster, K. A. 1993. "Exploring the Links between Political Structure and Metropolitan Growth." *Political Geography* 12 (6): 523–47.

Freire, S., and M. Pesaresi. 2015. "GHS Population Grid, Derived from GPW4, Multitemporal (1975, 1990, 2000, 2015)." European Commission, Joint Research Centre.

Fulton, W., R. Pendall, M. Nguyen, and A. Harrison. 2001. *Who Sprawls the Most? How Growth Patterns Differ across the United States.* Washington, DC: Brookings Institution.

Giacomin, David J., and David M. Levinson. 2015. "Road Network Circuity in Metropolitan Areas." *Environment and Planning B: Planning and Design* 42 (6): 1040–53.

Glaeser, E. L. 1998. "Are Cities Dying?" *Journal of Economic Perspectives* 12 (2): 139–60.

Glaeser E. L., and M. E. Khan. 2004. "Sprawl and Urban Growth." *Handbook of Regional and Urban Economics* 4: 2481–2527.

Grassmueck, G., and M. Shields. 2010. "Does Government Fragmentation Enhance or Hinder Metropolitan Economic Growth?" *Papers in Regional Science* 89 (3): 641–57.

Harari, M. 2016. "Cities in Bad Shape: Urban Geometry in India." Working Paper, The Wharton School, University of Pennsylvania, Philadelphia.

Henderson, J. V., A. Storeygard, and D. N. Weil. 2012. "Measuring Economic Growth from

Outer Space." *American Economic Review* 102 (2): 994–1028.

Hendrick, R., and Y. Shi. 2015. "Macro-level Determinants of Local Government Interaction: How Metropolitan Regions in the United States Compare." *Urban Affairs Review* 51 (3): 414–38.

Hsu, F. C., K. E. Baugh, T. Ghosh, M. Zhizhin, and C. D. Elvidge. 2015. "DMSP-OLS Radiance Calibrated Nighttime Lights Time Series with Intercalibration." *Remote Sensing* 7 (2): 1855–76.

Huang, J., and D. Levinson. 2015. "Circuity in Urban Transit Networks." Working Paper 201501, Nexus Research Group, University of Minnesota, Minneapolis.

Huang, J., X. X. Lu, and J. M. Sellers. 2007. "A Global Comparative Analysis of Urban Form: Applying Spatial Metrics and Remote Sensing." *Landscape and Urban Planning* 82 (4): 184–97.

Inostroza L., R. Baur, and E. Csaplovics. 2013. "Urban Sprawl and Fragmentation in Latin America: A Dynamic Quantification and Characterization of Spatial Patterns." *Journal of Environmental Management* 115: 87–97.

Jaffe, Adam, Manuel Trajtenberg, and Rebecca Henderson. 1993. "Geographic Localization of Knowledge Spillovers as Evidenced by Patent Citations." *Quarterly Journal of Economics* 108 (3): 577–98.

Kim, S. J., A. Schumann, and R. Ahrend. 2014. "What Governance for Metropolitan Areas?" Regional Development Working Paper, OECD, Paris.

Knaap, G., and A. C. Nelson. 1992. "The Regulated Landscape: Lessons on State Land Use Planning from Oregon." Cambridge, MA: Lincoln Institute of Land Policy

Knaap, G., C. Ding, and L. D. Hopkins. 2001. "Managing Urban Growth for the Efficient Use of Public Infrastructure: Toward a Theory of Concurrency." *International Regional Science Review* 24 (3): 328–343.

Litman, T. 2015. "Analysis of Public Policies That Unintentionally Encourage and Subsidize Urban Sprawl." Victoria Transport Policy Institute. Supporting paper commissioned by LSE Cities at the London School of Economics and Political Science, on behalf of the Global Commission on the Economy and Climate (www.newclimateeconomy.net) for the New Climate Economy Cities Program.

Lo, C. P. 2001. "Modeling the Population of China Using DMSP Operational Linescan System Nighttime Data." *Photogrammetric Engineering and Remote Sensing* 67 (9): 1037–47.

Lynch, K. 1981. *A Theory of Good City Form.* Cambridge, MA: MIT Press.

Ma, L., J. Wu, W. Li, J. Peng, and H. Liu. 2014. "Evaluating Saturation Correction Methods for DMSP/OLS Nighttime Light Data: A Case Study from China's Cities." *Remote Sensing* 6 (10): 9853–72.

Mills, E. S., and B. W. Hamilton. 1989. *Urban Economics, 4th Edition.* Glenview IL: Scott, Foresman, and Company.

Nelson, A. C., and K. A. Foster. 1999. "Metropolitan Governance Structure and Income Growth." *Journal of Urban Affairs* 21: 309–24.

Ostrom, E. 2010. "Beyond Markets and States: Polycentric Governance of Complex Economic Systems." *Transnational Corporations Review* 2 (2): 1–12.

Pandey, B., P. K. Joshi, and K. C. Seto. 2013. "Monitoring Urbanization Dynamics in India Using DMSP/OLS Nighttime Lights and SPOT-VGT Data." *International Journal of Applied Earth Observation and Geoinformation* 23: 49–61.

Parks, R. B., and R. J. Oakerson. 1989. "Metropolitan Organization and Governance." *Urban Affairs Quarterly* 25 (1): 18–29.

Parr, J. B. 1979. "Regional Economic Change and Regional Spatial Structure: Some Interrelationships." *Environment and Planning A* 11 (7): 825–37.

Partridge, M. D., D. S. Rickman, A. Kamar, and M. R. Olfert. 2009. "Agglomeration Spillovers and Wage and Housing Cost Gradients across the Urban Hierarchy." *Journal of International Economics* 78: 126–140.

Pesaresi, M., D. Ehrlich, A. J. Florczyk, S. Freire, A. Julea, T. Kemper, P. Soille, and V. Syrris. 2015. "GHS Built-Up Grid, Derived from Landsat, Multitemporal (1975, 1990, 2000, (2014)." European Commission, Joint Research Centre (JRC) [Dataset] PID: http://data.europa.eu/89h/jrc-ghsl-ghs_built_ldsmt_globe_r2015b.

Prosperi, D., A. V. Moudon, and F. Claessens. 2009. "The Question of Metropolitan Form: Introduction." *Footprint 3*(2): 1–4.

Quintero, L., and M. Roberts. 2017. "Explaining Spatial Variations in Productivity: Evidence from 16 LAC Countries." Working Paper, World Bank, Washington, DC.

Quíros, T. P., and S. R. Mehndiratta 2015. "Accessibility Analysis of Growth Patterns in Buenos Aires, Argentina: Density, Employment and Spatial Form." *Transportation Research Record: Journal of the Transportation Research Board* 2512.

Ríos, A. A. 2015. "Metropolitan Coordination in Mexico." *Current Urban Studies* 3 (1): 11–17.

Rosenthal, S. S., and W. C. Strange. 2004. "Evidence on the Nature and Sources of Agglomeration Economies." In *Handbook of Urban and Regional Economics, Volume 4,* edited by J. V. Henderson and J.-F. Thisse, 2119–71. New York: North Holland.

Shi, K., B. Yu, Y. Huang, Y. Hu, B. Yin, Z. Chen, L. Chen, and J. Wu. 2014. "Evaluating the Ability of NPP-VIIRS Nighttime Light Data to Estimate the Gross Domestic Product and the Electric Power Consumption of China at Multiple Scales: A Comparison with DMSP-OLS Data." *Remote Sensing* 6 (2): 1705–24.

Small, C., C. D. Elvidge, and K. Baugh. 2013. "Mapping Urban Structure and Spatial Connectivity with VIIRS and OLS Night Light Imagery." Paper presented at the Urban Remote Sensing Event (JURSE), São Paulo, April 21–23.

Squires, G. D. 2002. *Sprawl: Causes and Consequences and Policy Responses.* Washington, DC: The Urban Institute.

Stansel, D. 2005. "Local Decentralization and Local Economic Growth: A Cross-Sectional Examination of US Metropolitan Areas." *Journal of Urban Economics* 57 (1): 55–72.

Sutton, P. C., T. J. Cova, and C. D. Elvidge. 2006. "Mapping 'Exurbia' in the Conterminous United States Using Nighttime Satellite Imagery." *Geocarto International* 21 (2): 39–45.

Tewari, M., S. Alder, and M. Roberts. 2016. "Patterns of India's Urban and Spatial

Development in the Post-Reform Period: An Empirical Analysis." Working paper.

Tiebout, C. M. 1956. "A Pure Theory of Local Expenditures." *Journal of Political Economy* 64: 416.

Thompson, D. W. 1952. *On Growth and Form.* Second Edition. Cambridge: Cambridge University Press.

Wheeler, C. H. 2001. "Search, Sorting, and Urban Agglomeration." *Journal of Labor Economics* 19 (4): 879–99.

WHO (World Health Organization). 2016. *Urban Green Spaces and Health: A Review of Evidence.* Copenhagen: WHO Regional Office for Europe.

Whyte, W. 1968. *The Last Landscape.* Garden City, NY: Doubleday.

Wu, J., L. Ma, W. Li, J. Peng, and H. Liu. 2014. "Dynamics of Urban Density in China: Estimations Based on DMSP/OLS Nighttime Light Data." *IEEE Journal of Selected Topics in Applied Earth Observations and Remote Sensing* 7 (10): 4266–75.

Zhang, Q., and K. C. Seto. 2011. "Mapping Urbanization Dynamics at Regional and Global Scales Using Multi-Temporal DMSP/OLS Nighttime Light Data." *Remote Sensing of Environment* 115 (9): 2320–29.

Zhang, Q., C. Schaaf, and K. C. Seto. 2013. "The Vegetation Adjusted NTL Urban Index: A New Approach to Reduce Saturation and Increase Variation in Nighttime Luminosity." *Remote Sensing of Environment* 129: 34-41.

Zhou, N., K. Hubacek, and M. Roberts. 2015. "Analysis of Spatial Patterns of Urban Growth across South Asia Using DMSP-OLS Nighttime Lights Data." *Applied Geography* 63: 292–303.

Zhou, Y., S. J. Smith, K. Zhao, M. Imhoff, A. Thomson, B. Bond-Lamberty, and C. D. Elvidge. 2015. "A Global Map of Urban Extent from Nightlights." *Environmental Research Letters* 10 (5): 54011.